Simple, Clear, and Correct

Essays

William J. Kelly
Bristol Community College

Longman

Boston   Columbus   Indianapolis   New York   San Francisco
Upper Saddle River   Amsterdam   Cape Town   Dubai   London   Madrid
Milan   Munich   Paris   Montréal   Toronto   Delhi   Mexico City
São Paulo   Sydney   Hong Kong   Seoul   Singapore   Taipei   Tokyo

Acquisitions Editor: Matthew Wright
Senior Supplements Editor: Donna Campion
Marketing Manager: Thomas DeMarco
Production Manager: Ellen MacElree
Project Coordination and Text Design:
   Elm Street Publishing Services
Electronic Page Makeup: Integra Software Services Pvt., Ltd.
Cover Designer/Manager: John Callahan
Cover Image: Getty Images
Senior Manufacturing Buyer: Roy L. Pickering, Jr.
Printer and Binder: LSC Communications
Cover Printer: LSC Communications

For permission to use copyrighted material, grateful acknowledgment is
made to the copyright holders on page 324, which is hereby made part of
this copyright page.

Library of Congress Cataloging-in-Publication Data

Kelly, William J. (William Jude), 1953–
   Simple, clear, and correct: essays/William J. Kelly.
   p. cm.
Includes index.
ISBN 13: 978-0-205-56184-1
ISBN 10: 0-205-56184-5
1. English language—Rhetoric—Handbooks, manuals, etc.   2. English
   language—Grammar—Handbooks, manuals, etc.   3. Report writing—
   Handbooks, manuals, etc.   I. Title.
PE1408.K4756 2011
808.4—dc22

                                                          2010024780

14 18

Longman
is an imprint of

ISBN-13: 978-0-205-56184-1
www.pearsonhighered.com   ISBN-10: 0-205-56184-5

Dedication

To Michelle—
How do I start to thank you for all that you
have done, for all that you do?

The *Simple, Clear, and Correct* Series

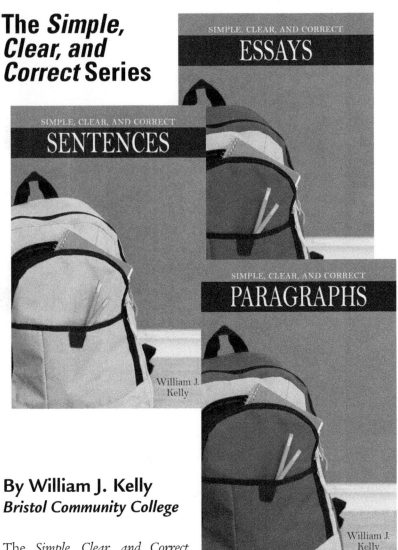

By William J. Kelly
Bristol Community College

The *Simple, Clear, and Correct* series includes three brief, very affordable books: one on *Sentences*, one on *Paragraphs*, and one on *Essays*. The presentation and features of the *Simple, Clear, and Correct* series ensure that the subject matter in all three books is appealing and easy to comprehend. The language is accessible and uncomplicated, and specific, relevant examples illustrate each principle. Meaningful writing activities, including plentiful topics for exploration, appear throughout each book. All three books feature an effective use of white space and gray-screen effects, plus a carefully designed system of headings to serve as a clear guide through the material. Presented in an easy-to-handle 6 by 9 trim size and a page count of around 350 pages, all three books follow the advice of the title: *simple, clear*, and *correct*.

Contents

CHAPTER 17 Subject–Verb Agreement 256

CHAPTER 18 Correct Verb Use: Irregular Forms, Tense, and Voice 263

CHAPTER 19 Pronoun Use 277

Preface

Overview

Think of an effective piece of writing you have encountered. Perhaps it was an article in a print or online periodical, a personal essay, a brochure, a chapter from a textbook, or a set of instructions. Or maybe it was an entry on a blog or even just an e-mail from a friend.

Now ask yourself: what about that document helped to make it effective? The truth is that there is no special system, no magic formula, no particular combination of elements that leads, every time, to a piece of writing that works. But here's something that you can be sure of every time: an effective piece of writing will be *simple, clear*, and *correct*.

These traits are the hallmarks of good writing—and your primary goal as a writer is to ensure that every document you create expresses your focus directly and communicates your ideas easily and in acceptable standard English. These hallmarks of good writing are also the foundation of *Simple, Clear, and Correct: Essays*.

You'll find that *Simple, Clear, and Correct: Essays* provides complete and engaging explanations and illustrations of the stages of the writing process, all in simple, clear, and correct terms. It also offers a thorough discussion of the rhetorical *modes*—the organizing strategies or patterns that writers use to fulfill their purpose or *aim* in a piece of writing—as well as specific approaches to research and documentation activities and multiple topics for writing that are both meaningful and relevant.

At the same time, *Simple, Clear, and Correct: Essays* offers thorough coverage of key elements of grammar and usage. This emphasis on these matters of *form* is crucial. Good ideas alone aren't enough to constitute an effective piece of writing. For readers to value the quality and validity of your message, your ideas must be expressed correctly, in complete sentence form, with all elements following the accepted rules of standard English. *Simple, Clear, and Correct: Essays* offers clear analysis of the most common problem spots in form. All these errors are thoroughly explained and illustrated, with concrete strategies provided to avoid or eliminate them.

Arrangement of the Text

Simple, Clear, and Correct: Essays is divided into four sections. Part I, "From Basic Ideas to Complete Draft," features four chapters. The first chapter, "The Essay: Process and Product," defines the essay and discusses the relationship between your *aims* in writing and the *modes* or writing techniques that help you fulfill those aims. It also provides the first of many annotated examples in the text. The next three chapters, "Prewriting," "Composing," and "Revising," introduce and explain the writing process in thorough detail, with plenty of specific examples and opportunities to practice and develop mastery of the concepts presented. Together, these chapters show how an essay—in this case, the essay introduced in the first chapter—evolves from initial promising but unfocused ideas to a polished, effective final draft.

Part II, "The Modes: Considering the Organizational Strategies and Approaches," includes nine chapters devoted to the rhetorical modes: *narration, description, example, process, definition, comparison and contrast, cause and effect, division and classification,* and *argument.* Each mode is presented as an organizing technique or pattern used to fulfill a specific purpose of a piece of writing and meet the reader's needs. The exception is argument, which is discussed as an intent—an aim or *purpose*—rather than a type.

Each chapter contains a thorough explanation of the characteristics of a particular mode, complete with a practical checklist, an essay with annotations illustrating the principles presented, and a published essay in which the mode dominates. The essays throughout the text serve as models for good writing, and they cover a wide variety of interesting, appealing, and relevant topics, including ways to live a greener life, a grizzly attack, the surprising ingredients in a common household product, a near drowning, a visit to a museum gone bad, the process of and devastation from a tsunami, and the geek within us all. The study questions and writing assignments that follow the essays enhance mastery of the material and provide an opportunity to apply the concepts discussed.

Chapter 13, "Argument," thoroughly explores and illustrates how a writer uses an appropriate combination of modes to persuade a reader. It also reinforces the importance of drawing support from experts and acknowledging this material properly. In addition, this chapter contains a valuable list of common logical fallacies, with specific examples of the errors and specific ways to avoid or eliminate them.

Part III, "Specific Applications: Issues of Research and Documentation," consists of one chapter. Chapter 14, "Research and Documentation Activities: A Brief Guide," discusses the process of completing a research paper or assignment, offering specific guidance in such areas as assessing the validity of traditional and electronic sources and avoiding plagiarism. It also illustrates the proper way to include—whether in the form of direct quotation, paraphrase, or summary—and document expert information both in the text of the paper and at the end in accordance with the latest Modern Language Association (MLA). Annotated pages from a research paper on solar energy, presented in MLA style, are also included.

Part IV, "Dealing with Matters of Form," consists of eight chapters devoted to those aspects of grammar and usage that writers must understand and master in order to present their ideas in acceptable standard English. These areas include recognizing parts of speech and parts and types of sentences (Chapter 15); avoiding sentence fragments, comma splices, and run-on sentences (Chapter 16); providing correct subject–verb agreement (Chapter 17); using verbs properly, including irregular forms and issues related to tense and voice (Chapter 18); using pronouns correctly, including proper pronoun–antecedent agreement (Chapter 19); using adjectives, adverbs, and other modifiers (Chapter 20); spelling (Chapter 21); and parallelism and punctuation (Chapter 22).

Presentation and Features of the Text

The presentation of *Simple, Clear, and Correct: Essays* ensures that the subject matter is engaging and easy to understand. Key features include

- accessible, straightforward, conversational language throughout
- specific, relevant examples to illustrate all aspects of the writing process
- numerous thought-provoking opportunities for writing

- annotated examples of all stages of the writing process, the modes, and the research paper
- practical checklists to evaluate progress with all aspects of writing
- simple, clear explanations of errors in form, making identification and elimination easy
- an attractive page layout, featuring an effective use of white space and gray-screen effects
- a carefully designed system of headings serving as a clear guide through the text
- an easy-to-handle 6-by-9-inch trim size

In short, *Simple, Clear, and Correct: Essays* is a book that embodies the principles outlined in its own title.

Supplements and Additional Resources

Pearson Writing Resources for Instructors and Students
Book-Specific Ancillary Material

Instructor's Exam Copy for *Simple, Clear, and Correct: Essays,* 1/e (ISBN 0-205-00087-8)

Instructor's Manual and Answer Key for *Simple, Clear, and Correct: Essays,* 1/e (ISBN 0-205-61982-7) The *IM* is designed to save instructors time and provide them with effective options for teaching their writing classes. It offers suggestions for setting up their course, provides additional teaching tips and activities, and supplies answers to the exercises found in the book. This valuable resource is exceptionally useful for adjuncts who might need advice in setting up their initial classes or who might be teaching a variety of writing classes with too many students and not enough time.

Additional Resources
The Pearson Writing Package   Pearson is pleased to offer a variety of support materials to help make teaching writing easier for teachers and to help students excel in their coursework. Many of our student supplements are available free or at a greatly reduced price when packaged with *Simple, Clear, and Correct: Essays.* Visit www.pearsonhighereducation.com, contact your local Pearson sales representative, or review a detailed listing of the full supplements package in the *Instructor's Manual* for more information.

MyWritingLab **MyWritingLab** (www.mywritinglab.com) is a complete online learning program that provides better practice exercises to developing writers.

What makes the practice in MyWritingLab better?

- **Diagnostic Testing:** MyWritingLab's diagnostic test comprehensively assesses students' skills in grammar. Students are given an individualized learning path based on the diagnostic's results, identifying the areas where they most need help.
- **Progressive Learning:** The heart of MyWritingLab is the progressive learning that takes place as students complete the Recall, Apply, and Write exercises within each topic. Students move from literal comprehension (Recall) to critical understanding (Apply) to the ability to demonstrate a skill in their own writing (Write). This progression of critical thinking, not available in any other online resource, enables students to truly master the skills and concepts they need to become successful writers.
- **Online Gradebook:** All student work in MyWritingLab is captured in the Online Gradebook. Students can monitor their own progress through reports explaining their scores on the exercises in the course. Instructors can see which topics their students have mastered and access other detailed reports, such as class summaries, that track the development of their entire class and display useful details on each student's progress.

Acknowledgments

I would like to acknowledge the assistance of a number of people as I worked on *Simple, Clear, and Correct: Essays.* First, thanks to John M. Lannon, University of Massachusetts, Dartmouth (retired), and Robert A. Schwegler, University of Rhode Island, for their guidance and also their wisdom—and also their friendship. Thanks also to Paul Arakelian, University of Rhode Island; Paul F. Fletcher, Professor Emeritus, Bristol Community College; and Jack R. Warner, Executive Director of the South Dakota Board of Regents for Higher Education, for their steadfast interest in me and my work.

I remain deeply grateful for the encouragement of a number of my colleagues at Bristol Community College, including Catherine Adamowicz, Gabriela Adler, Debbie Anderson, Denise DiMarzio, Michael Geary, Tom Grady, Jeanne Grandchamp, Farah Habib, Elizabeth Kemper French, Deborah Lawton, Arthur Lothrop, Diane Manson, Diana McGee, Linda Mulready, Jean Paul Nadeau, Joanne Preston, and Howard Tinberg.

I want to acknowledge the help of the following instructors from across the country whose insightful suggestions helped me shape the text: Shawn Adamson, Genesee Community College; Janna Anderson, Fullerton College; Elsie M. Burnett, Cedar Valley College; Cathy E. Fagan, Nassau Community College; Debra Farve, Mount San Antonio College; Ellen Gilmour, Genesee Community College; Ruth Hatcher, Washtenaw Community College; Sandra Hooven, University of Las Vegas; Noel Kinnamon, Mars Hill College; Kathy Parrish, Southwestern College; Rebekah J. Rios-Harris, Cedar Valley College; Cynthia VanSickle, McHenry County College; and William L. Young, University of Southern Alabama. I also offer special thanks to Nicole C. Matos, College of DuPage, and Timothy Matos, Truman College, who evaluated *Simple, Clear, and Correct: Essays* and drew on their background and teaching expertise to provide astute advice. It is truly my good fortune that Nicole and Tim are also my older daughter and son-in-law.

A number of people at Pearson Education deserve my thanks for their hard work on my behalf. First, I deeply appreciate the belief in and support for this project that Matthew Wright, Senior Acquisitions Editor, Basic English and Developmental Writing, has demonstrated from beginning to end. Thanks also to Jessica Kupetz, Assistant Editor, Developmental English, for marshaling the text through production and publication; to Sue Nodine, Project Editor for Elm Street Publishing Services; and to Ellen MacElree, Project Manager for Pearson Longman, for making the finished product look so good.

Most of all, I owe thanks to my family, starting with my late parents, Mary R. and Edward F. Kelly. Their lessons continue to influence my three brothers and me. I greatly appreciate the love and support of my parents-in-law, Flo and Leo Nadeau, and my sons-in-law, Jeremy Wright and Timothy Matos. I am immensely proud to be the father of Jacqueline M. Wright and Nicole C. Matos—and to be the grandfather of Alexander Owen Matos. Their love sustains me.

But the person who deserves my thanks most of all is my wife, Michelle Nadeau Kelly. For more than 37 years, she has supported my teaching and my writing, believing in me far more than I have ever believed in myself, and I am grateful beyond what words can express for her intelligence, her humor, and her love.

WILLIAM J. KELLY

PART I

From Basic Ideas to Complete Draft

1

1

The Essay: Process and Product

Understanding the Structure and Scope of the Essay

Writing is an activity that plays an important role in all academic and professional fields, and you can expect, on a regular basis, to deal with various writing tasks, both in school and beyond the classroom. Many of the assignments you will face will call for extended writings, and one of the most common of these longer documents is the **essay**.

With this kind of multiparagraph document, a writer expresses a reaction to or an opinion or attitude about a topic, providing plenty of supporting examples and details to create a document of about 500–700 words. Many of the selections that appear on the op-ed pages of newspapers and in print and electronic magazines and periodicals qualify as essays, as do many letters to the editor and columns and pieces labeled "Commentary" or "Analysis." Blog entries can often be classified as essays, too.

In many of your academic courses, you will be expected to write essays that address a variety of subjects. In a criminal justice class, for instance, you might be asked to offer an opinion about electronic monitoring as a substitute for imprisonment. In an ethics course, you might be asked to express your views regarding euthanasia.

One characteristic common to all essays is *scope*. A paragraph, for example, deals with a subject in a limited way. An essay covers a subject more thoroughly, exploring multiple facets and angles.

The Relationship between Your Aim and Your Approach in an Essay

As with all writing, your **aim**—the purpose or intent behind your essay—determines how you will approach the subject matter. In general, you will find that when you write, you fulfill one of three aims: to **inform**, to **entertain**, or to **persuade**.

For example, the aim of an essay about the popularity of zip lining, an activity during which people are harnessed to a cable that carries them along the tops of trees, would be to inform. If the focus were instead on the thrill you felt as you rode along a zip line, then the aim would be to entertain. And if the focus were on the need for greater safety regulations for potentially dangerous activities like zip lining, then the aim would be to persuade.

In most cases, an essay generally fulfills a **primary aim** and one or more **secondary aims**. Although the primary purpose of the essay about imposing additional safety regulations on zip lining would be to persuade, the explanation of what zip lining entails would make informing a secondary aim. In addition, the details and examples of this relatively new thrill ride would likely capture and hold the reader's attention, so entertaining would be another secondary aim.

The organizing approaches you use to fulfill your aim—*narration, description, example, process, definition, comparison and contrast, cause and effect,* and *division and classification*—are known as the rhetorical **modes**. For instance, if an assignment calls for you to explain distinctions between subjects, comparison and contrast, the mode that examines similarities and differences, would be your choice. If an assignment calls for you to tell the story of the funniest event that you have ever witnessed, then narration, the mode that presents episodes in sequence, would be the appropriate strategy. Chapters 5 through 12 define and illustrate the different modes in detail.

Chapter 13 covers *argument*. Unlike the organizing strategies presented in Chapters 5–12, argument is actually an aim, not a mode. With argument, you express a stance on a subject, and you employ the combination of modes that will convince your reader to accept the validity of your point of view.

1

Imagine you were writing an argument essay indicating that medical professionals should ignore the wishes of parents who want to deny medical care to their seriously ill children because of religious beliefs. You might use description to detail the ravages that a disease like leukemia can have on a child when it is untreated. You might also use definition to specify the extent of parental rights and cause and effect to detail the implications of such a decision, all to support your argument.

Understanding the Structure of the Essay

To create a successful essay, you need to understand and follow a simple structure. The typical essay consists of three parts: the *introduction*, the *body*, and the *conclusion*.

The Introduction

In most cases, the **introduction** of an effective essay is a single paragraph specifying the subject and providing a clear direction for the reader. The introduction does this through the **thesis**—a sentence that indicates the main point of the paper. This part of the essay sparks interest, compelling the reader to continue reading. Chapter 3 discusses the thesis in detail and presents proven strategies for developing introductions.

The Body

The part of your essay in which you develop your main point is the **body**. This section consists of several paragraphs, each fully amplified so that it supports and illustrates your thesis. The actual number of paragraphs comprising the body will depend on several factors, including the focus and direction of the essay and the length of the paragraphs themselves. With an essay of 500 to 700 words, the body will likely consist of four to ten paragraphs, but three is the minimum number. Chapters 3 and 4 explain in greater detail how to compose and revise the body of your essay.

A type of essay sometimes taught in writing classes features a three-paragraph body. This type of document, known as the **five-paragraph essay**, has five paragraphs total: an introductory paragraph, three body paragraphs, and a concluding paragraph. The introduction identifies three key features about the topic, each of the three paragraphs in the body discusses one of the points in detail, and then the conclusion restates the significance of the information presented, echoing the introduction. While this structure may be too rigid or limiting for some writing situations, the five-paragraph essay may prove particularly useful with some timed writing assignments like essay examinations and writing assessments.

The Conclusion

The part of an essay that brings the document to a complete and logical close is the **conclusion**. This element, generally a single paragraph, strengthens the overall message expressed by the thesis and developed in the body, summing up the *significance* of the essay. For the most part, conclusions don't introduce new ideas, since the place to raise new ideas is the body. Sometimes, however, a conclusion will ask a question or raise an issue for the reader to consider. Chapter 3 covers this element of the essay in greater detail and presents some strategies for creating effective conclusions.

Consider the following figure, which shows the structure of an essay:

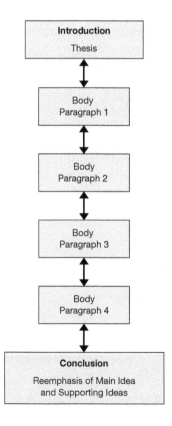

1

As you can see, the box representing the introduction is larger than the boxes representing the body paragraphs. That's because the introduction contains the big idea—the thesis. The arrows between the paragraphs point in both directions because the idea presented in each paragraph is related to the thesis as well as to the other supporting ideas. And the box representing the conclusion is the largest of all. That's because the conclusion reiterates the significance of all the information presented—the thesis *and* the supporting ideas.

Formatting Your Essay Properly

When it comes time to commit your essay to paper, follow these format guidelines, unless your instructor directs you otherwise:

- Double-space the various drafts of your essay, and make sure to provide adequate margins. The default margins in most word-processing programs are suitable for preparing an essay.
- In the upper right hand corner of the first page, supply a **running head**—your last name and the page number. With a word-processing program like Microsoft Word, include this information in the header, and the program will automatically repeat your name and the appropriate page number on all subsequent pages. Otherwise, repeat your last name and the appropriate page number in the upper right hand corner of every page of your essay.
- In the upper left hand corner, provide a **heading**, which consists of four lines of information—your name, your instructor's name, the full title of the course, and the date the paper is due. Finally, a full double space below, provide your **title**, centered from left to right, as this model shows:

Dorsey 1

Caitlyn Dorsey
Professor Michelle Nadeau
English 101—College Writing
October 15, 2009

Liberal Arts <u>Is</u> a Legitimate Major

Dealing with a Writing Assignment: Examining a Successful Essay

1

Consider the following writing prompt, typical of what students face in a writing class:

School isn't the only place where we learn lessons. The workplace is a source of many of the lessons that last a lifetime. Think of your first job—what lessons, positive or negative, did you learn? How has this experience affected the way you conduct your-self? In an essay of about 500 words, discuss what your first foray into the world of employment taught you.

Of course, the writing you will complete as a student will not be restricted to your composition class. For example, this variation of the same writing prompt could appear as a question on an essay test or as a journal topic in a sociology, business, or economics course:

Last week's readings and class discussions focused on challenges that many employees face when they first join the work-force. Chapter 4 illustrated several typical errors that new workers make and spelled out how such missteps affect their view of their jobs and of themselves as workers. What were the worst errors you made on your first job? How have these incidents helped to shape you as a person and as a worker?

Or you might face a writing task that isn't actually part of an academic course—for instance, an essay required as part of the application for a competitive student scholarship like this one:

Each year, the Tri-City Industry, Technology, and Business Cooperative (ITBC) offers a full tuition scholarship to a deserving second-year student. Applications must be received by May 30. In addition to transcripts and three letters of recommendation, applicants must include an essay of 500–700 words in response to the following topic:

> The ITBC strongly believes that successful professionals are people who assess their strengths and weaknesses on the job. Please write an essay in which you discuss an employment experience that helped you recognize your own strengths and capitalize on them or identify your weaknesses and develop strategies to eliminate them.

All three scenarios focus on the same basic topic, and all three call for the same general approach. The following essay responds to these assignments. Note the annotations accompanying the essay, which identify characteristics and features that contribute to its effectiveness:

The **title** prepares the reader by hinting at the focus of the essay.

Real World 101: What My First Job Taught Me

My first job was as a part-time clerk at a grocery store, and my experiences on the job taught me much more than how to maintain inventory and stock shelves. I learned how important it was to pay attention to directions and to be on time for every shift. I also learned that the way to earn respect and to make the job easier was to be a good co-worker. Most important, I learned that when it comes to work I'm responsible to complete, I shouldn't trust someone else to complete it. That mistake almost cost me my job.

My first week at GroceryWorld included three days of training during which the trainer explained various duties. For instance, I

The first paragraph in the body deals with the **first supporting idea**: the importance of listening carefully on the job. **Narration, description**, and **cause and effect** help to fulfill the aims of the essay.

The first sentence serves as the **thesis** and indicates the main point of the essay. The other sentences in the **introduction** indicate the **supporting ideas**. The thesis also indicates that the primary aim of the essay is to **inform**. The introduction also asserts that job can teach valuable lessons beyond the basic of a field, so its **secondary aim** is to **persuade**.

learned how to take the pallets of groceries from the delivery trucks and arrange them in the storage area of the store. The point was to set up the pallets so that the grocery crews could easily find what they needed, and they wouldn't have to waste time looking for what they needed for the shelves. During my first two weeks on the job, I failed to follow these directions on four occasions. After the fourth time, the crew chief came into the storage area to yell at me. Worse, he complained to my supervisor, who put a written warning in my personnel file. The truly embarrassing thing is that the whole problem was avoidable. The trainer had told me how important the arrangement of the pallets is in terms of productivity. I just hadn't listened very well.

The second paragraph in the body deals with the **second supporting idea**: the importance of being on time. This paragraph builds on the discussion in the previous paragraph about listening to directions. **Narration, cause and effect**, and **example** help to fulfill the aims of the essay.

Another important lesson I learned was about being on time. Before I started this job, lateness was a very bad habit for me. It didn't make any difference whether it was going to school or out with friends or on a date. I could be counted on to be five or ten minutes late, and for the first two weeks on the job, my bad habit continued. But when I received my first paycheck, I realized the immediate consequences of punching in late. Even when I was just a minute late, the company docked me a quarter-hour of my pay. Stapled to my pay

1

slip was a notice stating that if I continued to punch in late, I would be dismissed. When I saw how much money my bad habit was costing me, I changed my ways, both at work and in my personal life.

The third paragraph in the body deals with the **third supporting idea**: the importance of being an effective team member. This paragraph builds on the discussions presented in the previous body paragraphs about listening to directions and being on time. **Example, narration, description, process**, and **cause and effect** help to fulfill the aims of the essay.

Before I started that job, I never gave much thought to working as part of a team. But as a member of a five-person work crew, I learned how important good teamwork is. On many nights, for example, I was in charge of restocking the dairy case, which took about an hour. When I was done, I was supposed to join my crewmate in the frozen food aisle, a job that took one worker over two hours but much less with a helper. After the two of us finished there, we had to join the rest of our team, who were assigned to identify and fill gaps in the shelves and restock the end displays in different areas of the store. If any one of us didn't finish a job, the entire crew fell behind and had to face a very unhappy supervisor the next shift. That taught me that when you help teammates, you help yourself, and I keep this lesson in mind now whenever I face group work of any kind.

But I learned the most important lesson the hard way when I trusted someone who wasn't trustworthy, and I was almost fired as a result. When my supervisor went on vacation, a worker

The fourth paragraph in the body deals with the **fourth supporting idea**: the need to exercise good judgment in the people you trust. This paragraph builds on the discussions presented in the previous body paragraphs about listening to directions, being on time, and being a good team member. **Narration, example**, and **cause and effect** help to fulfill the aims of the essay.

1

from another crew, who seemed genuinely nice and easy going, became acting supervisor. One night, when I fell behind in my work, he told me not to worry, that he would finish up for me. The next day, I was called into the store manager's office. She held up the shift assessment sheet from the previous night. On this form, the acting supervisor had written that I had refused to complete my work for the night. I was shocked. I just couldn't believe that someone who appeared to be so nice would tell me to go home and then lie about it. I told the manager that I was sorry, that I must have misunderstood what the acting supervisor had said. The manager accepted my apology but warned me that I would be fired if there were any more problems. That incident taught me that first impressions aren't always accurate and that when something seems too good to be true, it probably is.

The **conclusion** restates the point expressed in the **thesis**— that this first job provided valuable lessons beyond basic knowledge of this industry. It also **reinforces** the **significance** of the **thesis** and the **supporting ideas**. The conclusion therefore helps to fulfill the **primary aim—to inform**—and the **secondary aim—to persuade**.

I work with kids at the local Boys and Girls Club now, and the lessons I learned on my first job are really helping me. Today, whenever someone gives me instructions, I listen carefully. I also make showing up on time a priority, and I do my best to be a good worker and dependable crewmember. But most important, I now try to use good judgment before I put my trust in someone because if the person isn't worthy of that trust, the consequences can be pretty severe.

1

As the annotations indicate, a number of elements combine to make this an effective essay. It has a clear main point, a **thesis**; several specific examples that offer support; and a conclusion that restates the significance of the entire document, all of which help to fulfill the writer's intent—the **aim**.

But how does an essay like this come to be? In other words, how do you go from a simple concept to a complete and successful piece of writing? The answer is the **writing process**, and the next three chapters will walk you through the stages involved: **prewriting**, **composing**, and **revising**.

Summary Exercise

1. Consider the discussion that opens this chapter about the writing in different academic disciplines. Think of your experiences in school, either in college or in your previous years in school, and list three writing tasks you have faced. Which of these writing assignments did you find easiest? Which did you find hardest? Explain your reasoning.

2. Choose an article of around 500 words from a newspaper, magazine, or the Internet or a passage of about 500 words from one of your other textbooks. Make a copy and exchange it with a classmate.

   a. Using the discussion on pages 3–4 about **aim**, identify the primary aim in the document you have chosen as well as in the document your classmate has given you. Specify what aspects or elements led you to your conclusions.

   b. Compare your analysis with your classmate's. If you disagree in any way, consider each other's responses to see if the additional information will influence your thinking.

3. Take another look at "Real World 101: What My First Job Taught Me," the annotated essay on pages 8–11. In your view, what is the strongest part of the essay? What about this element or aspect stands out from the rest?

4. Consider the three writing scenarios related to work (pages 7–8). Or if you'd prefer, think about another topic presented in the chapter (electronic monitoring rather than imprisonment, page 2; legalization of euthanasia, page 2; extreme sports or thrill rides like zip lining, page 3; the funniest situation that you have ever witnessed, page 3; or the degree that medical specialists treating severely ill

1

children should consider the personal or religious beliefs of the children's parents, page 4). Choose the topic that most appeals to you, identify what you think your primary aim would be, and jot down some examples or details that would help your reader understand your point. Save your work for later use.

2

Prewriting

Understanding Prewriting

It's a simple truth: before you can write an essay, you need to have something to write about—a specific topic and ideas and examples to support, illustrate, or explain that topic. You generate this material, the foundation for your essay, during **prewriting**, the first stage in the writing process. Any activity during which you plan, explore, or examine a subject—things like talking to others (or to yourself into a recording device), reading, seeing a video or film, or simply thinking—qualifies as prewriting.

But a number of more structured prewriting activities are also available to you, including *freewriting, brainstorming, clustering,* and *branching.* Each technique allows you to approach this vital part of the writing process in a slightly different way. What you need to do now is try each activity to see which technique—or which combination of techniques—best matches the way you prefer to work.

Freewriting

One proven prewriting activity is **freewriting**. This technique involves writing down everything that comes into your head on a subject without stopping for a set period of time—generally ten minutes or so. When you freewrite, you don't worry about making mistakes, expressing your ideas in complete sentences, repeating ideas, or drifting away from your original point. You just keep writing. If you can't think for a moment, write, "I'm stuck" or "Can't think" until another idea comes to mind. With freewriting, your goal is to get ideas flowing and to generate as much information as possible. You will sort through the material later.

Consider this freewriting on lessons learned from a first job, the subject of the model essay on pages 8–11:

My first job?—OK, that was GroceryWorld, Junior year in high school. Started with a bad attitude—not really bad, but I didn't know much about being a good worker. I showed up late in the beginning—docked my pay, put a letter in my file. Embarrassed and mad. Didn't know how to work on a team—I'd just concentrate on my own stuff, didn't help the other crewmates. Some of them didn't want to work with me—complained to the boss. The night when the guys helped me finish my aisle and I helped them—finally understood. Messed up on arranging pallets in the backroom—I didn't pay much attention during training. Still see some of those guys in the summer—most have other jobs now. Ava stayed, but she is training to be a manager now. What else did I learn? Compromise? Flexibility? I don't know. Maybe I didn't learn that stuff until I started with the Boys and Girls Club. That incident when the acting supervisor lied and told the boss that I had refused to finish my work

2

> *before going home. No way!! He said that he would take care of it and then wrote me up. The next day, boss calls me in and showed me the sheet. I almost got fired!!! I'll never trust someone like that again. A really big lesson.*

As this example illustrates, it's always a good idea to highlight, underline, or circle your best prewriting ideas, no matter what technique you use. Then you'll be prepared to develop those ideas more fully as you continue to work through the rest of the writing process.

MASTERY EXERCISE 1 Practice with Freewriting

1. Choose one of the following subjects and freewrite on it, using the model freewriting as a guide:
   - An experience on public transportation
   - Self-esteem
   - A campus frustration
2. Identify the most promising ideas in your freewriting by highlighting, circling, or underlining them.
3. Focus on one of the promising ideas and generate three details or examples about it.
4. What did you like most about freewriting? Explain your reasoning, indicating whether you will be likely to use this prewriting technique again.

Brainstorming

Another effective prewriting technique is **brainstorming**. When you brainstorm, you examine a subject over a period of time—perhaps fifteen minutes or longer, if necessary—in a careful, deliberate way in order to develop potential supporting ideas. Rather than recording all the ideas that come to mind, you list only those that are directly connected to your topic, as this sample brainstorming on the lessons learned from a first job illustrates:

> *Lessons from My First Job*
>
> - *First job—GroceryWorld*
> - *My cousin's friend got me the application*

- No sense of how to be a good worker
- Liked dealing with the customers
- Dress code wasn't too bad-collared shirts, no logos, no ripped or torn jeans
- Daydreamed during training-messed up a week later on pallets in the backroom
- Late for work more often than on time in the beginning-docked my pay!!
- Teamwork-didn't do my part to help the crew at first
- Only non-smoker on my team
- Alex and Owen now crew members with me at Boys and Girls Club
- The lie the acting supervisor told about me-it almost cost me my job!
- Big lesson-never count on anyone to do your own work

As you can see, you won't develop as many ideas when you brainstorm as when you freewrite. The good news is that your brainstorming ideas will be clearly connected to the topic, as the highlighted material in this example illustrates. In fact, sometimes they have such an obvious connection that they could be slightly rearranged to serve as a rough outline for an essay.

MASTERY EXERCISE 2 Practice with Brainstorming

1. Choose one of the following subjects and brainstorm on it, using the model brainstorming as a guide:
   - Stereotypes
   - High school pressures
   - Bad driving habits
2. Identify the most promising ideas in your brainstorming by highlighting, circling, or underlining them.
3. Focus on one of the promising ideas and generate three details or examples about it.

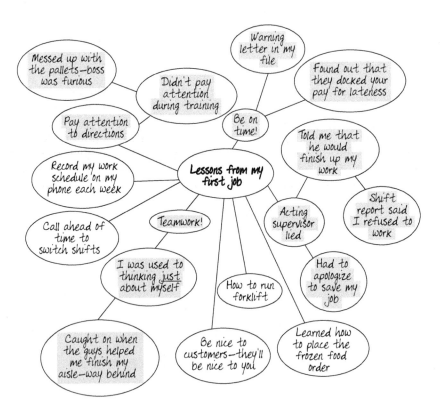

2

4. What did you like most about brainstorming? Explain your reasoning, indicating whether you will be likely to use this prewriting technique again.

Clustering

An effective prewriting technique with a visual twist is **clustering**. With clustering, instead of writing across a page or listing ideas in a column, you let your ideas spread out in multiple directions across a page. You write your subject in the middle of the page and circle it. Then, as a related idea comes into your head, you write and circle it elsewhere on the page, drawing a line back to the idea that inspired it, and continue this process until you have filled the page with examples and details to help you develop an essay. This sample clustering, also on the lessons learned from a first job, shows what happens when you follow this process:

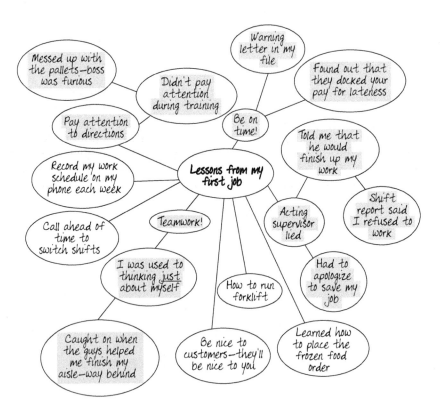

As you can see, the lines connecting the items make it easier to see the relationships among the ideas and to identify and emphasize the most promising points, as the highlighting illustrates.

MASTERY EXERCISE 3 Practice with Clustering

1. Choose one of the following subjects and create a clustering on it, using the model clustering as a guide:
   - Time management challenges
   - Your favorite childhood game
   - The emphasis on physical appearance in our culture
2. Identify the most promising ideas in your clustering by highlighting, circling, or underlining them.
3. Focus on one of the promising ideas and generate three details or examples about it.
4. What did you like most about clustering? Explain your reasoning, indicating whether you will be likely to use this prewriting technique again.

Branching

An additional prewriting technique that also has a visual element is **branching**. To create a branching, first list your subject on the left side of a piece of paper, roughly in the center. As related ideas come to mind, list them to the right of the idea from which they developed, connecting them with lines. Continue this process, listing new groups of ideas across the page from left to right, until you have filled the page. Take a look at this model clustering on the lessons from a first job:

2

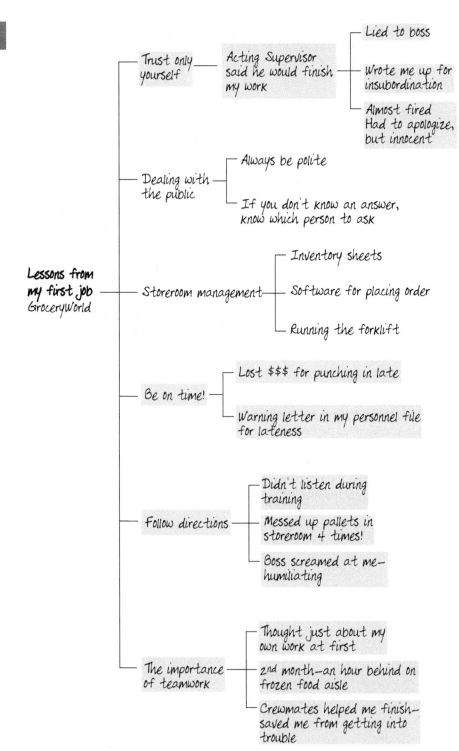

Lessons from
my first job
GroceryWorld

Trust only yourself
— Acting Supervisor said he would finish my work
  — Lied to boss
  — Wrote me up for insubordination
  — Almost fired Had to apologize, but innocent

Dealing with the public
— Always be polite
— If you don't know an answer, know which person to ask

Storeroom management
— Inventory sheets
— Software for placing order
— Running the forklift

Be on time!
— Lost $$$ for punching in late
— Warning letter in my personnel file for lateness

Follow directions
— Didn't listen during training
— Messed up pallets in storeroom 4 times!
— Boss screamed at me—humiliating

The importance of teamwork
— Thought just about my own work at first
— 2nd month—an hour behind on frozen food aisle
— Crewmates helped me finish—saved me from getting into trouble

An advantage of branching, as the highlighted material demonstrates, is that different segments contain related examples. This feature often makes it easier to organize information later in the writing process.

MASTERY EXERCISE 4 Practice with Branching

1. Choose one of the following subjects and create a branching on it, using the model clustering as a guide:
   - Your best-loved or most popular family member
   - Advantages of growing up in a small town or a big city
   - Social networking sites like Facebook and MySpace
2. Identify the most promising ideas in your branching by highlighting, circling, or underlining them.
3. Focus on one of the promising ideas and generate three details or examples about it.
4. What did you like most about branching? Explain your reasoning, indicating whether you will be likely to use this prewriting technique again.

Establishing Which Prewriting Technique Is Best for You

A successful essay begins with prewriting, so identifying the prewriting technique that works for you is crucial to your success as a writer. Ultimately, your decision will come down to your own comfort level: which technique matches your personal working style? In addition, you can adapt a technique or combine it with another. The point is that the strategy—or combination of strategies—that enables you to lay the foundation for an effective essay is always your best choice.

Summary Exercise

1. Of the prewriting techniques you tried, which technique did you like least? What is it about this planning strategy that doesn't match the way you prefer to work?

2. Now that you have prewritten on several topics, what has surprised you most about the prewriting process?

2

3. Using the technique you prefer, prewrite on one of the following topics:

   - The outdoor or sporting activity you most prefer as a participant or a fan
   - The impact of ignorance of any kind
   - A dangerous relationship
   - The source of genuine confidence
   - What awaits you in the future

4. After identifying the most promising ideas in your prewriting, create an essay of about 500 words that incorporates this material. Use "Real World 101: What My First Job Taught Me" (pages 8–11) as a model.

3

Composing

Understanding the Composing Stage

During the prewriting stage of writing, you consider a subject and generate examples and details about it. Once you have developed this material, you move to the second stage of the writing process, **composing**, during which you transform your preliminary ideas into a complete, correct **draft essay**. To accomplish this, you need to articulate a specific main idea—your **thesis**—which you express in your introduction. You must also develop **supporting paragraphs**, each of which explains or illustrates some point directly connected to or associated with your thesis, and create a conclusion that restates or emphasizes the significance of the thesis and supporting paragraphs. At the same time, you must concentrate on **form**, ensuring that the material you write is in **clear, complete sentences**. When you follow the process to its end, the result is a complete version known as a **first draft essay**.

3

Understanding the Nature of an Effective Thesis

As Chapter 1 explained, an essay is divided into three sections—**introduction**, **body**, and **conclusion**. The role of the introduction is to provide a clear direction for the reader, and a successful introduction does so through the **thesis**, the main idea of the essay. Think of a thesis as a billboard in sentence form that lets the reader know what is coming up ahead.

An effective thesis generally consists of two parts: a *subject* and the *writer's attitude about* or *reaction to* that subject. This structure clarifies the purpose of the essay and establishes the reader's expectation about the way the subject will be discussed.

For example, if you were writing an essay about the role that alternative energy sources are expected to play in our immediate future, your thesis would look something like this:

subject

Effective Thesis: *Companies proposing to build offshore wind farms*

attitude about the subject

must agree to pay a significant portion of their profits to the government and to adhere to strict environmental guidelines for the privilege of operating on public land.

As you can see, this thesis features both a subject and an attitude about or reaction to it, so it is effective. The thesis also suggests that the primary purpose of the essay is to persuade, so it's a fair assumption that the rest of the paper will provide reasons why companies looking to construct wind farms offshore should have to pay hefty fees and adhere to guidelines that would increase the cost of construction and operation.

At the same time, keep in mind what a thesis *isn't*. A good thesis is *not*

- an announcement of your intent, featuring words like *I plan, I intend,* or *This paper concerns,* expressions that merely repeat what you should make obvious in your thesis.

Ineffective Thesis: I want to explain about the needs to regulate wind farms on public lands.

- a statement of fact, which is a verifiable truth that leaves no room for discussion or debate:

Ineffective Thesis: Construction of wind farms off the U.S. coasts involves obtaining multiple complex government permits.

- a title, which is not usually a sentence and is generally intended to provide only a broad hint of the subject of your essay:

Ineffective Thesis: Wind Power: Doing It Right, Doing It Fairly

---

MASTERY EXERCISE 1 Distinguishing between an Effective and an Ineffective Thesis

1. Consider the following list of sentences. If the sentence would serve as an effective thesis, label it **E** in the space provided. If it is ineffective because it is an announcement, a statement of fact, or a title, label it **I**.

_____ a. Search engines like Google provide access to enormous amounts of information on a subject.

_____ b. The essay will concern the growing popularity of graphic novels.

_____ c. The Best Way to Improve Public Education.

_____ d. Unless many Americans change their exercise habits, they face a future of bad health.

_____ e. The best way to improve morale in the workplace is to reward people based only on their work performance.

2. Choose one of the sentences that you have identified as ineffective and explain what specific changes you would need to make in order for the sentence to serve as an effective thesis.

Drawing on Prewriting Material to Create a Draft Thesis

In many ways, the development of a draft thesis serves as the bridge between the prewriting and the composing stages of the writing process. Your thesis lets your reader know what is to come in the rest of the paper.

On occasion, you will know the main point of your writing right from the start. You might be asked to write on a particular subject that you already know well or choose one on the basis of your own interest or knowledge. That makes developing a thesis easy—just take the point you want to make and express it in complete sentence form.

More often, however, the actual focus for your essay will spring from your prewriting. Once you've highlighted the ideas that you initially felt held the most promise for development, you should *filter* this material. For instance, you may discover that several of the examples and details are closely connected, suggesting a direction

3

for your essay. Or one of the ideas may simply stand out from the rest, inspiring you to pursue it.

In any case, once you have identified your main idea, you need to develop a thesis that encapsulates this focus. At this point, your thesis is a **draft** that may or may not evolve as you work through the rest of the writing process.

In "Real World 101: What My First Job Taught Me," the sample essay in Chapter 1 (pages 8–11), the main idea came right from the following prewriting:

My first job?–OK, that was GroceryWorld, Junior year in high school. Started with a bad attitude–not really bad, but I didn't know much about being a good worker. I showed up late in the beginning–docked my pay, put a letter in my file. Embarrassed and mad. Didn't know how to work on a team–I'd just concentrate on my own stuff, didn't help the other crewmates. Some of them didn't want to work with me–complained to the boss. The night when the guys helped me finish my aisle and I helped them–finally understood. Messed up on arranging pallets in the backroom–I didn't pay much attention during training. Still see some of those guys in the summer–most have other jobs now. Ava stayed, but she is training to be a manager now. What else did I learn? Compromise? Flexibility? I don't know. Maybe I didn't learn that stuff until I started with the Boys and Girls Club. That incident when the acting supervisor lied and told the boss that I had refused to finish my work before going home. No way!! He said that he would take care of it and then wrote me up. The next day, boss calls me in and showed me the sheet. I almost got fired!!! I'll never trust someone like that again. A really big lesson.

The highlighted ideas identify specific incidents that have greater significance than simple experiences at a first job. Here is a draft thesis that represents this concept:

<table>
<tr><td></td><td>*subject*</td><td>*reaction to the subject*</td></tr>
</table>

Draft Thesis: *My first job at the grocery store* **taught me many important things that had nothing to do with the grocery business.**

MASTERY EXERCISE 2 Developing a Draft Thesis

1. For the Summary Exercise in Chapter 1 and Mastery Exercises 1–4 and the Summary Exercise in Chapter 2, you completed prewritings on a number of subjects. Choose the one that you liked best or that you feel holds the most potential for development. Using the example above to guide you, develop a draft thesis.
2. Create a listing of at least five details or examples that would be good support for your draft thesis. If you need additional details, prewrite again, this time on the main idea expressed in your thesis, to generate the information you need.

Focusing on Strong Supporting Details and Examples

With a draft thesis already created, you need to provide details and examples that offer the strongest support for your main idea. The following ideas, highlighted, circled, or underlined during prewriting, are a good starting point:

- GroceryWorld
- I didn't know much about being a good worker.
- I showed up late in the beginning-docked my pay, put a letter in my file.
- Didn't know how to work on a team
- The night when the guys helped me finish my aisle and I helped them-finally understood.
- Messed up on arranging pallets in the backroom-I didn't pay much attention during training.

3

> • That incident when the acting supervisor lied and told the boss that I had refused to finish my work before going home. No way!! He said that he would take care of it and then wrote me up. The next day, boss calls me in and showed me the sheet. I almost got fired!!! I'll never trust someone like that again. A really big lesson.

Of course, these ideas alone aren't enough to constitute an entire essay even once they are expressed in complete sentences. They are merely starting points to be explained in greater detail and combined with other ideas that you develop in order to support your thesis.

Once you have identified likely supporting ideas and details, you should combine any related points and then consider the best way to arrange the information so that it fully communicates your message to your reader. This order will serve as a tentative blueprint for the body of your essay. Common methods of arrangement, all discussed in greater detail in Chapter 4 (pages 45–49), include

- **chronological order**—arrangement on the basis of time
- **spatial order**—arrangement on the basis of physical proximity to something else
- **emphatic order**—arrangement on the basis of significance or importance relative to other supporting ideas

Here again is the draft thesis about lessons learned from a first job:

Draft Thesis: My first job at the grocery store taught me many important things that had nothing to do with the grocery business.

The thesis emphasizes that the lessons were important, so emphatic order, which involves ranking ideas from strong to stronger to strongest, would seem a good choice.

Among the supporting ideas, the information about the need to pay close attention to avoid repeatedly making mistakes is certainly important. More important is the material about the need to be punctual. Even more important are the ideas about the need to be a good team player. But most important of all—and already the most developed point in the prewriting—are the details concerning the need to be careful about whom you should trust while on the job. The following list reflects the preliminary order:

My first job at the grocery store taught me many important things that had nothing to do with the grocery business.

1. Messed up on arranging pallets in the backroom—I didn't pay much attention during training.
2. I showed up late in the beginning—docked my pay, put a letter in my file.
3. I didn't know much about being a good worker.

   Didn't know how to work on a team.

   The night when the guys helped me finish my aisle and I helped them—finally understood.
4. That incident when the acting supervisor lied and told the boss that I had refused to finish my work before going home. No way!! He said that he would take care of it and then wrote me up. The next day, boss calls me in and showed me the sheet. I almost got fired!!! I'll never trust someone like that again. A really big lesson.

Rather than being just an unfocused listing of ideas, these details now serve as a plan for an essay.

MASTERY EXERCISE 3 **Identifying Solid Supporting Ideas and Establishing a Preliminary Order**

1. For Mastery Exercise 2 (page 27), you developed a draft thesis and generated five details or examples that could be used as support. Now turn each of the details or examples into complete sentences.
2. Using the discussion on developing a preliminary order (pages 28–29) to guide you, arrange the details or examples in a way that you feel best communicates your meaning to your reader.

Amplifying: Transforming Writer-Centered Ideas to Reader-Centered Sentences and Paragraphs

With a plan for development in place, the next step is to **amplify** the prewriting ideas—to express them more completely, clearly, and correctly while adding other details, examples, and illustrations when appropriate. As you do so, you need to keep your reader's needs in mind.

At this point, the ideas you generated during prewriting are likely *writer centered*. In other words, because they are your ideas, they make sense to you in their current, limited form. They won't necessarily make sense to anyone else, however, until you make them *reader centered*—presented in correct sentence form, with enough detail that someone without your specific background and experience can understand the point you are making.

The secret to making your writing reader centered and meeting your reader's needs is to think of yourself *before* you learned what you now know about your subject. How much information did you need in order to understand this subject? What specific examples and details helped you make sense of it? Your reader will need at least the same amount and degree of information that you needed. Using a **Reader Evaluation Checklist** is a way to make sure that your supporting information meets the needs of your reader. To use the Reader Evaluation Checklist below, simply insert your topic in the blank spaces and then write your answers to the questions.

READER EVALUATION CHECKLIST

❏ What does the average reader need to know about _____?

❏ What does the average reader already know about _____?

❏ What information would help the average reader better understand _____?

❏ What did I find the hardest to understand about _____ at first?

❏ What helped me to figure out _____?

❏ What's the best example or explanation I can give the average reader about _____?

As you answer these questions, you will also focus on the examples or explanations that your reader will need in order to see your point.

Consider this detail from the prewriting on lessons learned from a first job:

Writer-Centered Information:	The night when the guys helped me finish my aisle and I helped them—finally understood.

As it currently stands, this material isn't clear, complete, or correct, and, as a result, it doesn't communicate its full meaning.

Now consider the same information, expressed in reader-centered form:

Reader-Centered Information:	On many nights, I was in charge of restocking the dairy case, which took about an hour. Then I would join my crewmate for another hour in the frozen food aisle. After we finished, we had to join the rest of our team to take care of stock shortages throughout the rest of the store. If any one of us didn't finish a job, the entire crew fell behind and had to face a very unhappy supervisor the next shift. That taught me that when you help teammates, you help yourself.

As you can see, this reader-centered version is vastly superior. It has been amplified and now includes additional sentences that explain the original information. As a result, it is far clearer and more complete than the writer-centered version. And the entire passage is expressed in correct sentence form, ensuring that a reader will be able to follow the point being presented.

MASTERY EXERCISE 4   Amplifying to Turn Writer-Centered Information into Reader-Centered Material

1. The following five statements are writer centered. Choose three and explain what specifically is needed to make each statement reader centered.
   a. I want a job in this field because of the rewards and challenges involved.
   b. Some urban legends seem almost believable.
   c. This activity holds more potential for injury than people think.

3

     d. Society has truly benefited from this technological innovation.

     e. Young people just don't seem as interested in it today as they used to be.

2. For Mastery Exercise 3 (page 29), you turned five previously generated details or examples into complete sentences. Now, using the discussion and examples above, including the Reader Evaluation Checklist, amplify to make each of these sentences more reader centered.

Creating an Effective Introduction and Conclusion

The ultimate success of an essay depends in part on the effectiveness of two specialized sections: the **introduction** and the **conclusion**. These parts of the essay provide vital context for the reader concerning the message and purpose of the document.

    The specific role of the introduction is to express the main idea of the essay—the thesis—while engaging the interest of the reader and indicating what will follow in the body. In terms of structure, making the thesis the first sentence of the introduction, with the sentences that follow it clarifying the point, is sometimes a good strategy. Other times, placing the thesis toward the end of the introduction, with the initial sentences stirring the reader's interest, works well. The ultimate decision always depends on what arrangement does the best job of establishing the subject and inspiring someone to continue reading.

    Consider this draft introduction for "Real World 101: What My First Job Taught Me," the essay developed from the freewriting on lessons from a first job (page 26):

> My first job at the grocery store taught me many important things that had nothing to do with the grocery business. I learned about paying attention to directions and punctuality. I also learned how important it is to be a team player. Most of all, I learned to be more careful about whom to trust on the job because of an instance that almost got me fired.

As you can see, the thesis opens this paragraph, letting the reader know the point of the essay right from the start.

When it comes to creating an effective introduction, you may also find a number of proven techniques useful. For example, to create reader interest, you can sometimes strengthen your thesis by including

- an **anecdote**—a brief, entertaining story that emphasizes the thesis
- **pertinent facts** or **statistics**
- a **relevant saying** or **quotation**
- a **rhetorical question**—a type of question not to be answered but to provoke thought or discussion

The job of the conclusion is to bring an essay to a logical and appropriate close, offering a last word on the subject while generally restating the significance of the thesis and the supporting paragraphs in the body. In general, conclusions don't present new information in detail. The place for the presentation of new ideas and examples is in the body of the essay.

Here's the draft conclusion for "Real World 101: What My First Job Taught Me":

The lessons I learned on my first job are really helping me now. Whenever someone gives me instructions, I now listen carefully. I also show up on time and try my best to help my co-workers. Most important, I never depend on anyone else to complete my work. I made the mistake of trusting someone, and I almost lost my job as a result.

Even in draft form, this conclusion is effective, restating the significance of the thesis and the supporting ideas and echoing the points presented in the introduction and the body.

A number of other techniques are available to create an effective conclusion. For example, you might include

- an anecdote that embodies the emphasis of the introduction and body
- a question that requests additional examination or analysis of the subject

- a quotation that encapsulates the point that has been made in the essay
- a list of ideas or issues related to the point of the document

As with an effective introduction, the exact technique—or combination of techniques—that you use to create a solid conclusion always depends on what does the best job of helping you impress your point on your reader one last time.

MASTERY EXERCISE 5 Working on Introductions and Conclusions

1. Using the discussion and examples of effective draft introductions above to guide you, create a draft introduction for the essay you have been developing as you've worked through the various Mastery Exercises in this chapter.
2. Of the alternate techniques for developing a conclusion (pages 33–34), which one do you think might prove useful as you develop a draft conclusion for your essay? Why? Explain your reasoning.

Creating a Rough Draft and a First Draft

With a thesis and promising supporting ideas developed, the next step is to create a **first draft**—a complete version of the essay. A first draft essay doesn't have to be perfect. Rather, it just needs to be complete and ready for the next stage in the writing process: **revision**.

Actually, you should always create two initial versions of an essay: a *rough draft* and a *first draft*. The rough draft is the first complete version, but it is for your eyes only. Once this rough draft is complete, take a brief break and then check it quickly for any obviously awkward or unclear spots and any noticeable errors in form. Address these problems, and you will have your first draft.

You should use a computer to prepare your rough and first drafts. The various word-processing tools make it easier to eliminate problem spots as you work through the writing process. You might consider double- or triple-spacing your draft to leave room to make corrections or add information by hand. If you can't use a computer, write on every other line, again with the idea that you can more easily make adjustments.

So what happens when you follow these steps? Here is the first draft of "Real World 101: What My First Job Taught Me," with the key ideas from the prewriting, some of them adapted a bit, highlighted:

Real World 101: What My First Job Taught Me

My first job at the grocery store taught me many important things that had nothing to do with the grocery business. I learned about paying attention to directions and punctuality. I also learned how important it is to be a team player. Most of all, I learned to be more careful about whom to trust on the job because of an instance that almost got me fired.

I had three days of training during my first week at GroceryWorld. The training instructor lectured us about the right way to arrange the grocery pallets in the warehouse. But I didn't pay attention to the instructions, and I made so many mistakes that the crew chief yelled at me publicly and put a warning letter in my file. It was a really embarrassing situation.

My first job taught me the importance of being on time. I used to be late for everything before I got this job. I even showed up late for my grandparents' anniversary party. They had been married for 55 years. My grandfather, who had been in the Air Force until he retired, died last year. Anyway, when I got my paycheck for my first two weeks of work, I found out that my pay was docked a quarter hour of my pay for every time I was late. A note was also stapled to my check that said I would be fired if my lateness continued. From that time on, I began to make being on time a priority.

On many nights, I was in charge of restocking the dairy case, which took about an hour. Then I would join my crewmate for another hour in the frozen food aisle. After we finished, we had to join the rest

3

of our team to take care of stock shortages throughout the rest of the store. If any one of us didn't finish a job, the entire crew fell behind and had to face a very unhappy supervisor the next shift. That taught me that when you help teammates, you help yourself.

The most important lesson I learned was not to trust someone else to finish up my own work. One night, when I fell behind in my work, the acting supervisor told me that he would finish up for me. The next day, I was called into the store manager's office. She held up the shift assessment sheet for the previous night where the acting supervisor had written that I had refused to complete my work for the night. I told the manager that I was sorry, that I must have misunderstood what the acting supervisor had said. I never made that mistake again.

The lessons I learned on my first job are really helping me now. Whenever someone gives me instructions, I now listen carefully. I also show up on time and try my best to help my co-workers. Most important, I never depend on anyone else to complete my work. I made the mistake of trusting someone, and I almost lost my job as a result.

This first draft essay is not perfect, but it doesn't have to be at this stage. Instead, a first draft just needs to be a complete version—a document with an introduction that directs the reader, a series of paragraphs in the body offering support for the thesis, and a conclusion. Like any first draft, this one holds promise. Before it fulfills this promise, however, the remaining weaknesses and errors need to be identified and addressed. In other words, it is ready for the next stage in the writing process: **revision**.

MASTERY EXERCISE 6 **Evaluating a First Draft Essay**

1. Take another look at the first draft of "Real World 101: What My First Job Taught Me." In your view, which of the paragraphs is most effective? Why? And which paragraph is least effective? Why?

2. Like most first drafts, the first draft of "Real World 101: What My First Job Taught Me" has some weaknesses to be addressed. What section of this essay needs the most attention? What about this detail, example, or paragraph leads you to this conclusion?

Summary Exercise

1. For Mastery Exercise 2 (page 27), you developed a draft thesis for an essay and generated some potential supporting ideas. Then for the rest of the Mastery Exercises in the chapter, you continued work on different aspects of this draft essay. Now, following the discussion and examples throughout this chapter, develop a rough draft of about 500 words. Or, if you'd prefer to start work on another essay, choose one of the following subjects, prewrite on it, and follow the steps outlined in Mastery Exercises 2–5 to create a rough draft.

- Professional sports and performance-enhancing drugs
- An activity or hobby that you wish you had more time for
- Cheating in the classroom

2. Review the material on amplifying to create reader-centered material (pages 30–31). Put a checkmark next to the detail or example that is most reader centered in your rough draft, and circle any detail or example that needs to be more reader centered.

3. In your view, which is more effective in your rough draft, your introduction or your conclusion? What about this section makes it more successful?

4. Take a break of at least several hours, and then scan your rough draft again for any obviously awkward or unclear spots and any noticeable errors in form. Eliminate these problems and create the first draft of your essay.

Revising

Understanding the Revising Stage

Once you have completed a draft of your essay, you need to take a break of a day or so. This way you will bring a rested and refreshed eye to the final stage of the writing process, **revising**, during which you *refine* and then *polish* your draft. Think of this stage as what the word itself says, as *re-vision*, that is, as seeing again. Revision consists of three phases:

- *reassessing*, examining your first draft to see what already works and what still needs work
- *redrafting*, addressing remaining problem spots by adjusting existing material and generating new material
- *editing*, tightening and then proofreading your essay to eliminate errors in form that would distract your reader from your subject

When you follow these three steps, the result is a greatly improved version of your initial draft.

Take a look at the following figure of the writing process, which illustrates how revision works:

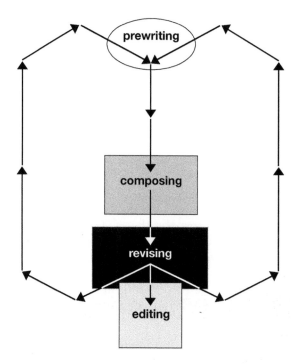

As the previous chapters indicate, after you prewrite, you move to composing and completing a draft essay. Next, as the arrows in this illustration show, you move on to revising.

But notice that the arrows flow from revising back to prewriting. That's because the writing process is *recursive*, which means that you move back through steps as you complete the process. It works this way: You first **reassess** your first draft to identify areas that still need work. Once you identify any gaps and weaknesses, you will often need to head back to prewriting to generate additional information so that you can **redraft** and address these problems. The arrows then continue back through composing, leading you eventually to **editing**. The result is a polished draft.

4 Reassessing for Unity, Coherence, and Effective Language

When you reassess an essay, you reexamine it closely, focusing on several factors that influence its ultimate success. In particular, you need to evaluate your draft for

- unity
- coherence
- effective language

Evaluating Unity

An essay is **unified** when all the examples, illustrations, and details work together to support the thesis. Therefore, when you reassess your first draft, check each element and section to make sure it is directly connected to your main idea—your thesis—and offers specific support.

Consider again the third paragraph of the first draft of "Real World 101: What My First Job Taught Me":

My first job taught me the importance of being on time. I used to be late for everything before I got this job. I even showed up late for my grandparents' anniversary party. They had been married for 55 years. My grandfather, who had been in the Air Force until he retired, died last year. Anyway, when I got my paycheck for my first two weeks of work, I found out that my pay was docked a quarter hour of my pay for every time I was late. A note was also stapled to my check that said I would be fired if my lateness continued. From that time on, I began to make being on time a priority.

The topic sentence—*My first job taught me the importance of being on time*—is certainly directly connected to the thesis. But the details about the grandparents, including the number of years they had been married, the grandfather's time in the Air Force, and his death the previous year, take the paragraph in a different direction. As a result, they disrupt the unity and need to be eliminated and replaced with details and examples that are specifically related to the thesis.

4

Now take a look at the final draft version of the same paragraph:

Another important lesson I learned was about being on time. Before I started this job, lateness was a very bad habit for me. It didn't make any difference whether it was going to school or out with friends or on a date. I could be counted on to be five or ten minutes late, and for the first two weeks on the job, my bad habit continued. But when I received my first paycheck, I realized the immediate consequences of punching in late. Even when I was just a minute late, the company docked me a quarter-hour of my pay. Stapled to my pay slip was a notice stating that if I continued to punch in late, I would be dismissed. When I saw how much money my bad habit was costing me, I changed my ways, both at work and in my personal life.

As you can see, this paragraph, like the first draft version, acknowledges that being late was a widespread problem for the writer. But instead of veering off into the story of the grandparents, this paragraph presents brief examples of non-work-related tardiness and then turns to the effects of failing to be on time at work. Note that this material has also been **amplified**—additional specific information about the episode has been provided to make the picture even clearer for the reader.

MASTERY EXERCISE 1 Considering Unity

1. Read the following passage and identify any sentences that disrupt its unity:

> Several construction projects going on simultaneously around the city have made getting to school a nightmare. For one thing, the highway exit nearest my house has been blocked off for a month./Many accidents occur because drivers don't observe the speed limits on highway exits./The detour to get on the highway forces drivers to go in the opposite direction for almost five miles, which adds almost 15 minutes to my trip. In addition, three main streets that run across town are being widened

4

and repaved, so only one lane is open on each road. ⟨Nobody seems concerned that the trees that were cut down to make room for the project were estimated to be 100 years old.⟩On most days, traffic backs up for almost a mile on each of these routes, especially during the early morning rush hour, delaying drivers for at least 10 minutes.⟨To make things even worse, three of the parking lots at the college are being reconstructed. Students who don't arrive by 7:30 have to park in the annex parking lots, and these lots are twice as far from the academic buildings as the other lots are.⟨Apparently city and state transportation officials failed to check with each other about their construction plans. As a result, my normal 20-minute commute to school now takes me almost a full hour.

2. Briefly explain how the directly related information in the paragraph provides support for the main idea expressed in the topic sentence.

Evaluating Coherence

When an essay is **coherent**, each idea flows smoothly to the next within a framework that is appropriate for the situation. To reassess a first draft for coherence:

- Check for adequate **transition** within and among paragraphs.
- Evaluate the **order of presentation**.

Transition   Think of transition as a bridge that connects or an echo that traces an idea or detail from one sentence, unit, or section to another. You can provide transition for your reader in one of three ways:

- repeating key words and phrases
- using *synonyms*—words with a similar meaning
- including transitional words or expressions

When you repeat a key word or use a synonym in its place, you emphasize it for your reader. Take a look at the following passage, which illustrate how these transitional techniques work:

EXAMPLE: *Representative Grace Waterman* was first elected to *Congress ten years ago. In this decade, she* has addressed the *House* on multiple occasions about the need for

> *greater funding* for *middle school education*. This *money*
> would be used to enhance *basic language and*
> *mathematical skills.*

The italicized words in these sentences show the transitions at work. *She* takes the place of *Representative Grace Waterman, decade* replaces *ten years,* and *House* refers back to *Congress.* In addition, *money* takes the place of *greater funding,* and *basic language and mathematical skills* refers back to *middle school education.* Thanks to these transitions, the ideas flow from one sentence to the next with no needless repetition in phrasing.

You can also use the following transitional expressions, grouped according to the types of relationships they indicate, to strengthen transition:

TO ILLUSTRATE OR SUGGEST CAUSE AND EFFECT

accordingly	for example	indeed	particularly
after all	for instance	in fact	specifically
as a result	for one thing	of course	therefore
because	if	overall	thus
consequently			

EXAMPLE: As the forward kicked the ball, the goalie lunged to the right. **As a result**, she was able to deflect the ball as time ran out.

TO ADD, RESTATE, OR EMPHASIZE

again	finally	in conclusion	next
also	further	in other words	too
and	in addition	moreover	to sum up
besides			

EXAMPLE: The number of people beating the high cost of fuel by choosing public transportation has risen in the last two months. **Moreover**, sales of bicycles are at their highest level in 20 years.

TO SHOW TIME OR PLACE

above	currently	once	to the right (left)
after	earlier	presently	under
as soon as	here	since	until
before	immediately	soon	when
below	lately	then	whenever
beyond	now	there	where

4

EXAMPLE: The people waiting for security screening at the airport were initially confused about the delay. **After** TSA officials began to move people to another line, they understood that one of the screening machines had stopped working.

TO COMPARE OR CONTRAST

although	despite	likewise	though
and	even though	nevertheless	yet
as	however	on the other hand	
at the same time	in contrast	regardless	
but	in spite of	still	

EXAMPLE: The bookstore wasn't sure it would be able to get what I had ordered by Wednesday. **However**, I received a call this morning saying that my books were in.

In "Real World 101: What My First Job Taught Me," the third paragraph talks about the importance of being on time for work, and then the fourth paragraph covers the importance of being a good team member. Take another look at the opening sentences of the final draft version of paragraph 4:

Before I started that job, I never gave much thought to working as part of a team. **But** as a member of a five-person work crew, I learned how important good teamwork is. On many nights, **for example**, I was in charge of restocking the dairy case, which took about an hour. **When** I was done, I was supposed to join my crewmate in the frozen food aisle, a job that took one worker over two hours but much less with a helper. **After** the two of us finished there, we had to join the rest of our team, who were assigned to identify and fill gaps in the shelves and restock the end displays in different areas of the store. **If** any one of us didn't finish a job, the entire crew fell behind and had to face a very unhappy supervisor the next shift. That taught me that when you help teammates, you help yourself, and I keep this lesson in mind **now whenever** I face group work of any kind.

This paragraph is effective in part because the transitional words, shown in boldface print, provide connections and keep the ideas flowing smoothly.

MASTERY EXERCISE 2 Considering Coherence

1. Identify the transitions in the following paragraph. Make two lists, one of transitional expressions and the other of any synonyms, pronouns, or repeated words:

   After a 10-year absence, I recently visited the small town where my grandparents lived when I was a child, and I couldn't believe how changed the place was. For one thing, the population has almost doubled, with new houses taking the place of wooded areas and other open spaces. The big dairy farm next to the house my grandparents lived in, for example, is gone, replaced with a housing development containing over thirty homes. During my childhood, there was so little traffic that the town didn't have a single traffic light. Today, so many vehicles are on the roads that the administration installed two round-a-bouts and four sets of traffic lights along Main Road. Near the town square where a beautiful wooded park used to be, a huge shopping plaza has been built, with several national retailers, including a major department store, a well-known electronics store, and a "big box" hardware store. Across the street, the building that used to contain several small businesses is now mostly empty, with only a neighborhood bakery still open. I guess this kind of growth is inevitable, but I was really saddened to find that the town of my childhood has changed so dramatically.

2. Take two of the transitional expressions you have identified and briefly explain how these words connect ideas in the paragraph.

Order of Presentation   How you organize your essay has a great deal to do with how effective it will be. The key is to choose the method of arrangement that makes it easy for your reader to follow and comprehend the point you are making in your essay. Three common methods of organization are *chronological order, spatial order,* and *emphatic order.*

Chronological order is order based on time. This method of arrangement is appropriate any time you need to present events or episodes in the order in which they occurred. On those occasions when you need to provide additional context for your reader, you can use a **flashback**, an episode deliberately presented out of order to give your reader some necessary background to understand the entire event. Sets of instructions, recipes, and other similar documents rely on a variation of chronological order called **linear order**. With linear order, you list the steps involved in the order in which they occur or must be completed.

Look at this paragraph about an upsetting experience at a water park:

A few months ago, I briefly lost sight of my four-year-old daughter, Jacqueline, at a water park, and I am still having nightmares about it. She and I were in the kiddie area, enjoying the wading pool and the small tube ride. After about a half an hour, she wanted to go for a ride on the water slide in this part of the park, so I walked her over to the entrance. The ride consists of a small covered area on top of a platform, with slides coming out in three different directions. I watched as she climbed up a small ladder leading to the covered area, and then I went around to the slide that I assumed she was coming down. When two other children came down instead, I began to panic. Then I heard this shriek from the slide to the right. Too impatient to wait for the main slide, she had gone down the right slide. At the bottom, she went completely under the water and got a mouthful, which startled her, and not seeing her father when she expected to made things worse. I stepped around the corner and hugged her, and the whole event was over. Still, I can't seem to get that minute when I couldn't find her out of my mind, and I guess maybe I never will.

4

As you can see, chronological order makes it easy to make sense of the experience. The writer was at a water park with his daughter *a few months ago*. *After* spending half an hour in one part of the kiddie area, they headed to another ride. He watched his daughter climb up the ladder to ride the slide and *then* went around to the front of the slide. *When* his daughter didn't immediately emerge, he started to panic and *then* heard his daughter's scream. His daughter, not wanting to wait for the main slide, had gone down the slide on the right. The writer stepped to the other slide and hugged his daughter, ending the event.

Spatial order involves presenting details and examples as they physically appear in relation to each other. Whenever you need to explain where one object, person, or place exists relative to other objects, persons, or places, spatial order is crucial. The key to spatial order is presenting the details in a logical, easy-to-follow way—top to bottom, back to front, left to right, and so on.

Consider the use of spatial order in this paragraph about a campground:

The tornado that struck Springfield last week, the first in the history of the city, caught the area residents completely off guard. People living near the harbor first spotted a waterspout moving across the water toward the shore and alerted city officials. The tornado hit the picnic grove behind the beach dead on. It knocked down, uprooted, or shredded all the trees, leaving an enormous pile of trunks and branches on the edge of the beach. Directly behind the grove, the building containing the changing and shower facilities looked like a bomb had hit it. The roof had ripped open lengthwise, with a huge section of it lying to the right of the structure, and the back wall had blown out. In the parking lot to the left of the building, a small pickup truck had been tossed, upside down, on top of an SUV, and debris a couple of feet deep covered the surface of the lot. All in all, an area the size of two football fields was just completely destroyed.

4

Spatial order makes it easy to visualize the destruction caused by the tornado. The tornado first appeared as a waterspout *moving across the water.* The grove *behind* the beach received a direct hit, resulting in a huge pile of tree trunks and branches *on the edge of the beach.* The building *directly behind the grove* was heavily damaged, with part of the roof, which had *ripped open lengthwise,* lying *to the right of the structure,* and the back wall had smashed to bits. In the parking lot to the *left of the building,* one vehicle lay *upside down on top of an SUV,* and a pile of rubble *a couple of feet deep* covered *the surface of the lot.* In total, the area of destruction was the *size of two football fields.*

Emphatic order involves arranging the various supporting ideas and details so that they provide the most impact. This organization builds and holds the reader's interest in your subject. Typically, you begin with a strong supporting point, move to a stronger point, move to an even stronger point, and save your strongest example for last.

The first draft of "Real World 101: What My First Job Taught Me" is arranged in emphatic order. Take a look again at the supporting ideas for this essay:

Draft Thesis: My first job at the grocery store taught me many important things that had nothing to do with the grocery business.

- The importance of paying attention to instructions
- The importance of being on time
- The importance of being a good member of a team
- The importance of trusting only those workers who have earned that trust

Paying attention to instructions is important, and being on time is even more important. Being a good crew member is more important still, but learning to judge the honesty and dependability of coworkers is most important of all.

Keep in mind that the importance of supporting examples relative to each other in emphatic order will often be something of a judgment call. In terms of the lessons learned from a first job, for instance, some people might feel that paying attention to details is more important than being on time. The key word here is *judgment*:

4

take the time to consider your way through your supporting examples and have a rationale for the final order you establish.

You may also opt to use more than one method of organization in one essay. For example, in both the first draft and final draft of "Real World 101: What My First Job Taught Me," chronological order plays a role within the paragraphs of the body. This approach makes perfect sense. These paragraphs all feature brief episodes illustrating the lesson learned, episodes that must be presented in the order in which they occurred in order to communicate their full meaning. Therefore, like many things in writing, a combination of approaches is the best choice because it does the best job of expressing the main idea and meeting the needs of the reader.

MASTERY EXERCISE 3 Considering Order

1. For each of the following topics, explain what method of organization—chronological order, spatial order, or emphatic order—you would be likely to employ and why you would make this choice.
   - Public service as a graduation requirement
   - Your dream house
   - A shocking discovery you made
   - Annual mandatory testing of drivers over the age of 65
   - A night out gone wrong
2. A topic can be explored—and organized—in more than one way. In addition, as page 49 explains, sometimes you'll use more than one method of organization to make your ideas more accessible to your reader. Choose one of the subjects above for which you have already identified a likely order of organization, and briefly explain what other method of arrangement or combination of methods could be used to present the material and why you feel this way.

Evaluating Language

The effectiveness of the language you use directly affects your essay. Your goal is to employ *clear* and *specific* terms, phrasing that captures your full meaning. Therefore, check for any vague, general, or nonprecise language as well as for any wording that would be more effective if it were more fully supported with an additional

4

example or detail. When you write, "A nice little dog," your reader has only a general idea of what you mean. But when you write, "An excitable, grayish-tan pug puppy named Mugwump that loves to lick everyone's hands and ears," you create a far more precise picture for your reader.

At the same time, be on the lookout for any indirect or overly wordy expressions. Your goal is writing that is *concise*—brief but to the point. Check for any **deadwood**, vague or general words that add no real meaning to your writing. Common examples of deadwood include *definitely, quite, extremely, somewhat*, and *a lot*. General words such as *very* and *really* are also deadwood, particularly when they are combined with general or subjective words—for instance, *quite warm* or *somewhat difficult*. Replace any expressions from the following list of deadwood with the concise version to its right:

Deadwood	Improved Version
due to the fact that	because
the majority of	most
has the ability to	can
in the near future	soon
prior to	before
completely eliminate	eliminate
come to the realization that	realize
with the exception of	except for
in order that	so
at the present time	now
take action	act
the month of October	October
give a summary of	summarize
mutual cooperation	cooperation
make an assumption	assume

Another way to keep your writing concise is to choose the **active voice** over the **passive voice** when appropriate. With the active voice, the subject does the action:

                          subject   *verb*

Active Voice: The *administration agreed* to the workers' demands.

With a passive voice version, the order of the sentence is reversed, with the subject *receiving* the action:

Passive Voice: The *workers' demands were agreed* to by the

administration.

Both versions are correct, but with the active voice, the reader knows, right from the start and in fewer words, who had agreed to the demands.

Consider the underlined phrases in paragraph 2 of the first draft of "Real World 101: What My First Job Taught Me":

> I had <u>three days of training</u> during my first week at GroceryWorld. The training instructor lectured us about <u>the right way</u> to arrange the grocery pallets in the warehouse. But I didn't pay attention to the instructions, and I made <u>so many mistakes</u> that the crew chief yelled at me publicly and put a warning letter in my file. <u>It was a really embarrassing situation.</u>

This language needs to be adjusted because the wording is vague, general, and nonspecific. What kind of training occurred? What was the right way to arrange the pallets? How many mistakes were made? What made the situation so embarrassing?

Now take a look at the final draft version, with the changes highlighted:

> My first week at GroceryWorld included three days of training during which the trainer explained various duties. For instance, I learned how to take the pallets of groceries from the delivery trucks and arrange them in the storage area of the store. The point was to set up the pallets so that the grocery crews could easily find what they needed, and they wouldn't have to waste time looking for what they needed for the shelves. During my first two weeks on the job, I failed to follow these directions on four occasions. After the fourth time, the

4

crew chief came into the storage area to yell at me. Worse, he complained to my supervisor, who put a written warning in my personnel file. The truly embarrassing thing is that the whole problem was avoidable. The trainer had told me how important the arrangement of the pallets is in terms of productivity. I just hadn't listened very well.

With the language adjusted, there is no longer any question about the training, the correct way to arrange pallets of groceries, the number of mistakes, or the reason for embarrassment. As a result, the paragraph effectively communicates its message to the reader.

MASTERY EXERCISE 4 Considering Language

1. Make the following phrases clear and specific:
   a. an unattractive shirt
   b. a bad storm
   c. a beautiful painting
2. Revise the following passage to make it more direct and concise:
   > Finding the sternum is a very crucial step when you are trying to perform the lifesaving act of giving CPR. The sternum is essentially between the breasts, and you find it by using the fingers on your hand to trace the sternum. Once you find the sternum, you need to find its tip, which is at is end, which you can find just above where the rib cage starts. Once you have found the tip, use two fingers on your hand to help you to measure back from the tip. This is the point at which you will begin the process that will help the unfortunate individual, woman, man, or child who needs your help.
3. Convert the following sentences from passive to active voice and then briefly explain which version of the three sentences—the passive version or the active version—is correct and why you feel this way:
   a. The delicious meal was prepared by student chefs from the nearby culinary school.
   b. The new Stephen King novel was read by me in two days.
   c. The elderly woman's flat tire was changed by a kind truck driver who pulled over in the pouring rain.

Seeking Help from an Objective Reader

4

You are writing your essay to communicate your ideas to someone else, so it makes perfect sense to ask an objective reader to assess it. Anyone who will respond to your writing honestly and fairly—a classmate, a friend, a family member, and so on—is a good choice. The following **Reader Assessment Checklist** will help your reader evaluate your essay and provide useful feedback:

READER ASSESSMENT CHECKLIST

❑ Do you understand the point I am making? Does my thesis clearly state the topic along with my perspective on it? (thesis)

❑ Do I stick to that point all the way through? Does each paragraph relate directly to the thesis? (unity)

❑ Are all my ideas and examples clearly connected and easy to follow? (coherence)

❑ Are the words I've used clear, specific, and concise? (effective language)

❑ Are my introduction and conclusion effective?

❑ What changes do you think I should make?

Take a look at these reader comments in response to the first draft of "Real World 101: What My First Job Taught Me":

> Your essay is good. I know just what you mean—my first job taught me a lot, too. The thesis makes sense, and the paragraphs in the body are all connected to it. I like the introduction because it let me know what you were going to discuss in the rest of the essay. In terms of ways to improve it, maybe you could add some specific details. I was curious about the kind of training you had, and I really wondered about the incident when someone promised to do something and then lied about it. I'd really like to know more about that. I was also confused with the information about your grandparents in the third paragraph. I wasn't sure of the connection of this material to the rest of the essay—should it be eliminated? I work on a team at work, so I liked the stuff about being part of a crew. I am also interested in knowing more about that part of your job. I think these kinds of changes would make your paper even better than it already is.

With your own reassessment and suggestions like these, you are prepared for the next part of the revising process: redrafting.

4 Redrafting

Once you have identified what works in your first draft and what still needs work, you are ready to **redraft** to address the problem spots. Your primary goal at this point is to create a new and improved version. You do this by bringing your ideas into even greater focus for your reader by eliminating all weaknesses in unity, coherence, and language.

You also **amplify** by providing additional specific examples and details to support your ideas and fill any gaps. Keep the transitional expressions *for example* and *for instance* in mind as you amplify. Even if you don't actually include them in the material you add, these expressions will remind you to supply a specific supporting example. They also cue your reader that a specific illustration will follow.

The reader's comments in response to the first draft of "Real World 101: What My First Job Taught Me" indicated interest in the episode concerning an untrustworthy coworker, which appears in the fifth paragraph. The reader suggests explaining this event in greater detail as a way to improve the essay. Now consider the final draft version of this paragraph, which, as the highlighted areas show, has been amplified so that it covers the episode in far more specific detail:

But I learned the most important lesson the hard way when I trusted someone who wasn't trustworthy, and I was almost fired as a result. When my supervisor went on vacation, a worker from another crew, who seemed genuinely nice and easy going, became acting supervisor. One night, when I fell behind in my work, he told me not to worry, that he would finish up for me. The next day, I was called into the store manager's office. She held up the shift assessment sheet from the previous night. On this form, the acting supervisor had written that I had refused to complete my work for the night. I was shocked. I just couldn't believe that someone who appeared to be so nice would tell me to go home and then lie about it. I told the manager that I was sorry, that I must have misunderstood what the acting supervisor had said. The manager accepted my apology but warned me that I would be fired if there were any more problems. That incident taught me that first impressions aren't always accurate and that when something seems too good to be true, it probably is.

This newer version of the paragraph is without question more effective. Rather than just telling about the episode, it uses additional specific details and examples to **show** it to the reader.

You will find redrafting different each time you write. Sometimes you will need to make small adjustments in a number of paragraphs, and other times you will concentrate on a single paragraph or section of your essay. Just remember not to lose sight of the value of redrafting: it helps you make your essay as thorough and informative as possible.

MASTERY EXERCISE 5   Using Redrafting to Improve a Draft

1. The following sentences are too limited in the current form to be effective. Amplify them by adding specific details and examples in the form of a complete sentence or two, after the transitional expressions *for example* or *for instance*.
   a. That YouTube video was the strangest one I have ever seen. For example, _____.
   b. My neighborhood has a lot of things going for it. For instance, _____.
   c. The shutdown of the office computer system created many problems. For example, _____.
2. Using the Reader Assessment Checklist on page 53, evaluate the following brief passage.
   > Sexual abuse is among the worst things that could happen to children. A lot of people don't realize that they come from all over. When I started reading about it, I was surprised. It's important that the public recognize this, too, so that people can do more to support the victims. They have developed a number of techniques to make it easier for them to talk about the abuse. These techniques have been tested and even used in some courtrooms. We need more of these.
3. Using the sample peer response on page 53 to guide you, write a brief note (100–105 words) to the writer indicating what works and what still needs improvement in this passage.

4 Editing: Eliminating Errors

The final step in revision is **editing**, during which you eliminate any remaining errors in form—spelling, punctuation, grammar, usage, and format. Of course, editing isn't a one-time thing. It is likely that you have identified and eliminated obvious errors at every stage of the writing process. But before you hand in your final draft, you need to do a more systematic check, called **proofreading**.

The secret to effective proofreading is to perform this step when you are well rested and free from any distractions. If you are tired or not concentrating fully, you may miss errors that will distract your reader from your good ideas and therefore make your final draft far less successful than it could be.

When you proofread, use the following checklist, which lists the most common writing problems and the abbreviations generally used to identify them in a piece of writing:

PROOFREADING CHECKLIST

❑   Have I eliminated all sentence fragments (*frag*)?

❑   Have I eliminated all comma splices (*cs*)?

❑   Have I eliminated all run-on sentences (*rs*)?

❑   Is the spelling (*sp*) correct throughout?

❑   Is the verb tense (*t*) correct throughout?

❑   Do all subjects agree with their verbs (*s/v agr*)?

❑   Do all pronouns agree with their antecedents (*pro/ant agr*)?

As you do more writing, it won't take you long to discover what errors you are prone to making. For example, you may not have difficulty with sentence fragments or verb tenses but may instead have problems with errors not currently listed, for instance, double negatives or misused modifiers. By the way, don't worry if you do not yet understand these problems or how to solve them. Chapters 15–22 in this book focus on how to recognize and correct various errors in form. In any case, to create a truly useful personal proofreading checklist, simply replace the listings of errors you don't regularly make with the errors that you do tend to make.

Having someone else proofread your final draft is another proven strategy to eliminate errors in form. You might even work with a proofreading partner, checking each other's essays. In addition, take full advantage of any spell-checking or style-checking features on your computer, but *never* rely exclusively on these tools. Despite great advances, computers still don't reason the way humans do, especially in terms of context. If you use the wrong word—"brake" when you actually need "break"—the computer may not catch the error because both words are spelled correctly. Therefore, *always* proofread your paper one more time after using these functions to make sure that you have corrected all the errors.

MASTERY EXERCISE 6 **Correcting Errors through Proofreading**

1. Of the errors in form listed on the **Proofreading Checklist** on page 56, which do you find most difficult to avoid? Why do you think this particular problem troubles you more than the others on the list?

2. Proofread the following passage using the Proofreading Checklist on page 56 as a guide. Make a list of the various errors in form, and provide a corrected version of each.

   Americans and their interactions with nature have changed involvement in such activities as hiking, camping, and hunting have slowly but consistently declined. Of course, early in the history of the United States. People did not generally seek out adventures in nature. But in more modern times, people begin to view nature as a place of beauty to be enjoyed. Though much of the 20th century, for example, recreational hunting and fishing remained popular sports. Backwoods camping trips was mainstays for many families, over the last 25 years, however, participation in such activities has apparently waned. In some cases, their has even been a decline in vacation trips to well-known U.S. National Parks. Such as Yellowstone or the Grand Canyon. The exact reason for this shift away from these kinds of outdoor pursuits aren't clear. Although some people point to the emergence of such innovations as the Internet and video games. Regardless of the cause, a person in the United States is less likely to place a trip into the wilderness at the top of their vacation wish list today.

   Check your answers against the corrected version on page 63.

4   Looking Again at the Final Draft

So what results when you follow the steps in the revising process? The first draft of "Real World 101: What My First Job Taught Me" appeared in Chapter 3 (pages 35–36), and several of the paragraphs have appeared in this chapter in both first draft and final draft forms. Here again is the complete final draft. The highlighted areas indicate material that has been adapted or added, and the annotations accompanying the essay explain how the changes transformed something good into something better, which is always the goal of revising:

Real World 101: What My First Job Taught Me

This new material in the introduction clarifies the focus of the fourth supporting idea and makes the introduction stronger as a result.

My first job was as a part-time clerk at a grocery store, and my experiences on the job taught me much more than how to maintain inventory and stock shelves. I learned how important it was to pay attention to directions and to be on time for every shift. I also learned that the way to earn respect and to make the job easier was to be a good co-worker. Most important, I learned that when it comes to work I'm responsible to complete, I shouldn't trust someone else to complete it. That mistake almost cost me my job.

My first week at GroceryWorld included three days of training during which the trainer explained various duties. For instance, I learned how to take the pallets of groceries from the delivery trucks and arrange them in the storage area of the store. The point was to set up the pallets so that the grocery crews could easily

These new details specify the correct way to arrange the pallets, the exact number of mistakes made, and the reason for embarrassment. The point of the paragraph is now clearer for the reader.

4

find what they needed, and they wouldn't have to waste time looking for what they needed for the shelves. During my first two weeks on the job, I failed to follow these directions on four occasions. After the fourth time, the crew chief came into the storage area to yell at me. Worse, he complained to my supervisor, who put a written warning in my personnel file. The truly embarrassing thing is that the whole problem was avoidable. The trainer had told me how important the arrangement of the pallets is in terms of productivity. I just hadn't listened very well.

These new examples of non-work-related tardiness replace the details that disrupted the unity of the paragraph.

Another important lesson I learned was about being on time. Before I started this job, lateness was a very bad habit for me. It didn't make any difference whether it was going to school or out with friends or on a date. I could be counted on to be five or ten minutes late, and for the first two weeks on the job, my bad habit continued. But when I received my first paycheck, I realized the immediate consequences of punching in late. Even when I was just a minute late, the company docked me a quarter-hour of my pay. Stapled to my pay slip was a notice stating that if I continued to punch in late, I would be dismissed. When I saw how much money my bad habit was costing me, I changed my ways, both at work and in my personal life.

This new material at the end underscores to a greater degree the effect that this experience has had on the writer's behavior.

4

Before I started that job, I never gave much thought to working as part of a team. But as a member of a five-person work crew, I learned how important good teamwork is. On many nights, for example, I was in charge of restocking the dairy case, which took about an hour. When I was done, I was supposed to join my crewmate in the frozen food aisle, a job that took one worker over two hours but much less with a helper. After the two of us finished there, we had to join the rest of our team, who were assigned to identify and fill gaps in the shelves and restock the end displays in different areas of the store. If any one of us didn't finish a job, the entire crew fell behind and had to face a very unhappy supervisor the next shift. That taught me that when you help teammates, you help yourself, and I keep this lesson in mind now whenever I face group work of any kind.

These two sentences provide the transition needed to eliminate the abrupt opening of the first draft version of this paragraph.

This new sentence underscores the effect that this experience has had on the writer.

But I learned the most important lesson the hard way when I trusted someone who wasn't trustworthy, and I was almost fired as a result. When my supervisor went on vacation, a worker from another crew, who seemed genuinely nice and easy going, became acting supervisor. One night, when I fell behind in my work, he told me not to worry, that he would finish up for me. The next day, I was called into the store manager's

These details help to reinforce how serious the consequences might have been while also adding information that provides necessary background and explains why the writer was willing to put faith in the acting supervisor.

The additional details and examples paint a clearer picture for the reader of the seriousness of the situation.

office. She held up the shift assessment sheet from the previous night. On this form, the acting supervisor had written that I had refused to complete my work for the night.

I was shocked. I just couldn't believe that someone who appeared to be so nice would tell me to go home and then lie about it. I told the manager that I was sorry, that I must have misunderstood what the acting supervisor had said. The manager accepted my apology but warned me that I would be fired if there were any more problems. That incident taught me that first impressions aren't always accurate and that when something seems too good to be true, it probably is.

ese details lp to reinforce w serious the nsequences ght have been ile also adding ormation that ovides cessary ckground and plains why the iter was lling to put th in the acting pervisor.

I work with kids at the local Boys and Girls Club now, and the lessons I learned on my first job are really helping me. Today, whenever someone gives me instructions, I listen carefully. I also make showing up on time a priority, and I do my best to be a good worker and dependable crewmember. But most important, I now try to use good judgment before I put my trust in someone because if the person isn't worthy of that trust, the consequences can be pretty severe.

This new opening sentence clarifies where the writer is applying these lessons, and the rephrased final sentence strongly reiterates the point of the strongest of the supporting paragraphs.

Keep in mind that effective revision involves working through multiple drafts before your essay is as effective as it could be. But as the final draft of "Real World 101: What My First Job Taught Me" demonstrates, the work involved in revision is always worth it.

4   MASTERY EXERCISE 7   **Evaluating a Final Draft**

1. Consider the various changes in the final draft of "Real World 101: What My First Job Taught Me," which have been highlighted. In your view, what is the single most effective change? Explain why you have made this choice.
2. Imagine that a classmate is the author of this essay and has asked you to review the paper before handing it in for grading. Using the Reader Assessment Checklist, page 53, evaluate the essay and then write a brief note (100–150 words) to the writer in which you provide your reaction.

Summary Exercise

1. For the Summary Exercise at the end of Chapter 3 (page 37), you created a first draft essay of about 500 words on one of the topics presented. Now you need to revise that essay. Or, if you'd prefer, choose one of the following topics, work your way through the writing process, and develop a first draft essay of about 500 words:

   - Your stand on a controversial issue in the news today
   - How kids' pastimes and hobbies have changed since you were a child
   - How to remain calm during a stressful time

2. Reassess your first draft essay considering its unity, coherence (including transition and order of presentation), and language, using the explanation and examples in this chapter to guide you.

3. Ask an objective reader, perhaps a classmate who is also working on an essay, to use the Reader Assessment Checklist (page 53) to evaluate your first draft.

4. Consider your own assessment and your reader's evaluation, and redraft to address problem spots.

5. Check your essay for any remaining errors in form, using the Proofreading Checklist (page 56) as a guide, and then ask another reader to do the same.

6. After taking a break of a day or so, correct any remaining errors, producing a final draft essay that is *simple* and *clear* in terms of content and *correct* in terms of form.

Correcting Errors through Proofreading, page 57

4

Americans and their interactions with nature have changed.
rs Involvement
~~involvement~~ in such activities as hiking, camping, and hunting have

slowly but consistently declined. Of course, early in the history of the
frag ,people
United States~~.~~ ~~People~~ did not generally seek out adventures in nature.
t began
But in more modern times, people ~~begin~~ to view nature as a place of
sp Through
beauty to be enjoyed. ~~Though~~ much of the 20th century, for example,

recreational hunting and fishing remained popular sports. Backwoods
s/v agr were   *cs . Over*
camping <u>trips</u> ~~was~~ mainstays for many families, ~~over~~ the last 25 years,
sp apparently
however, participation in such activities has ~~apparantly~~ waned. In
sp there
some cases, ~~their~~ has even been a decline in vacation trips to well-
frag ,such
known U.S. National Parks. ~~Such~~ as Yellowstone or the Grand

Canyon. The exact <u>reason</u> for this shift away from these kinds of
s/v agr isn't frag ,although
outdoor pursuits ~~aren't~~ clear. ~~Although~~ some people point to the

emergence of such innovations as the Internet and video games.
pro/ant agr people   *are*
Regardless of the cause, ~~a people~~ in the United States ~~is~~ less likely to

place a trip into the wilderness at the top of <u>their</u> vacation wish list

today.

PART II

The Modes: Considering the Organizational Strategies and Approaches

5

Narration

Understanding Narration

When you need to tell a story—to relate a sequence of events making up an entire episode—**narration** is the mode that you turn to. Narration encapsulates time and incidents while focusing on the key moments that a reader needs to know to understand the full significance of the incident or occurrence.

An essay concerning a workplace encounter with an out-of-control patron would call for narration. So would an elementary school field trip to a museum during which you became separated from your classmates. Because it creates involvement, narration is an important technique to master.

The Elements of an Effective Narrative Essay

To make your narrative essay effective, be sure to include the elements described on the following pages.

Sufficient Transition

As you are developing a narration essay, you will find the following transitional expressions particularly useful:

after	during	later	soon
before	first (second, etc.)	meanwhile	then

Chronological Order

The order in which you present your information directly affects your reader's ability to make sense of it. With narration, **chronological order** is often the ideal method of arrangement to use. Chronological order, as Chapter 4 (pages 46–47) explains, involves presenting a series of events as they actually occurred in time so that your reader can more easily follow and understand the significance of the entire episode.

Appropriate Flashbacks and Flashforwards

When the situation calls for it, flashbacks and flashforwards can help give your reader insight to understand a situation more fully. These devices interrupt the narrative flow to provide the reader with information necessary to understand the point being made.

With a flashback, you include an event that occurred *before* the incident you are relating in order to emphasize or explain the importance of that particular point. Imagine you are writing an essay about a time you went to pay the restaurant bill while on a date and discovered to your horror that your wallet was empty. To make it easier for your reader to understand what happened, you might include a flashback in which you remember taking out your cash to count it at home and then leaving the bills on your bureau.

With a flashforward, you interject information about something that occurred *after* a part of the episode in order to accentuate or explain the significance of some point within the sequence. Think of an essay about a camping trip during which you woke up to discover a garter snake sharing your sleeping bag. You might include a flashforward detailing how, at a cookout a few months after this experience, you dumped a plate of food on a relative when you saw a similar snake under your chair.

An Effective Point of View

Point of view refers to the perspective from which you relate the experience. With narration, you will likely turn to either *first-person point of view* or *third-person point of view*.

Employ the first-person point of view when you write from the vantage point of a participant, for instance, in an essay about your first trip to a hospital emergency room. With first person, you will use the personal pronouns *I, me, my*, and *mine* as you discuss your actions.

Use the third-person point of view when you write from the vantage point of an observer of others, for example, in an essay about an argument you witnessed at a restaurant that turned violent. Because you focus on others with third-person narration, you will use pronouns like *she, her, he, him, they, them*, and so on.

A Thorough Presentation

With a narrative essay, you have two important, interrelated objectives concerning your supporting examples and details: including sufficient information while not getting off-subject. You fulfill these two goals by keeping your focus on your intent as indicated in your thesis.

An essay about the problems you faced when you put off a school project until the night before it was due, only to encounter complication after complication, might feature a thesis like this:

From a two-hour power failure to a computer meltdown that destroyed all my notes and visuals, the business law project that I tried to complete at the last minute quickly became a nightmare.

The body of the essay should contain specific examples of the problems as they occurred. *First*, the power went out, and *then* when the power came back on, you were unable to find hard copies of two of the articles that you had intended to use as support. *Next*, you received a call from a friend who had broken down on the highway and who was desperate for a ride. *Finally*, your computer screen went blank—the motherboard had failed.

But including additional information about your later discussion with the customer service department of the computer manufacturer would be inappropriate. As interesting as this conversation might have been, it is only marginally connected to your struggle to finish the project for your business law class and thus would take your essay offtrack. Therefore, because it isn't directly connected to your thesis, you shouldn't include this material.

A Narrative Essay Checklist

Once you complete a draft of a narrative essay, use the following **Narrative Essay Checklist** to evaluate it and then ask an objective reader to do the same.

NARRATIVE ESSAY CHECKLIST

❏ Does the introduction set the scene for the sequence of events to follow?

❏ Is there sufficient transition to guide the reader?

❏ Does the document employ chronological order to make the time frame of the events clear for the reader?

❏ Are flashbacks and flashforwards provided whenever information from outside the primary sequence is needed?

❏ Is the point of view—first or third person—appropriate for and consistent with the document's purpose?

❏ Does the document supply a sufficient number of examples and details to keep an audience engaged without becoming side-tracked?

5

Use the answers to these questions to help you revise your essay and create an effective final draft.

Analysis: Examining an Annotated Narrative Essay

This introduction sets the scene for the sequence of events to follow. It offers details that create context in terms of the nature of the trip. In addition, the final sentence serves as the thesis, indicating the specific focus.

The Mummy and Me: My Misadventure at the Art Museum

A tradition for all fourth graders at my elementary school was a spring field trip to the Metropolitan Museum of Art in Center City. The journey from my town to the museum took almost an hour and a half, and for most of us, it was the longest we had ever traveled. When that big yellow school bus pulled up to the school door to take my fourth-grade classmates and me to the museum on that May morning, I was so excited I almost couldn't catch my breath. Little did I know that a few hours later, I would also find it difficult to catch my breath, this time for an entirely different reason.

Note that the essay is told from the **first-person point of view**.

Thesis Statement

On the long ride to the museum, my classmates and I had a great time, singing, yelling back and forth, and laughing. We got so loud at one point that Mrs. Moore, the school's art teacher, threatened to make the bus driver turn around and head home. After we quieted down, she talked to us about the different exhibits and works of art that we would see in the museum. She also stressed the importance of not wandering away from our classmates, reminding us all, "It's a big place. Stay with the group!"

As this paragraph indicates, the essay is arranged in **chronological order**. The story begins in the morning and moves forward in time through the rest of the day.

5

Note how **transitional words and expressions**—*at one point, After also*—keep the sequence flowing.

When we arrived, I could see that Mrs. Moore wasn't exaggerating. The museum building, which reminded me of a castle, covered almost two full city blocks. The lobby where we picked up our admission passes was the largest room I had ever been in. As I waited to get my pass, I looked around and noticed five or six corridors

The **thorough discussion**, with plenty of **specific details and examples**, draws the reader into the story.

Note how **transitional words and expressions**— *When, As I waited*—keep the sequence flowing.

leading to different areas of the museum, and all of these corridors looked pretty much the same. Directly behind the huge mahogany desk at the entrance was a marble staircase leading up to the other four floors of the museum. Overwhelmed by the sheer size of the place, I promised myself that I would do exactly as Mrs. Moore said and stay with the group.

For the rest of the morning, we looked at the paintings in the different rooms on the first floor. While we moved from area to area on the first floor, Mrs. Moore told us stories and told us details to look for in particular works. We would then crowd around the works she had discussed, looking for the features she had identified. I was shorter than most of my classmates, so I often had to wait until the rest of them had looked at a painting before I could get a good look at it. As a result, I quickly found myself at the very end of the group.

After eating our lunch in the museum cafeteria at the back of the first floor, we headed up to the second floor to look at the artwork from ancient civilizations. I was especially interested in this part of the museum because the Egyptian exhibits were there, including an actual mummy. In fact, I was so excited about seeing a mummy

The level of **specific detail** here makes it easy to understand what the morning was like for the students on the field trip. The writer's height, important to the story, is also emphasized.

Note how **transitional words and expressions**— *For the rest of the morning, While, then*—keep the sequence flowing.

5

Key details concerning interest in mummies and the second staircase appear here, giving the reader needed background to understand the events to follow.

up close that I didn't take the time to pay attention to my surroundings. If I had, I would have realized that although the staircase we were using looked exactly like the one I saw when we entered the museum, this one was at the opposite end of the building.

Our first stop on the second floor was the Egyptian displays. I wasn't the only one fascinated by the mummy. In fact, just about everyone from my school was crowding around the display, and for quite a while, I couldn't get much of a look. While I was waiting for my classmates to finish examining the artifact, I kept busy by looking at the elaborate sarcophagus across from the mummy.

The **thorough explanation** of the difficulty the writer initially faced in seeing the mummy makes it easy for the reader to understand the events that follow.

5

Note how **transitional words and expressions**— *After what seemed like an hour, When, then*—keep the sequence flowing.

After what seemed like an hour, the crowd moved on and I could finally get a close look at the mummy. When I reached the display, I was instantly mesmerized. I couldn't believe that I was looking at someone who had lived thousands of years ago. I read and reread the card that explained who the mummy was, where he had lived, and what he likely died from, and then I just stared at the dark, leathery face.

Chronological order continues to guide the reader through the different elements making up the story, and **specific examples and details** make the situation clear for the reader.

When I finally looked up, I was shocked. All of my classmates were gone. I immediately headed out of the room and down the corridor

The **specific examples and details** here explain how the writer became separated from the rest of the group, at the same time explaining the feelings this separation created. The **flashback** takes the reader back to the original warning, presented in the second paragraph, emphasizing the fear the writer felt.

As **chronological order** brings the story to a close, the **key examples and details** here explain how the writer avoided being left behind at the museum.

toward the stairs, but as I reached the open area, everything looked different. The stairs and the different corridors seemed backward, and I couldn't tell where I had been and where my classmates might have gone. I was so confused and scared that I couldn't think clearly, and I didn't know what to do. I just stood there, trying not to cry while also trying to catch my breath. In my head, over and over, I could hear the words, "It's a big place. Stay with the group!"

Just when panic was about to consume me completely, a museum guide noticed me and asked if I was with the group from the Truman School. After I nodded, she said that I was at the wrong staircase, that the group had just headed down the front stairs to the waiting bus. She pointed me in the right direction, and I just sprinted down the hallway to the correct set of stairs. From the top of the stairs, I could see the last of the group, with Mrs. Moore at the very end, heading out the door, so I ran down the stairs two at a time to catch up. When I reached Mrs. Moore, I mumbled something about having had to go the bathroom and re-joined the group.

Everybody was tired, so the bus ride back to school was much quieter. For most of the trip, I kept my eyes closed and tried to

Note how **transitional words and expressions**— *Just when panic was about to consume me completely, After I nodded, When*—help to complete the sequence.

5

This conclusion restates the significance of the episode by again including the teacher's warning that the writer accidentally violated and that led to some moments of intense fear. ⟶ sleep. Mrs. Moore probably thought that I was happily dreaming about the mummy or some of the works of art she had exposed us to. Instead, I kept seeing myself standing at the top of the stairs with no idea what to do or where to go, hearing her say over and over, "It's a big place. Stay with the group!"

MASTERY EXERCISE 1   Responding to the Annotated Essay

1. The second paragraph includes a direct quotation from the teacher leading the field trip: "It's a big place. Stay with the group!" How would the effect have been different if a paraphrase had been used rather than the teacher's exact words? And do you agree with the choice to repeat the same quotation in two other places, in paragraph 8 and in the final paragraph?
2. In your judgment, which paragraph in the body does the best job of offering support for the main idea presented in the thesis? What about this paragraph leads you to this conclusion?
3. Chronological order is clearly the dominant order of arrangement, a logical choice for a narrative essay. But what role does *spatial order*—the method of arrangement stressing the relative physical relationship among people, places, and things—play in the essay? (For more on spatial order, see pages 46–47.)

WRITING A NARRATIVE ESSAY A

This essay tells the story of the complications involved in getting separated from classmates, teachers, and chaperones on a school field trip to a museum. Consider field trips that you experienced during your career as an elementary or secondary student. What was the most unusual, humorous, sobering, or surprising event that occurred during one of those trips? Now use narration to tell that story in an essay of about 500 words.

WRITING A NARRATIVE ESSAY B

As this essay clearly shows, the experience of being separated from a group and being lost in an unfamiliar place can be terribly upsetting and stressful, especially for a young child. How upsetting, then, must it have been for the adults in charge of the group? Have you ever been among the people in charge of a gathering, event, meeting, or group when something went wrong for which you were in some way responsible? For this assignment, use narration to tell the story in an essay of about 500 words, being sure to explain in detail what role you played, what you expected would happen, and how things went wrong.

Illustration: Considering a Narrative Essay
TREADING THOUGHTFULLY
Liliana Ibara

When most people think of islands in the South Pacific, their first thoughts likely turn to images of swaying palm trees, golden sands, and crystal blue waters. Behind such idyllic scenes, however, danger sometimes awaits, as Liliana Ibara underscores in the following essay, which originally appeared in the Los Angeles Times. *In her essay, she recounts an experience during a simple visit to a beautiful, secluded spot on the Hawaiian island of Maui, her father's birthplace, that took a dramatic and terrifying turn.*

What goes through a person's mind when what is needed to survive is tantalizingly close but ultimately still out of reach?

People who might drown are advised to kick off their shoes. People who have merely fallen into the water and are going to hop back onto land keep their shoes on. This is why I was clinging to my flip-flops.

I had just left the tide pool where we'd been swimming and was about to sit down and pee when I was swept into the ocean. We were miles from a bathroom—to get here we had taken a dirt road through silver-green pineapple fields and then clambered down a steep path into a cove. At the bottom was a deep pool of still water fed by ocean surges, apparently protected from waves by a natural rock wall. The only other person nearby was a woman videotaping the waves.

My husband Jeremy was still in the tide pool when I knew I was in real trouble. The waves were lifting and lowering, not crashing, so at first I thought I could ride one up to the rocks I'd just left and then scramble to higher rocks. But each time a wave lifted me gently up and in and I curled my fingers around a rock's edge, the retreating wave would pull me back down so hard and fast I couldn't make myself understand it was just the force of water. And then everything was bright white water and I was struggling to get up to the air again, spitting out water, bewildered and terrified.

Finally, Jeremy saw me. I let go of whatever calm I'd been trying to maintain, and of my flip-flops too. I remember Jeremy's face right then—actually I don't know if I'm remembering his face, or his voice, or something else, but I sensed complete helplessness and terror.

Panicked, needing to say something, he told me to swim over to some of the lower rocks. They looked very close, and if you weren't in the water feeling the strength of the surges, it looked doable. It was impossible. The woman on the cliff spotted me and threw a rope down. Jeremy couldn't find it, but he found another and tied one end to a rock, throwing the other in the water. I told him to call 911 and reluctantly, afraid to leave, but helpless if he stayed, he went to retrieve the cell phone from our car. Then it was just me and the bright yellow rope and the rise and fall of the waves. I tried to coordinate myself with the bobbing and keep my head above water.

I am not interested in adrenaline highs. I buckle my seat belt, I don't ride on roller coasters, I stay out of the water when the ocean looks rough—my favorite outdoor adventure is floating down gentle rivers on an inner tube. I was raised by Safety Dad. When we were young my father skipped the drug talk, and instead gave my sister

and me the tsunami talk, telling us we should run to high ground if
we ever saw the ocean retreating. And at that time, when all I knew
of tsunamis came from Japanese woodblock prints, such a warning
seemed like the epitome of a father's unending crazy worry. He
informed us too about various riptides and currents and horrible
things that had happened to little girls who hadn't heeded their
fathers' warnings. His tours of Maui were full of tidbits about
honeymoon couples who had died by falling off cliffs (backing up
to take pictures, picking fruit on overhangs, diving off waterfalls
into shallow pools). Where others saw wonderful black cliffs and
sparkling deepest blue water, we saw the aloha-shirted bodies of
drowned tourists among the rocks.

   Now, treading water, I thought of all those warnings and his
mandate not to panic, ever. I thought of the water safety class I'd
taken at the YWCA when I was ten. I tried to remember if certain
movements attracted sharks. I thought about how pretty the cliffs
looked and about a neighbor's daughter who'd been swept out to
sea and never found. For the first time in a long while I didn't worry
about not having a job or a life plan. Instead, I just thought about
how nice it would be to be out of the water and how little I wanted
to die just then.

   I tried to breathe in and out deliberately, slowly. I finally
caught the end of that yellow rope. I pulled up the slack and held
on as the waves pushed me up one more time, and then I tugged
hard on the rope. It slipped into the water.

   I was very tired and baffled to still be bobbing about in the
water, still struggling with each wave. It was too hard and I wanted
to float instead. Just float. So I swam out to calmer water and set-
tled in to a very slow tread.

5

I looked up to see the videotape woman talking to Jeremy. She was talking into a cell phone. Jeremy walked back to the rocks, a good ten feet above the highest surges. Someone would come get me in ten minutes, he said. I told him to keep talking to me. Tried to joke, asked him if we needed to tell my dad, told him I loved him, explained how to use a visual marker to locate me should I slip under (I was not planning to go under, but it never hurts to show off one's level-headedness).

And then Jeremy was gone. Where he'd been standing white water was flowing down the rocks. He'd been washed over and I couldn't make it back to help him. I knew all of this, and was reduced to a strange kind of selfish anguish that I wouldn't get to see him again, that I'd met someone so good for me and now he was gone. But just a minute later I saw his head above the rocks. He'd been knocked backwards by the wave, tumbled over, and finally, thankfully spit out into the tide pool.

A few minutes later a helicopter arrived and lowered down a little net basket. A man popped out, helped me get seated and we floated magically up. Ascended, I might say, the motion being so gentle and the cliffs so beautiful and the grass on top of the cliffs getting closer and closer.

I have never been so overjoyed to sit on grass.

Shock is a wonderful thing. It was what allowed me to talk reasonably to my rescuers—Maui Fire Department Rescue 10 and the woman with the camera, a painter named Diana Lehr—to give them my address and chat about other rescues in that area (very few as lucky as mine I later discovered).

Jeremy and I discussed details on the drive home, debated telling my parents, squeezed hands. All the what-if's came later, when we told my parents and friends. When we washed the sea out of our cuts. When my mother hugged me. When I tried to sleep and instead thought of all those people in the tsunami with no helicopters coming to get them, without calm water to float in, their husbands, friends, neighbors failing to reappear on the dry land, above the water's edge.

MASTERY EXERCISE 2 **Considering Significance and Meaning**

1. After Liliana Ibara was swept into the ocean, what kept her from simply climbing back onto the shore?
2. How did the lessons Ibara's father had taught her and her sister help during her ordeal?
3. After returning from retrieving their phone, what happens to Ibara's husband, Jeremy?

MASTERY EXERCISE 3 **Analyzing Method and Technique**

1. Here again is the final sentence of Liliana Ibara's introduction: "This is why I was clinging to my flip-flops." Why do you think she ends her opening paragraph in this fashion? Do you agree with her strategy? Explain your reasoning.
2. Midway through her essay, Ibara employs an extensive flashback. In your view, how does her decision to interrupt chronological order influence the effectiveness of her essay?
3. Ibara is finally rescued by helicopter, a point she raises in paragraph 12. Why do you think she chose not to discuss in greater detail the experience of being lifted from the ocean to the helicopter and brought to shore, something that in itself must have been exciting? Would adding such material strengthen her essay—or weaken it? Why do you feel this way?

WRITING A NARRATIVE ESSAY C

Liliana Ibara's essay focuses on an apparently safe situation that suddenly turned potentially lethal. Have you ever had an experience that took a dramatic turn? For example, have you ever taken a hike in a wooded area, missed a turn, and ended up lost? Have you ever been stuck outside, unprepared for a sudden shift to extreme weather, or have you ever experienced an injury or accident with help not immediately available? For this assignment, focus on one of these topics or another related subject and use narration to tell your reader the story in an essay of about 500 words.

WRITING A NARRATIVE ESSAY D

In the second paragraph, Liliana Ibara mentions the only person who witnessed her being washed into the ocean, "a woman videotaping the waves." Have you ever been witness to a shocking, memorable, or otherwise remarkable scene? What was happening? Who was involved? Were other people around? How did they behave? For this assignment, use narration to tell that story, employing third-person point of view, in an essay of about 500 words.

Summary Exercise

1. Prewrite on one of the following topics, revisiting the events involved in that episode:

   - An incident during which you challenged authority
   - A time when you were caught in a lie
   - An incident of random kindness—or of random violence— that you witnessed

2. Create a draft essay of about 500 words in which you use narration to discuss the various stages involved in the event.

3. Using the Narrative Essay Checklist, page 69, as a guide, revise your draft. Make sure you provide an introduction that sets the scene for the sequence of events to follow and sufficient transition to keep your ideas flowing. In addition, check that you have followed chronological order, with any appropriate flashbacks or flashforwards, and that you have included multiple examples and details that don't deviate from your main point. Finally, be sure to have an objective reader evaluate your essay in terms of these points.

4. Addressing any problems you and your reader have identified, create a final draft of your narrative essay.

6

Description

Understanding Description

When you need to provide a detailed account of an item, event, or experience, drawing on perceptions and reactions resulting from your five senses, **description** is the mode you need. As a developmental strategy, description animates and re-creates abstract and concrete subjects, making situations, impressions, and experiences almost tangible for your reader.

Description would be the mode to turn to in an essay concerning a place from your childhood that no longer exists. It would also be the ideal organizing strategy for an essay about an encounter with severe weather. Description is an important mode to master because it creates a sense of authenticity and credibility, conveying to your reader vivid experience and lasting memory.

The Elements of an Effective Descriptive Essay

To make your descriptive essay effective, be sure to include the elements described on the following pages.

Sufficient Transition

The following transitional words and expressions will be especially useful as you develop a descriptive essay:

above, below	in front of, behind	toward, away
close, far	next to, near, between	up, down

Appropriate Sensory Details

What does milk taste like? What does velvet feel like? What does thunder sound like? Good answers to these questions—answers that paint a clear picture for your reader—require **sensory details**, phrasing that captures what you perceive through your five senses: hearing, sight, smell, taste, and touch.

One way to communicate sensory experiences to your reader is to express them in concrete language. Don't just say that your family dog, after an unfortunate encounter with a skunk, smelled terrible. Instead, say the odor was *acrid and caustic, causing you to choke and your eyes to water.*

Another technique, especially effective when you are describing an unusual or unfamiliar experience or sensation, is to compare it to something more ordinary or familiar. To describe the pain you felt when you severely sprained ligaments by rolling your ankle while running, you might say that the injury felt like a *sudden electric shock* or *an intense, localized fire in your lower leg.*

Both Objective and Subjective Description

Descriptive writing can be divided into two general categories: **objective description** and **subjective description**. Objective description refers to observable or verifiable characteristics such as size, shape, color, speed, weight, and so on. Subjective description concerns reactions to or impressions of details, experiences, and situations.

Think of a place you were frightened to go as a child—a cellar in your grandparents' house, for example. This cellar was about *ten by fifteen feet* with *unfinished, whitewashed walls* and a *dirt floor*, lit by *a single bulb hanging on a wire from the ceiling.* Contained in the area was *a two-foot-square wooden shipping crate* filled with everything from *decades-old magazines* to *broken small appliances* to *rusty tools.* All in all, it was a fairly typical cellar.

But now think of how that room used to make you feel. For one thing, it was *cold and clammy*, and although you never saw any, *you were sure giant insects or rats lived in the shadows.* And the *smell was musty,* like *what you imagined a mausoleum smells like.* To a ten-year-old, it was simply creepy.

The first paragraph about the cellar is largely objective, covering its actual features. The second paragraph, however, is mostly subjective, focusing on the impressions, not facts. Expect to use the combination of objective and subjective description that helps communicate your point to your reader.

A Thoroughly Developed and Focused Presentation

A successful descriptive essay requires a thoroughly developed and focused presentation. Ensuring that your presentation is thoroughly developed involves anticipating your reader's questions, concerns, and interests relative to your topic and then providing the specific details and examples that address these questions and concerns. Keeping your presentation focused involves following through on your purpose as identified in your thesis and the supporting sentences in your introduction.

With an essay concerning a visit to Yellowstone National Park, your reader would likely be quite interested in the specific scenes and sensations you experienced during your trip to this extraordinary place, so you should provide details like *spectacular geysers blasting into the brilliant blue sky,* filling the air with *moisture that smelled like steam leaking from an old pipe,* and *ponds and water holes with fluorescent reds, blues, greens, yellows, and oranges glowing* beneath the surface of *crystal clear boiling water.* You should also note the wildlife that you came upon as you toured the area—*a gangly young moose, groupings of shaggy bison* that stood *taller than your rental car,* and a *single juvenile black bear doing its best to open up a bear-proof trash container.* Finally, you should mention the scene as you drove through the park on *a moonlit night—the 100-foot sheer drop from the road* winding down a mountain and *the panorama of clouds of steam rising above pine trees against a violet sky.*

However, you should include only those details that are directly related to the main idea spelled out in your thesis. Therefore, you wouldn't mention U.S. Department of the Interior budget cuts that may reduce access to parts of Yellowstone or reference a recent study indicating that fewer people are now choosing national parks as vacation destinations. While such details may be accurate, they simply don't have a direct connection to the main idea of the essay.

Spatial Order or Some Other Appropriate Method of Arrangement

To arrange a descriptive essay, you'll find a couple of methods useful. With a paper that focuses largely on visual information, for example, you would likely turn to **spatial order** to communicate the scene to your reader. Spatial order helps your reader visualize the details of the scene as they actually exist in relation to each other. Consider an essay concerning the controlled chaos in a busy restaurant kitchen. Spatial order would enable you capture the layout of the kitchen itself: the long row of ovens, burners, and grills *against the right wall*, with a shiny exhaust hood *suspended above it*; a series of shiny metal prep stations, with storage shelves *underneath*, in the *middle of the room*; and a line of deep, industrial-grade sinks, with tall, curving faucets and heavy-duty side sprays *against the left wall*.

If your purpose is to explain what your first night working in that busy kitchen was like, however, chronological order would enable your reader to follow your experience. But if your goal is to discuss the various duties, from simplest to most complex, performed by the kitchen staff, then emphatic order would make it easy for your reader to understand the relative significance of each of these tasks.

6 A Descriptive Essay Checklist

Once you complete a draft of a descriptive essay, use the following **Descriptive Essay Checklist** to evaluate it and then ask an objective reader to do the same.

DESCRIPTIVE ESSAY CHECKLIST

❏ Does the introduction engage the reader and lay a clear foundation for the condition, phenomenon, or situation to be illustrated?

❏ Is there sufficient transition to guide the reader?

❏ Are there enough sensory details to support the thesis?

❏ Are both objective and subjective description used at appropriate spots in the essay?

❏ Is the description fully developed and focused, anticipating audience interests, concerns, and questions?

❏ Has spatial order or some other appropriate method of organization been used to make the description easy for the reader to follow?

Use the answers to these questions to help you revise your essay and create an effective final draft.

Analysis: Examining an Annotated Descriptive Essay

Weather Alert: My Blizzard Experience

This **introduction engages the reader** and **lays a clear foundation** for the phenomenon to be discussed.

Exaggeration seems a natural part of the description of weather events. Ask what a heavy rain was like, and you'll likely get an answer that includes words like *monsoon* or *flood*. Ask somebody what a hot summer day was like, and you'll probably hear words like *blowtorch* or *oven*. But a year ago, I experienced my first blizzard, and in this case, that term was no exaggeration.

Note the **thesis**, which identifies the **specific focus** of the essay.

The **objective description** regarding what constitutes a blizzard—wind speed, temperature, visibility, amount of snow—helps to ensure that the **presentation is fully developed and focused**.

The National Weather Service reserves the word *blizzard* for a special kind of weather event. The wind must be blowing over 35 mph, with overall visibility reduced to under a quarter of a mile for three or more hours. A significant amount of snow must also fall, as much as several inches an hour, often with heavy drifting. Finally, the temperature has to be cold, several degrees below freezing at the least. This surprise early December storm fit this description perfectly.

The **objective description** concerning the rarity of blizzards in this area and the incorrect weather forecast helps the reader understand why no one was prepared for the severe storm.

Here in the southeastern part of the state, we hadn't experienced a blizzard in more than forty years, and when the storm hit, everybody,

6

was caught off guard, including the television meteorogists. The actual prediction had been for heavy flurries, with slight accumulation, a common forecast for that time of year, so schools were in session and businesses and government offices were all open for business.

Note how the **objective description** makes it easy for the reader to appreciate the intensity of the storm.

But at about 11 a.m., the storm suddenly intensified. The temperature dropped to 20 degrees, almost 10 degrees lower than it had been an hour earlier, the wind picked up dramatically, and the gentle snow flurries turned to heavy snow. Within a half hour, the wind was blowing so strongly that the windows in my classroom were creaking and whining, and it was a near whiteout. A sense of excitement at what we were seeing and hearing swept across the room as we wondered what would happen next.

The **sensory details**—in this case, what was heard and seen—bring the storm into focus, and the **subjective description** about its effect on the classroom emphasizes its effect on the students.

6

Objective description—the amount of snow that had already fallen—and **sensory details**—the sensation of freezing snow on skin—bring the scene to life for the reader.

City officials responded to the dramatic worsening of the weather by announcing that all schools and government offices would close by 12:30 p.m. As I joined the rest of my classmates in the school parking lot, I could see that at least three inches of snow had already fallen, and the wind-whipped snow stung my skin.

I brushed off my car and then joined the long line of traffic leading from the school to Brayton Avenue, the road that led to my

Sensory details—a pounding heart, steaming breath, sweating—bring the reader into the situation.

neighborhood four miles away. I had only driven in the snow a couple of times before this storm, so when I hit the brakes and skidded a little, my heart began to beat rapidly. It was cold enough inside the car for me to see my breath, but I could still feel myself starting to sweat.

I soon found that skidding wasn't really going to be a problem. So many cars, trucks, and buses were on the road that I couldn't get up enough speed to skid. Under normal circumstances, my entire drive home from school would take me about 20 minutes. On this day, the first mile alone took me almost 45 minutes, with the wind and snow picking up the whole time. I had to stop five separate times to get out of the car and clean my windows, and each time the amount of snow I cleaned off was greater than the last time.

Over the next hour, the line of vehicles in front of me traveled at a crawl, with the weather conditions worsening all the while. All I could see were the glowing red brake lights of the car in front of me. Eventually, the flow of traffic stopped completely and just never started up again. At that point, I figured the best thing to do was walk the rest of the way home, so I pulled my car onto the sidewalk

bjective escription—the *length* of time *involved* in the *trip* on an *ordinary* day and on this day as well as the severe weather conditions— *paints* a clear *picture* of how *bad* the storm *was*. As a result, *the* presentation *remains* both **developed and focused**.

6

Notice how **spatial order** helps the reader visualize the scene—the writer pulls the car *onto the sidewalk in front of a small strip mall several blocks* from home to begin the half-mile walk home.

in front of a small strip mall several blocks from my house, locked it, and stepped out into the fiercely blowing snow.

The trip should have taken me at the most 10 minutes. Instead, it was 40 minutes before I reached my door. Almost a foot of snow had fallen, and deep drifts had formed on the sidewalks. At least 20 cars, some of them at odd angles, had been abandoned in the middle of the street. As a result, walking was so difficult that I actually fell three times. The blowing snow felt more like tiny pellets of ice hitting my face, and because I hadn't dressed for temperatures in the teens, I couldn't feel my hands and feet. When I finally reached my house, I felt as if I had climbed across a glacier instead of simply walked a few blocks.

After that blizzard, life didn't go back to normal for a week, and it was actually March before the last of the huge piles of snow left by the snowplows finally disappeared. This year, the city's historical society is selling calendars with pictures taken during the blizzard, but I don't need to see a picture to remember the storm. All I have to do walk down my street, and the whole experience comes rushing back.

Note how **spatial order**—drifts of snow on the sidewalk, cars abandoned in the middle of the road—makes it easy to visualize the chaos.

6

—The presentation here is **fully developed and focused**, thanks to an effective combination of **objective description**—the amount of snow, the temperature; **sensory details**—the feeling of the snow against the face; and **subjective description**—the walk was like crossing a glacier.

—The **conclusion** brings the essay to a complete and logical close, reemphasizing the impact of the entire experience.

MASTERY EXERCISE 1 Responding to the Annotated Essay

1. In your view, is the introduction effective as it is, or would you recommend some changes to the writer? Regardless of your opinion, explain your reasoning thoroughly.
2. As the annotations indicate, objective description appears more often than subjective description. Do you feel that this disparity is appropriate, or do you think more subjective description would have made the essay even better? What in the essay leads you to this belief?
3. Sensory details appear in several paragraphs of this essay. Which of these instances does the best job of capturing the experience? Why do you feel this instance is superior to the others? Is there any point in the essay where additional sensory details would make the overall description even more effective?

WRITING A DESCRIPTIVE ESSAY A

Because it is such a departure from what we are used to, a severe weather event often serves as an excellent subject for writing. As the annotated essay clearly demonstrates, descriptive details and examples abound when it comes to recording the power of nature in its rawest form. For this assignment, think of the most severe weather experience that you have ever had to deal with or that you were able to observe from the safety of your home or some other haven. Use different aspects of description, including objective and subjective description and sensory details, to write an essay of about 500 words in which you bring that experience to life for your reader.

WRITING A DESCRIPTIVE ESSAY B

No doubt some die-hard fans of winter would consider a blizzard a perfect weather day. How about you—what would your perfect weather day be like? During what season would it occur? What makes this season superior to the other three? What would the temperature be? Where would you be most likely to spend such a day? What kinds of activities would you enjoy? What in particular would distinguish this day from other good-weather days you have enjoyed? For this assignment, write an essay of about 500 words in which you address the ideas raised by these questions and others that these questions lead to. Create a fully developed and focused presentation for your reader by employing objective and subjective description and sensory details.

Illustration: Considering a Descriptive Essay
NIGHT OF THE GRIZZLIES
Jack Olsen

On August 12, 1967, two campers were killed by grizzly bears in separate incidents in Montana's Glacier National Park. These attacks marked the first recorded fatal encounters between humans and North America's largest carnivore in that region. The grizzly bear is a fearsome creature, an extremely fast, extremely powerful animal weighing in at between 300 and 800 pounds, with a standing height of 7 feet. Perhaps the most remarkable thing is that no previous fatalities had occurred at Glacier National Park, since many visitors to at that time routinely ignored rules concerning proper disposal of garbage in an attempt to draw bears out where they could be seen. The following passage, from Jack Olsen's The Night of the Grizzlies, *a book that grew out of a series of investigative articles on the killings for* Sports Illustrated, *places us in the middle of the attack that led to the death of 19-year-old Michele Koons.*

What do you imagine the scene was like when a group of campers discovered that they were the prey being stalked by a 500-pound grizzly bear?

Sometime between two and three in the morning, Denise Huckle found herself awake and listening intently to a splashing sound that was coming from the shallow water alongside the camp at Trout Lake. Squirt pushed himself up on his front paws and peered into the night toward the sound, and when a low growl began to issue from the puppy's throat, Denise grabbed him and stuffed him under her sleeping bag. She thought she could make out the silhouette of a bear, and she did not want Squirt to antagonize the animal. When the sounds seemed to move out of the water and down toward the original camp, Denise awoke the others and told them what she had heard. After a few minutes of silence, the Noseck brothers scrambled out and rebuilt the fire, by now only a bed of dull embers. They set the sack of cookies on the edge of a driftwood log, fanned up the fire once again, and returned to their bags. Within a few minutes, the bear had walked to the edge of the camp, grabbed up the cookie bag in a huge paw, and disappeared. Paul Dunn, the deepest of the sleepers, was up now, and the five frightened campers decided to lie awake, feed the fire, and wait for dawn. It was 3 o'clock; first light would be about 5:30 or 6. Paul Dunn inched his sleeping bag closer to the roaring fire but inched it back when his toes became too hot.

Once again, the bear began splashing in the shallow water below the camp, and almost simultaneously a woofing sound seemed to come from the woods above. For a few minutes, the companions of the night discussed whether bears attacked in packs or couples and finally decided that they did not. By 4 a.m., the noises had stopped, and most of the campers had pulled the bags over their heads and gone back to sleep.

Denise comforted Squirt, imprisoned for his own safety under the sleeping bag, and tried to stay awake. Dawn was not far off. More than once, Denise thought she heard noises around the edge of the campsite, and each time she patted and stroked the dog to keep him from making a sound. Except for the single low growl earlier when the bear had been wading around the edge of Trout Lake, Squirt's behavior had been perfect, but there was no doubt that the dog's scent was on everything in the camp, and especially on the two girls, Denise and Michele, who had spent more time than the others babying him in their arms. Denise tucked her pet farther under the bag till he was completely hidden.

It was 4:30, and the fire had fallen to low flames and embers again when she heard a splash and narrowed her eyes to peer into the night and saw a bear coming at a lope straight from the shoreline toward the center of the camp. When the bear was four or five feet away and she could make out its head and upper body clearly, Denise pulled the sleeping bag over herself and Squirt just as the dog began a high-pitched squeal. Lying perfectly still inside the warm bag, the terrified girl heard a ripping noise that sounded like shredding canvas, but then there was a silence broken only by the deep breathing and grunting of the grizzly. She held Squirt tightly in her arms and felt his trembling mingle with her own. She tried to keep the dog from bawling out its fright, as the bear sniffed rapidly at the bag.

Paul Dunn woke up and peeped from his own sleeping bag to see the huge wet form of the bear standing next to him. Noiselessly, the boy slithered into his bag and tried to remain absolutely still. He heard the bear making more sniffing sounds, and suddenly he realized that the sniffs were getting closer and closer. Then something crunched into his sleeping bag and took a firm grip on his sweatshirt. Instinctively, the boy threw back the flap of the bag and scrambled to his feet, slamming into the bear in the process and shouting to no one in particular, "The goddamn bear tore my shirt!" When the grizzly reared up on its hind feet as though to attack, Paul dashed to a tree and climbed thirty or forty feet in a matter of seconds, ripping and cutting his chest and his legs on the desperate ascent. When he reached the safety of the top, he looked down and saw the bear circling lazily below.

Lying in bags side by side, Denise and Ron Noseck saw the bear amble over to Paul Dunn's tree, a few feet outside the semicircle of campers, and Ron decided that the time had come to run for trees of their own. "We have to get out of here!" he yelled, and Denise replied, "I can't. I've got to undo the collar around Squirt's neck." Once again, Noseck told his girlfriend to run, and when she did not move, the 21-year-old dental student yanked the girl full-length from her sleeping bag and gave her a shove toward the southern end of the lake. The couple ran about fifty yards in the direction of the original camp, and as they ran, they heard Paul Dunn shouting down from his treetop. He seemed to be telling Ray and Michele to get out of their sleeping bags and make a break for it, but in their own headlong flight down the lakeline, Denise and Ron could not be sure. They reached a slight incline, and as they stopped, gasping for breath, the puppy came bounding up. Ron boosted the girl up a tree, threw the dog after her, and shinnied up a tree of his own. Neither one could see distinctly to the new camp fifty yards away, but they could still hear Paul Dunn shouting, and they added their own cries to the pandemonium. "Get out!" they yelled toward the camp. "Find a tree!"

6

From his observation point almost directly above the camp, Paul Dunn saw everything that happened within the small circle of reddish light thrown off by the dying fire. He saw Ron and Denise run down the shoreline, followed by the puppy, and then he saw the grizzly walk toward Ray Noseck's sleeping bag and begin sniffing rapidly. When the bear turned momentarily toward Michele's bag, Ray came out of his own as though shot from a gun and headed down the lake toward Denise and Ron, shouting as he ran, "Get out of your bag and run for it!"

Paul hollered at Michele, "Get out! Get out! Unzip and get out!"

The bear clamped its jaws on the side of the sleeping bag, and Paul heard the girl begin to scream. When the animal raked the bag with its claws, Paul heard Michele cry out, "He's ripping my arm!"

"Michele!" Paul shouted. "Get out of your bag! Run and climb a tree!"

"I can't," the girl screamed. "He's got the zipper!"

Then the defenseless girl shouted, "He's got my arm. . . . My arm is gone! Oh, my God, I'm dead!"

Paul Dunn saw the bear lift the sleeping bag in its mouth and drag it out of the circle of fire and up the hillside into the darkness. He heard a sound like bones crunching and shouted down the lake to the other three, "He's pulling her up the hill!" and then, "She's dead! She's dead!"

In the hysteria of the moment, it seemed to the 16-year-old boy that he must get dressed and join his friends, and when he figured that the bear and its helpless bundle were at least fifty yards up the hill, he scrambled down the trunk and slipped his trousers over his underclothes. Then he sprinted along the lake to the others and climbed another tree, and the four survivors of the attack comforted one another and waited for the dawn. It came at 6 a.m., an hour and a half after the attack, and while Ray attended to Denise and the dog, the two younger men ran back to the campsite and gathered up shoes and jackets.

They listened for any sounds coming from the dark woods that might indicate Michele was still alive. From somewhere up the hill in the direction the bear had taken, Ron was sure he could hear the sound of bones being snapped. The four terrified campers yanked on their shoes and ran down the trail toward the turnoff that led up and over Howe Ridge. Denise thought she saw the bear in the brush as they ran, but she said nothing, and two hours later, after running and stumbling and lurching four miles up and down the 2,000 feet of hill, the campers burst out on the road that ran from Going-to-the-Sun Highway along the northern edge of Lake McDonald to Kelly's Camp. A fisherman and his wife had parked at the trailhead and were just starting to hike in, but they took one look at the panicky group coming out and urged them into their car. When they pulled up at the path that led to the lake and the small ranger station, the four refugees from Trout Lake asked their benefactors to keep the dog in the car. Then they rushed off to tell their story to the ranger.

MASTERY EXERCISE 2 Considering Significance and Meaning

1. Once they heard the first sounds of the grizzly bear, what immediate steps did the campers take to try to keep themselves safe?
2. After camper Paul Dunn had escaped from the grizzly by climbing to the top of a tree, what did he see by the light of the waning fire?
3. As dawn came and the survivors of the bear attacks were fleeing their camp, what did they experience that led at least two of the campers to believe that the bear was still near?

6

MASTERY EXERCISE 3 Analyzing Method and Technique

1. Because this document is an **excerpt**—a piece of writing taken from a larger document—it doesn't include a traditional introduction. However, what details in the first paragraph prepare the reader for the events to follow?
2. At which point in the excerpt do you think that Jack Olsen most effectively uses sensory details? Why do you think this example is more powerful than the others?
3. In your view, does Olsen rely more on objective description or on subjective description in this excerpt? Explain what leads you to this conclusion.

WRITING A DESCRIPTIVE ESSAY C

Fortunately, the overwhelming majority of people in this world never have the kind of encounter with an animal that Jack Olsen recounts here. Most of us, however, have had some kind of run-in with a domesticated or wild animal in our lives. Some of these experiences are frightening or painful (coming face-to-face with a potentially rabid raccoon or fox, for instance, or being bitten by a dog) or humorous (being chased by an aggressive goat at a petting zoo or interacting with a vocal parrot or cockatoo). For this assignment, use different aspects of description, especially objective and subjective description and sensory details, to prepare an essay of about 500 words that shows your reader what you went through during this encounter.

WRITING A DESCRIPTIVE ESSAY D

The campers who were attacked by the bear had apparently felt that the beauty of Glacier National Park was worth the risk of a chance encounter with a grizzly bear. Is there a place that you have visited—or would like to visit—that would be worth this kind of risk? For this assignment, write an essay of about 500 words in which you use elements of description to capture the essence of a place that you believe has extraordinary beauty.

6

Summary Exercise

1. Prewrite on one of the following topics, focusing in particular on the various descriptive details and examples involved:

   - The scene at a concert, sporting event, water park, or some other place where crowds of people gather
   - What distinguishes a place where you spend a good deal of time—your room, your neighborhood, your gym or practice field, your place of employment, and so on
   - The filthiest you have ever become at work or at play

2. Create a draft essay of about 500 words in which you use the various aspects of description to communicate the vivid and unique nature of your topic to your reader.

3. Using the Descriptive Essay Checklist, page 84, as a guide, revise your draft. Make sure that you include an engaging introduction that gives your reader a clear foundation for the condition, phenomenon, or situation to be presented plus plenty of transition to guide your reader. At the same time, be sure to include key sensory details and appropriate objective

and subjective description. Finally, check that your overall presentation is thorough, focused, and arranged in spatial order or another suitable method of arrangement. Don't forget to have an objective reader evaluate your essay in terms of these points as well.

4. Addressing any problems you and your reader have identified, create a final draft of your descriptive essay.

6

7

Example

Understanding Example

When you need to make some concept, situation, or condition lucid and easy for your reader to understand, the answer is the mode of **example**. This organizing strategy fosters comprehension of a point by illustrating, clarifying, or supporting it. Think of your intent when you say or write, "For example." Your goal is to make your point powerfully by using a particular instance to illustrate or explain it.

If you were writing about the different lessons that children can learn from being part of a team or learning to play a musical instrument, example would be the technique to employ. Example would also be the dominant mode in an essay about ways that modern life affects the environment. Because this technique sheds light on the meaning or significance of a topic, example is an important developmental strategy to master.

The Elements of an Effective Example Essay

To make your example essay effective, be sure to include the elements described on this and the following pages.

Sufficient Transition

You will find the following transitional words and expressions especially useful as you develop an example essay:

after all	for instance	indeed	moreover	particularly
for example	in addition	in other words	of course	specifically

Specific Supporting Examples

The secret to making your assertions convincing to your reader is to make sure that the supporting examples you use are *specific*—precise, exact, and detailed—rather than general. Specific examples address the reader's needs by providing answers to the key questions *who, what, when, where, why*, and *how*. Merely saying that many people are wasteful when it comes to money, true though it may be, doesn't meet your reader's needs. This statement lacks the kind of detail that spells out exactly what you mean by "wasteful." Here's a more specific version:

> Many people waste money every day without seeming to be aware of it. Financial writer David Bach even coined a name for this kind of unnecessary spending: the Latte Factor. This terms refers to all the seemingly insignificant things that people purchase on a daily basis, for example, expensive coffee drinks, bottled water, snacks, and so on. Although the price for any one of these things may seem small, the total price tag for them over a single day may exceed $10. Over a year, that's $3,650, money that could be used for things that are actually needed or put into a savings account or invested.

This specific example directly addresses the reader's need, outlining in exact terms what wasteful spending means in this context.

Relevant Examples

In order to understand the point you are making, your readers depend on you to make your examples *relevant*—appropriate and directly related to your subject and purpose for writing. Relevant examples are also commonplace and easily understood. In an essay about issues that create great anxiety for today's high school students, relevant examples would include *fears about violence, worries about being accepted by peers, pressure to achieve in the classroom or on the athletic field*, and *issues involved in dating*. However, examples about changes in state licensing guidelines for teachers or insufficient funding for federal initiatives like No Child Left Behind, would not qualify as relevant for the vast majority of high school students.

Multiple Examples

No simple formula exists to determine the ideal number of examples to include in your essay. Instead, your intent will dictate the correct number of examples. In some cases, a series of short examples might powerfully illustrate a single concept or assertion. In other cases, fewer, more extended examples—in the form of anecdotes, case studies, or other scenarios—might enable you to make your point effectively.

In an essay about challenges that first-semester college students often face, for instance, you can think of at least four solid supporting points without much difficulty: *adapting to college-level work, setting and sticking to a study schedule, maintaining physical health through appropriate diet and regular exercise*, and *developing your ability to work independently*. With these examples—and, if the writing assignment allowed for it, even another example like *enjoying at least a limited social life*, discussed in a full paragraph—the resulting essay would clearly illustrate what awaits first-semester students.

Perhaps the only guideline to remember here is to provide at least three examples. In fact, this is the formula for an essay form known as the **five-paragraph essay**, sometimes used as a practice activity or as a technique during timed writing tasks such as essay examinations and writing assessments. As the name suggests, the five-paragraph essay features five paragraphs total. The introduction presents a thesis that identifies three main supporting ideas. Three body paragraphs, each discussing one of the supporting points, follow. Finally, a conclusion restates the significance of the thesis and the three supporting points. The annotated essay in this chapter, "The Other Side of Progress" (pages 102–105), is an example of the five-paragraph essay.

Effective Arrangement of Examples

How to arrange an essay is always an important consideration. With an example essay, the arrangement you choose will depend on the significance of the examples themselves. Sometimes, as with the proposed essay about the different anxieties many of today's high school students face (page 100), the examples are about equal in importance. In that case, it makes sense to experiment a bit from one draft to the next to see which order seems most logical.

Other times, however, some of the examples will carry more weight than others, and in those cases, you will find **emphatic order** especially useful. Consider the proposed essay on challenges that first-semester college students may face (page 100). *Maintaining physical health through appropriate diet and regular exercise* is certainly important, as is *enjoying at least a limited social life.* But *adapting to college-level work* is more crucial to success, and *setting and sticking to a study schedule* is even more crucial. Most important of all, though, is *developing your ability to work independently*, the hallmark of the thriving college student. Arranged this way, these examples attract and maintain the reader's interest.

An Example Essay Checklist

Once you complete a draft of an example essay, use the following **Example Essay Checklist** to evaluate it, and then ask an objective reader to do the same.

7

EXAMPLE ESSAY CHECKLIST

- ❏ Does the introduction indicate the concept or principle that the examples will support and illustrate?
- ❏ Is there sufficient transition to make it easy for the reader to follow the points you are making?
- ❏ Are the examples sufficiently specific to clarify meaning?
- ❏ Are the examples relevant—appropriate, commonplace, and directly related to your subject and purpose in writing?
- ❏ Are multiple examples that offer support for the thesis provided?
- ❏ Are the examples effectively arranged, with emphatic order employed when some examples carry more weight than others?

Use the answers to these questions to help you revise your essay and create an effective final draft.

Analysis: Examining an Annotated Example Essay

The Other Side of Progress

Here in the 21st century, Americans have benefited from enormous and extraordinary technological advances. These developments have helped to provide a lifestyle that our grandparents could probably have only imagined. But modern life is not without problems, some of which are the result of the very technology that has done so much to improve life. Take some basic examples like air-conditioning, wireless communication devices, and artificial outdoor illumination. Without a doubt, these innovations have made modern life easier, faster, and safer than at any other time in history, but they have also produced some unexpected and detrimental side effects.

Life for many people in the United States would be a good deal less pleasant without modern air-conditioning systems. In areas of the country where summer heat is occasionally oppressive, air-conditioning makes living comfortable. But in southern and western states, where fiercely hot weather for long periods of the year is the norm, air-conditioning makes a normal life possible. There are downsides, however. For one thing, air-conditioning saps precious

This introduction identifies the idea that the examples in the body will support and illustrate. Note that three modern innovations are identified: air-conditioning, wireless communication devices, and artificial illumination. With each subject covered in its own paragraph, plus this introduction and a conclusion, the resulting document is a five-paragraph essay.

The final sentence in the introduction serves as the thesis, identifying the specific point of the essay.

This first supporting example—the modern air-conditioning system—is both specific—detailed and exact—and relevant—directly connected to the thesis.

energy resources, in some cases leading to rolling brownouts and power failures across states and entire regions during especially warm periods. Furthermore, the improved weatherproofing and insulation intended to make air-conditioning systems more efficient have led to increases of dead air and mold in homes, schools, and businesses, resulting in increased respiratory illnesses and conditions, including asthma.

The **second supporting example**—the widespread availability of wireless communication devices—is both **specific** and **relevant**. Transitional **words**—*for example, Furthermore,* and *In other words*—help to emphasize the point being made.

Today, people enjoy access to afford-able and readily available wireless devices like cell phones, BlackBerries, and laptop computers that provide instantaneous connection to the rest of the world all day, every day. But this immediate and complete access has consequences that people a decade ago never had to deal with. Many workers, for example, report that because of these devices, they feel tethered to the workplace even when they are off the clock, including during weekends and vacations. Furthermore, while online games and social networking sites like MySpace and Facebook provide opportunities for virtual interactions, this time does not involve the actual company of others. In other words, the increase in access through electronic means can lead to social isolation that few would have anticipated.

Multiple examples of drawbacks of the growth of online communication, including added pressure on workers and potential social isolation, make it easy for the reader to understand the negative side of this innovation.

The **third supporting example**—extensive artificial outdoor lighting in U.S. cities and towns—is both specific and relevant.

Anyone who has ever flown at night across just about any area of the United States can attest to how thoroughly residential areas are lit. Even small towns and villages across the U.S. are aglow after sunset, and areas without exterior lighting are practically impossible to find in major cities like Chicago, New York, and Los Angeles. But there is a surprising negative side to this welcome hallmark of our modern society: light pollution. Sadly, the truth is that in many parts of the United States, people no longer have an unobstructed view of the night sky. Estimates from groups like the International Dark-Sky Association are that about a third of the artificial light visible at night simply shines upward and disperses. This light pollution unfortunately prevents about half of all Americans from doing what humans have been doing for thousands of years: simply standing outside at night and seeing our own galaxy, the Milky Way.

A greatly reduced view of the night sky, the unintended consequence of an innovation that most people see as essential, is the most surprising of the three supporting examples. **Emphatic order**—a strong example followed by a stronger example followed by the strongest example—creates and sustains interest for the reader.

In so many ways, the quality of life that people enjoy in 21st-century America is amazing. Homes and businesses are now often climate controlled, and wireless communication keeps people connected with whom they want, when they want. In addition, brilliant artificial illumination makes living, working, and traveling easier and safer. But it's still not a perfect world. Those carefully

The **conclusion** of this five-paragraph essay restates the thesis and the three supporting examples to emphasize that even innovations offering tremendous benefits have drawbacks.

sealed building have led to respiratory problems due to dead air and mold, and cyber connections are not substitutes for in-person interactions.

Most of all, the bright lights that cut through the darkness of night unfortunately make it impossible for some Americans to view one of nature's most beautiful sights: the stars.

MASTERY EXERCISE 1 Responding to the Annotated Essay

1. The focus of the essay is on the negative aspects of some modern innovations, yet each of the supporting examples in the essay opens with a discussion of the positive aspects of the advancement being illustrated. Do you agree with this strategy or would you suggest concentrating entirely on the drawbacks? Why do you feel this way?

2. The third paragraph offers two examples of problems stemming from today's wireless world of communication: workers unable to leave the office behind and social isolation because of people's involvement with online relationships rather than in-person contact. As you see it, are both examples necessary, or would the paragraph be more effective if it concentrated on one or the other? What about the paragraph leads you to this conclusion?

3. As the annotation next to paragraph 4 indicates, this essay is arranged on the basis of emphatic order. In your view, does the current order effectively draw and maintain the reader's interest, or would you recommend changing the order of any of these examples to create an even stronger presentation? Explain your reasoning.

7

WRITING AN EXAMPLE ESSAY A

Despite the downsides that can sometimes accompany progress, few people would choose to live without the kinds of modern innovations enjoyed in the 21st century. But imagine that you had to make some choices—what modern devices, adaptations, services, institutions, and so on, would you forego if it were absolutely necessary? For this assignment, identify at least three and then put the example mode to work. In an essay of about 500 words, explain your choices to your reader, being sure to address in specific terms how your life would differ without these innovations.

WRITING AN EXAMPLE ESSAY B
It is undeniable and perhaps unavoidable: progress has an impact on the environment, on the natural world, forever changing landscapes and affecting us in ways that we don't always recognize immediately. Sometimes it's an enormous matter, something affecting the entire planet, for instance, global climate change. But the impact of progress can be smaller, more local—for example, the filling in of a wetland for a housing development or business in your city or town. Consider this subject and identify at least three different ways that modern life has collided with and altered the world around you. Putting the example mode to work for you, write an essay of around 500 words in which you specify these changes for your reader, explaining the significance of their impact.

Illustration: Considering an Example Essay
THE NOSE KNOWS AFTER ALL
Bernice Kanner

7

When it comes to our senses, smell is far stronger than many of us realize. In fact, some studies suggest that the human olfactory system is more capable of creating enduring memories and triggering recollections than any of our other senses. Step into an indoor pool area, for instance, or break the seal on a bag of ground coffee or cut into a lemon, and the distinctive odors, aromas, or fragrances can bring scenes or events back into our consciousness in full and vivid detail. With the kind of power that scent has, it should surprise no one that the corporate world would attempt to capitalize on its evocative power, as Bernice Kanner recounts in the following essay. The author of 12 books, Kanner wrote on marketing, advertising, and other subjects for a number of periodicals, including the New York Times, *the New York* Daily News, *and* New York *magazine, during her career. In this essay,*

Kanner uses example to illustrate how companies and organizations have put the power of smell to work.

In what ways can exposure to particular scents affect the behavior, productivity, and attitude of those exposed to them?

Marketers have long known that customers browse longer and buy more in shops with floral fragrance, and that supermarkets whose bakeries emit the scent of fresh-baked bread sell more of everything.

The smell of peppermint is known to stimulate, lavender to relax and citrus to uplift. Nowadays, casinos are playing a good bet by piping in not only oxygen to keep gamblers awake, but also a whiff of peppermint and vanilla to keep them enthralled. Their chips have come in: Slot machine play is up.

Smell is the most evocative of the senses and until recently, the least utilized. Years ago Vance Packard, author of "The Hidden Persuaders," the most famous book about marketing hijinks in history, would have decried using the old schnoz as a malicious mind game, subliminal weaponry that posed a threat more dire than the Evil Empire.

Today, we accept being led by the nose as the common course, as prevalent and unnoticed as acid rain.

Researchers at the University of Liverpool recently discovered that scents such as those of ink, cheese, fruit and wine elicit far more detailed memories than do words or pictures.

British Airways injects the subtle scent of new-mown grass into passenger lounges at its terminals, so as to bring the outside inside to frazzled and cynical flyers.

Luxury automaker Rolls-Royce has taken the scent-sational step of treating its new cars with a chemical solution that mimics the scent of its illustrious 1965 Silver Cloud—the new-car smell isn't what its caliber of buyer wants. The vintage model smell suggests the automaker hasn't replaced much of the wood once used in the cars' interiors with molded plastic.

However, acknowledging the regional preferences of smell, automakers in Japan try to eliminate the smell of fine leather interiors because many Japanese people dislike the smell of leather.

"Odors alter brain wave activity and produce emotional responses that can influence us positively or negatively," says Sarah Harrop, director of the Aroma Co. in the United Kingdom, which scents the British Airways lounges. Scents can do more than put shoppers in the mood to buy. They can increase brand value by creating a more pleasant environment.

Indeed, a study by the Smell & Taste Treatment and Research Foundation in Chicago determined scent can often mean the difference between a browser and a buyer.

Eighty-four percent of consumers [were] asked to rate two identical pairs of Nike sneakers—one showcased in an unscented room and the other in a room that had been sprayed with floral scent. They claimed that the sneakers in the scented room were superior to the others.

They even admitted they would be willing to pay $10 more for the sneakers that didn't smell like, well, sneakers.

Annette Green, president of the New York–based Fragrance Foundation and Olfactory Research Fund, says marketers now recognize the nose can improve our whole quality of life and are learning to use scents in very innovative ways.

Automakers, for example, are testing the power of scents to prevent road rage and perk up weary drivers. Other companies are investigating behavioral aromatherapy to calm stressed workers.

In New Zealand and Europe, companies have trademarked product scents and even sued makers of smell-alikes.

There's even talk down the road of tampering with the human genome to alter our natural aromas genetically, so that we'll be able to smell younger, fresher or sexier naturally.

Perhaps sooner than that, scents will emerge from the Web. DigiScents, of California Technologies, has created the iSmell device. This device plugs into a computer and offers 128 basic smells, intact or blended, and wafted through via fan.

DigiScents plans to begin marketing this device to consumers soon, and has signed a deal with Procter & Gamble to scent its site. Cyrano Sciences, also based in California, is marketing a similar "portable nose" to the food industry.

Something else to sniff out: personalized scents. The latest status symbol is a unique signature fragrance, instead of a designer brand found in department stores. At the Paris-based House of Creed, perfumers customize fragrances after in-person consultations about one's lifestyle. The deal is that Creed won't sell that scent to anyone else for five years.

But not everyone is sniffing pretty. Anti-fragrance activists in North America are irked by what they call the invasiveness of secondhand scents and are moving to limit their use, claiming they threaten sufferers of asthma, allergies and chemical sensitivities.

Some institutions such as the University of Minnesota's School of Social Work and Denver's National Jewish Medical and Research Center have declared themselves fragrance-free. In Halifax,

Nova Scotia, every public building and many private businesses have voluntarily gone fragrance-free.

7

MASTERY EXERCISE 2 Considering Significance and Meaning

1. What has the gambling industry done to take advantage of the concept that what we breathe in can affect our behavior?
2. What do British Airways and the makers of Rolls-Royce automobiles hope to accomplish by employing scents in their operations?
3. In what ways are entrepreneurs using computer technology and the World Wide Web to harness the power of scent?

MASTERY EXERCISE 3 Analyzing Method and Technique

1. How do the examples in the first two paragraphs help Kanner prepare her audience for the discussion to follow in the body of the essay?
2. At only one point in the essay—the ninth paragraph—does Bernice Kanner include a direct quotation. Throughout the rest of the essay, she relies upon paraphrase. Why do you think Kanner chose to use Ms. Harrop's actual words at this one point? Do you agree with this strategy? Why or why not?
3. The last two paragraphs specifically focus on the downside of the pervasive presence of aromas and scents. Why do you think Kanner chose to place these examples at the end of her essay? How would her essay have been different if she had begun with these examples?

WRITING AN EXAMPLE ESSAY C

In her essay, Bernice Kanner focuses on a number of ways that companies use aromas and fragrance to help sell their products. But, of course, she hasn't covered all the approaches that marketers use to convince customers to buy. In your experience and from what you've seen on billboards, in print, on television, in the movies, on the Internet, and so on, what other techniques do companies use to hawk their products and services? For this assignment, write an essay of about 500 words in which you turn to example to explain at least four different marketing strategies to your reader.

Writing an Example Essay D

Kanner opens her essay with two examples—floral fragrances and fresh-baked bread—that create positive impressions so strong that they encourage people to purchase more when they encounter the scents. In your life, what aromas or fragrances rank as the most pleasant and positive you have experienced? What kind of effect or influence do they have on you? For this assignment, write an essay of about 500 words in which you use example to specify for your reader at least four of these scents and the power they wield.

Summary Exercise

1. Prewrite on one of the following topics, concentrating on specific and relevant instances and illustrations:

   - Pet peeves
   - A first-year college student's FAQ
   - The best sites on the Web for connecting with other people

2. Create a draft essay of about 500 words in which you use example to explain and clarify your meaning for your reader.

3. Using the Example Essay Checklist, page 101, as a guide, revise your draft. Make sure your introduction indicates the principle to be supported and illustrated. In addition, check that you have enough examples to strongly back up the concept you are discussing. Also, be sure that the examples themselves are both specific and relevant and that you have included enough transition to keep your ideas flowing smoothly. Finally, be sure that you have chosen an effective order of presentation for your examples. If the examples differ in significance, consider employing emphatic order to capture and hold your reader's attention. Remember to seek the assistance of an objective reader to evaluate your essay relative to these points.

4. Addressing any problems you and your reader have identified, create a final draft of your example essay.

8

Process

Understanding Process

When you need to explain the *how* of something—how to reach a goal, how a natural or man-made phenomenon occurs—**process** is the organizing strategy you rely on. Process freeze-frames function, making the steps and stages easier to understand.

Process is a versatile mode, with three variations to help you meet the needs of your reader. When your goal is to provide directions on how to do something such as a basic move in tae kwon do, you turn to *how-to writing*. When your intent is to record how you did something, for instance, performed an experiment in your psychology class, you use *process narrative*. And when your objective is to detail how something happens—how a tsunami occurs, for example—you employ *process analysis*. Because process plays such an important role in simplifying complexity in procedures and occurrences, it is a valuable mode to master.

The Elements of an Effective Process Essay

To make your process essay effective, be sure to include the elements described on this and the following pages.

Sufficient Transition

The following transitional words and expressions signaling time order and general sequence will be particularly useful as you complete a process essay.

TRANSITIONAL EXPRESSIONS FOR PROCESS WRITING

Beginning	Continuing			Ending
begin by	as soon as	second step, etc.	until	finally
initially	next	then	while	last

The Imperative Mood When Appropriate

The primary goal of process writing, especially sets of instructions, is to make unfamiliar steps or stages easier to understand. Therefore, with how-to writing, you should use the **imperative mood** (you), often informally called the **command**, to address your reader directly. In the imperative mood, the subject is not stated but is *understood* to be the person being directly addressed.

If you were writing about adding photos or video clips to a Facebook page, you could write:

> To add photos or videos to a Facebook page, the user should first log onto his or her account. When the page appears, the next step for the user is to find the photo link and click on it.

But it would be better to write:

> To add photos or videos to a Facebook page, first log onto your account. When your page appears, find and click on the photo link.

The passage is now shorter (25 words versus 39). More important, it is clearer and more direct, thanks to the use of the imperative mood.

8

Division of the Process into Simple, Logical Steps

The gap between what you know about your subject and what your reader knows looms large with process, which focuses on often-intricate procedures and occurrences. The secret to meeting your reader's needs is to separate the process into small, manageable steps. The more complicated the process is, the more you should break it down.

Imagine that your subject is how a handheld or automobile Global Positioning System, or GPS, functions. The science behind these increasingly common devices is complex, so it makes sense to break the process down to its basics, as this informal outline shows:

- GPS devices depend on satellites circling the earth. When a device is activated, it first sends a signal out into space to establish communication.
- A GPS device actually communicates with at least three satellites to identify a location accurately.
- These paths of communication enable the device to calculate the exact distances to and between the satellites.
- On the basis of this calculation, the device identifies a precise position.
- With this locale identified, the GPS device can draw on information in its memory to specify prospective routes, distances, times of arrival, and so on.

Broken down in this fashion, this complicated process is far easier for the average person to understand.

Clarity in What to Expect and What to Avoid

With process, as with all writing, you want to make sure that nothing distracts your reader from your main point. Therefore, be sure to emphasize or alert your reader to potentially confusing or especially complicated steps or stages. For example, the widespread and cumulative environmental damage that would occur following a decline in the population of honeybees can be hard for nonexperts to comprehend. Corners can challenge even the most experienced wallpaper hangers. It therefore makes sense when you write to call attention to these points in order to reassure your reader. When it's appropriate, offer an additional alternative explanation of that part of the process.

Linear Order

For much process writing—for example, how Supreme Court justices are confirmed or how you organized a cleanup of local wetlands— **linear order** is the ideal method of arrangement. Linear order is a variation of chronological order through which you present the steps in their functional order—in a direct line, step by step, as they must be performed to complete the process. Transitional words such as *first, second, next, then, afterward, finally*, and so on, direct the reader through the steps.

If you were dealing with a how-to subject such as how to make a kill shot in volleyball, you would employ linear order to present the process. *First*, as you anticipate a shot heading your way at the net, jump straight up. *Once* your arms are above the net, wait until the ball is slightly lower than your hands. *Then* quickly assess the best spot to send your shot. *Finally*, as strongly as you can, smash the ball downward in the direction you have identified.

A Process Essay Checklist

Once you complete a draft of a process essay, use the following **Process Essay Checklist** to evaluate it, and then ask an objective reader to do the same.

8

PROCESS ESSAY CHECKLIST

❏ Does the introduction identify the procedure or technique to be presented?

❏ Is sufficient transition to guide the reader through the steps and stages supplied?

❏ If it's appropriate for this essay, is the imperative mood (*you*) used to address the reader directly?

❏ Is each step simple and clear, or should some steps be divided or explained more fully?

❏ Are the steps presented in correct linear order or in some other appropriate method of arrangement?

Use the answers to these questions to help you revise your essay and create an effective final draft.

Analysis: Examining an Annotated Process Essay

Tsunami—When the Ocean Rises and Destroys

This **introduction** identifies the subject, spurring the interest of the reader.

This **thesis** specifies that the essay will explore how a tsunami occurs.

8

On December 26, 2004, more than 200,000 people in several South Asian countries, including Sumatra, Indonesia, Sri Lanka, and India, died as a result of a single natural disaster: a tsunami ("Asian Tsunami Death Toll"). People sometimes mistakenly call such an occurrence a tidal wave, but no tides are actually involved. The name *tsunami* comes from Japanese, and it means harbor wave. Actually, a tsunami is a series of waves that begins well beneath the surface of the water, sometimes hundreds or thousands of miles away from the point at which the huge volume of water reaches any harbor.

Note the **parenthetical documentation** for factual information taken from another source.

Note the **parenthetical documentation** for factual information taken from another source.

Scientists have identified several triggers for a tsunami. For example, an eruption of an undersea volcano can set off a tsunami, as can a coastal landside or a meteor strike. In the case of the 2004 tsunami in South Asia, two plates of the earth shifted deep beneath the ocean near Sumatra (Bonincontro). The result was an underwater earthquake, which is considered the most common cause of a tsunami.

This paragraph establishes **linear order**, presenting the **first step in the process**—a significant event creates a disturbance deep beneath the ocean's surface.

The energy generated by the impact or pressure of the initial events leads to a dramatic change in the ocean. Water moves upward and then outward in all directions. The resulting waves are massive and powerful. They can be as long as 100 miles from end to end and travel at enormous speed, sometimes hundreds of miles an hour, as they head for landfall and unsuspecting residents and tourists.

From the shore, one telltale sign of the onset of a tsunami is an unexpected and severe draining of beaches and harbors. Sometimes people, unaware of the powerful force heading toward them, walk out where the waters have receded, assuming they are looking at an extremely low tide. When the tsunami waters finally arrive, these victims are swept up and drowned.

As the speeding water reaches land, the upward slope of the shore causes the water to gather even greater strength and height. Depending on the degree of the slope and force of the original underwater event, a tsunami wave can reach heights of 50 feet or more, and successive waves can be larger than the first. As these powerful waves roar inland, they do enormous damage to anyone or anything in their path. The destruction is not just along the shoreline, either. In one area of Indonesia hit in the 2004 tsunami, water actually traveled 2.5 miles inland

Note how this use of transition emphasizes what happens as a result—a huge volume of water heads toward land.

Continuing the adherence to linear order, this paragraph presents the third step—water drains out to an extreme degree before crashing back ashore.

Continuing the adherence to linear order, this paragraph presents the next stage—the surge of water hits the slope of the shore, leading to huge waves that rush inland far beyond normal ranges.

Continuing the adherence to linear order, this paragraph presents the second stage of the process—the underwater disturbance forces water up and outward, generating powerful waves that move out in all directions.

Note how this use of transition clarifies the change in focus to the view from the shore as a tsunami approaches.

8

Note how this use of transition carries forward the discussion of the process.

Note the parenthetical documentation for factual information taken from another source.

This **concluding paragraph** restates the significance of the thesis and brings the essay to a logical close.

8

(*Managing Tsunami Risk*). Each wave then does additional damage as it recedes, drawing back the debris from the structures and vehicles it carried or damaged on the way in.

Before the 2004 catastrophe, acknowledged as perhaps the most destructive tsunami in modern times ("The Deadliest Tsunami Ever?"), the public knew little about how this powerful force of nature occurs. The stunning photos and video clips of this tsunami shot by tourists and residents certainly raised the world's awareness of the raw power and danger of this natural phenomenon. These images show the ocean crashing and devastating everything in its path. But the wall of water is just the last part of the process, which begins deep in the ocean, far away from that point of impact.

Note how this **use of transition** helps to signal the movement from the body of the essay to the conclusion.

Note the **parenthetical documentation** for factual information taken from another source.

Works Cited

"Asian Tsunami Death Toll Tops 226,000." *chinadaily.com*. China Daily. File last modified on 19 January 2005. Web. 15 Sept. 2010. < http://www.chinadaily.com.cn/english/doc/2005-01/19/content_410485.htm >.

Bonincontro, Aldo. "Causes of the December 2004 Tsunami." *Helium.com*. Web. 16 Sept. 2010. < http://www.helium.com/Items/1253796-causes-of-the-december-2004-tsusami >.

Because information from other sources has been included in the essay, the **full citation** for each source, arranged in accordance with **MLA guidelines**, follows the essay, under the heading **Works Cited**.

"The Deadliest Tsunami Ever?" *nationalgeo
graphic.com.* National Geographic News.
File last modified on 7 Jan. 2005. Web.
15 Sept. 2010. < http://news.national
geographic.com/news/2004/12/1227_
041226_tsunami >.

*Managing Tsunami Risk in the Aftermath of
the 2004 Indian Ocean Earthquake &
Tsunami. www.rms.com.* Risk
Management Solutions, Inc., 2006.
Web. 16 Sept. 2010. PDF file, page 6.
< http://www.rms.com/Publications/
IndianOceanTsunamiReport.pdf >.

MASTERY EXERCISE 1 Responding to the Annotated Essay   **8**

1. The essay begins with the disturbing statistic that the 2004 tsunami killed more than 200,000 people. Why do you think the writer uses this startling fact to open the essay? Do you agree with this strategy?

2. The scope of the tragedy of the Southeast Asian tsunami is almost unfathomable. How does the step-by-step discussion of its process help to bring about a greater understanding of what happened on December 26, 2004?

3. As is often the case with process writing, this essay deals with a subject about which the writer likely knows far more than the reader. What aspect of the overall discussion of how a tsunami occurs does the best job of bridging this gap of knowledge between writer and reader? Explain your reasoning.

WRITING A PROCESS ESSAY A

As this essay makes clear, much more is involved in a tsunami than the average person realizes. Now consider another natural phenomenon, one about which you already know something or about which you would like to learn. For instance, how does a thunderstorm occur? How does the Gulf Stream or an atmospheric condition such as El Niño change weather patterns? What do various animals in extremely cold climates do to prepare for winter? How does the aurora borealis occur? What is the life cycle of salmon? What happens to the earth after a wildfire or volcanic eruption? Using the essay about tsunamis as a model, write an essay of about 500 words in which you use process to explain how the phenomenon occurs or takes place. If the process is unfamiliar to you, do some research, and be sure to document your essay correctly, in accordance with MLA guidelines, as the tsunami essay does. As you write, be sure to discuss the phenomenon in linear order, breaking the process into simple, easy-to-understand steps and providing plenty of transition throughout to keep your reader on track.

WRITING A PROCESS ESSAY B

The fourth paragraph of the sample essay points out that many victims of a tsunami drown, at least those who unwittingly put themselves in a dangerous situation from which they can't escape. Most of us have been luckier. Even though we've faced treacherous situations, we've managed to survive. Consider your own experiences: What is the most dangerous situation you have ever faced? What brought you to this dangerous situation? How did you escape from it? For this assignment, write an essay of about 500 words in which you discuss this experience. Turn to process to record the steps you followed to extricate yourself. Remember to provide an introduction that directs your reader and to present the steps you took in clear, complete form, with plenty of transition to guide your reader.

Illustration: Considering a Process Essay

GROWING A LOYAL CUSTOMER

Jill Griffin

When it comes to purchasing goods and services, U.S. consumers almost always have a choice. Think of the brand-name items you buy, credit card companies you do business with, restaurants you patronize. What made you select these companies? What keeps you going back? Courting a customer base and then maintaining and increasing it does not happen by accident. As this brief excerpt from Jill Griffin's Customer Loyalty: How to

Earn It, How to Keep It *explains, success in this area occurs when companies systemize their approach. Note how heavily Griffin relies on process, specifically a carefully outlined set of stages, effectively arranged to show what a business should do to stay in business.*

What steps should a company take to cultivate and hold the interest of its customers?

How can other companies engender the same loyalty that Harley-Davidson has developed? To understand the process, consider nature and the lessons it provides. In my seminars, I show a slide of an acorn and ask my participants what an acorn becomes over time. An oak tree, of course. It doesn't happen in a day, a week, a month, or even a year—it's a long, step-by-step progression.

People grow into loyal customers by stages as well. The process is accomplished over time, with nurturing, and with attention to each stage of growth. Each stage has a specific need. By recognizing each of these stages and meeting those specific needs, a company has a greater chance of converting buyers into loyal customers and clients. Let's look at each of these stages one by one:

Stage 1: SUSPECT. Suspects include everyone who might possibly buy your product or service. We call them suspects because we believe, or "suspect," they might buy, but we don't know enough yet to be sure.

Stage 2: PROSPECT. A prospect is someone who has a need for your product or service and has the ability to buy. Although a prospect has not yet purchased from you, he or she may have heard about you, read about you, or had someone recommend you to him or her. Prospects may know who you are, where you are, and what you sell, but they still haven't bought from you.

Stage 3: DISQUALIFIED PROSPECT. Disqualified prospects are those prospects about whom you have learned enough to know that they do not need or do not have the ability to buy your products.

Stage 4: FIRST-TIME CUSTOMER. First-time customers are those who have purchased from you one time. They can be customers of yours and still be customers of your competitor as well.

Stage 5: REPEAT CUSTOMER. Repeat customers are people who have purchased from you two or more times. They may have bought the same product twice or bought two different products or services on two or more occasions.

Stage 6: CLIENT. A client buys everything you have to sell that he or she can possibly use. This person purchases regularly. You have a strong, ongoing relationship that makes him or her immune to the pull of the competition.

Stage 7: ADVOCATE. Like a client, an advocate buys everything you have to sell that he or she can possibly use and purchases regularly. In addition, however, an advocate encourages others to buy from you. An advocate talks about you, does your marketing for you, and brings customers to you.

Stage 8: INACTIVE CUSTOMER OR CLIENT. An inactive customer or client is someone who was once a customer or client but has not bought from you in a period of time longer than the normal purchase cycle.

The Profit Generator System and the Customer Stages

How the Profit Generator System Works

In my marketing seminars, I use the image of the Profit Generator system to illustrate the marketing challenges every company must address to be profitable.

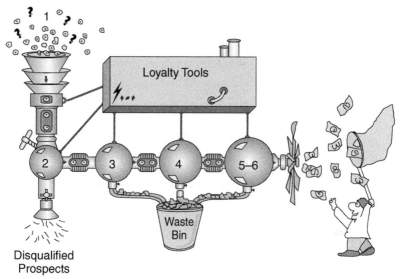

The Profit Generator System

8

The Profit Generator system works like this: An organization funnels *suspects* into its marketing system, and these people are either qualified as high-potential *prospects* or disqualified. Disqualified prospects are filtered out of the system, while qualified prospects remain inside. The sooner a disqualified prospect is filtered out, the better for you. Wasting time and money on suspects who will not buy or are unable to buy cuts dramatically into your profits, so you want to identify disqualified suspects as quickly as possible. Qualified prospects are then focused upon with the goal of turning them into *first-time customers*, then *repeat customers*, and eventually *clients* and *advocates*. While moving them through the Profit Generator system into higher levels of loyalty, you also want to encourage customers to buy regularly from you and stop buying from your competition. Without proper care, first-time customers, repeat customers, clients, and advocates can become *inactive*, causing a company substantial losses in sales and profits. You'll notice that the globes representing each customer stage become progressively larger. This is because, despite the fact that the number of customers in each stage is smaller than that in the preceding stage, the further along in the system the customer gets, the more bottom-line profit the organization can enjoy.

Every business has customers and clients that fall into some if not all of these categories. A residential real estate company has homeowners as clients. These homeowners could transition through five stages: suspect, prospect, lister, seller, and advocate. A hotel chain catering to corporate travelers has the travel departments of major corporations as clients. Their customer stages could be suspect, prospect, first-time booker, repeat booker, client, and advocate. While the actual names of the customer stages may be modified, most organizations have customers that evolve through a similar transition.

Other applications to the Profit Generator system vary as well. For example, in many industries buyer monogamy (i.e., whether that person is buying only from you or is also buying from a competitor) is the client-stage litmus test. In some sectors like state government that cannot buy exclusively from one seller, this may not be a reasonable requirement. In those situations, the best a company can hope for is that it is one of two or three sellers used exclusively by that buyer. Depending on the nature of your business, these stages can be modified to address the specifics of your own buying situation.

The rule of thumb in working within the Profit Generator system is that the goal for you within each stage of development is to "grow" the relationship into the next stage of development. The goal of interacting with a prospect is to turn a prospect into a first-time customer, a repeat customer into a client, a client into an advocate.

Once you reach the advocate stage, your job is to keep that person buying and referring..., a company can enjoy real profits when the customer has evolved into the latter stages of the Profit Generator process. Failure to "grow" customers to those advanced stages robs the company of profits and valuable referrals.

MASTERY EXERCISE 2 **Considering Significance and Meaning**

1. As Griffin explains it, how does an *advocate* differ from a *client*?
2. In her discussion of the Profit Generator system, Griffin states that disqualified prospects should be filtered out of the system as quickly as possible to avoid "[w]asting time and money." In what ways could a disqualified prospect cost an organization money?
3. What does Jill Griffin want her audience to understand about the ways successful companies do business? What aspects of or examples in the document have helped you reach this conclusion?

8

MASTERY EXERCISE 3 **Analyzing Method and Technique**

1. Griffin opens this excerpt with a rhetorical question. Why do you think she chose this way to introduce her process? Do you agree with her strategy? Explain your reasoning.
2. In Stage 1, according to Griffin, a potential customer is a *suspect*. This term usually carries a negative connotation. How does her explanation help create a positive connotation?
3. The excerpt features a visual entitled "The Profit Generator System." In what ways does this visual enhance the document, making it easier to understand the process?

WRITING A PROCESS ESSAY C

In a way, Jill Griffin's excerpt really concerns how to cultivate and maintain interest in a particular subject. For this assignment, first focus on one of your own hobbies or interests, carefully considering how you came to develop your interest in it. Then use process to outline steps that you believe would help someone else develop the same level of interest in the subject that you have.

WRITING A PROCESS ESSAY D

In this excerpt, Jill Griffin presents a strategy to help businesses attract and hold onto customers. If you were going to offer a similar strategy to help people become better customers, what would you suggest? Using the Griffin excerpt as a guide, write an essay of about 500 words in which you lay out a process that will turn people into more careful consumers.

Summary Exercise

1. Prewrite on one of the following topics, focusing on the steps or stages comprising it. Consult additional sources if necessary and correctly document any information you draw from these sources:

   - How to avoid panic
   - How performance-enhancing substances affect the body and give people an edge in competition
   - How to perform a complex move in a sport, dance, chess, video game, and so on

2. Create a draft essay of about 500 words in which you identify for your reader the steps making up the process.

3. Using the Process Essay Checklist, page 115, as a guide, revise your draft. Check that your introduction identifies the process and sets a clear direction for your reader. Make sure that have divided the process into manageable, easy-to-understand steps. At the same time, be sure that you have presented the process in linear order or some other appropriate method of arrangement, with sufficient transition to keep your meaning flowing for your reader. Finally, seek the guidance of an objective reader to evaluate your draft concerning these points as well.

4. Addressing any problems you and your reader have identified, create a final draft of your process essay.

9
Definition

Understanding Definition

Whenever your intent is to explain, delineate, or clarify the characteristics of some item, location, individual, and so on, the organizing strategy to turn to is **definition**. This mode crystallizes the meaning of both abstract and concrete subjects, spanning the gap between writer and reader.

Definition enables you to spell out the characteristics or elements necessary to be truly successful in life. This mode would also be the natural choice for an essay exploring the inner eccentric or geek within most people. Effective communication depends in large part on shared understanding, especially of general, complex, or abstract subjects. Definition is therefore an important mode to master.

The Elements of an Effective Definition Essay

To make your definition essay effective, be sure to include the elements described on the following pages.

Sufficient Transition

The following transitional words and expressions will help you specify the unique qualities or elements constituting your subject:

accordingly	indeed	in other words	on the whole	therefore
in addition	in fact	in the same way	specifically	thus

Both Limited and Extended Definitions

In general, you should provide both a **limited** and an **extended definition** in a definition essay. Think of a limited definition as a working explanation or characterization of the term you are discussing. It often makes sense to present this limited definition as the thesis in the introduction:

> True charisma, that trait that attracts and inspires admiration and devotion of others, is so easily recognizable because it is such a rare quality.

An extended definition is a fully developed explanation, complete with multiple supporting examples. With an essay on charisma, the extended definition would constitute the body, in which you would discuss charisma in fuller detail, dealing with ideas such as how people have been affected by specific individuals who possess this quality. The body might also cover the ways that famous—and infamous—popular-culture, political, and religious leaders use their special gift.

The Elements of an Effective Dictionary Definition

As you begin working on a definition essay, keep the basic pattern of a dictionary definition in mind: it identifies the general class to which the term belongs and then gives the special or distinguishing characteristics that set the word apart, as this example shows:

                                    class
EXAMPLE: Twitter is a **social networking service** *through*

           distinguishing characteristics
           which users connect to their followers by creating micro-blogs
           or "tweets" of no more than 140 characters that answer the
           question "What are you doing now?"

With an essay devoted to definition, consider using this kind of pattern, but on a far greater scale. In addition to class and distinguishing characteristics, provide several specific, concrete supporting examples.

To expand and enhance your definition, consider employing *synonyms, negation,* and *etymology*:

- *Synonyms* are words that hold a similar meaning. If you write that a computer game must be *entertaining* to be effective, including synonyms like *engaging* and *absorbing* would help to clarify your meaning and prepare your reader for the discussion to follow.
- *Negation* is a technique through which you define something by explaining what it *isn't*. When you write that intelligence isn't just the knowledge of a great volume of facts, you are suggesting that being intelligent also involves understanding the significance of and connections among these facts.
- *Etymology* is the origin and historical development of a word. You can find the etymology of a word as part of its definition in print and online abridged dictionaries and in a number of online language sites. An unabridged dictionary such as the *Oxford English Dictionary (OED)* is the best place to find extensive etymological information. Consider a common word like *music*. It descends from an ancient Greek expression meaning "art of the muses," the nine goddesses of inspiration, poetry, science, and the arts. Or consider the common adjective *bizarre*. One path of this word's development points to a French word meaning "odd" and a Basque word meaning "beard," the suggestion being that the bearded Spanish soldiers struck the French who saw them as strange or peculiar.

Denotation and Connotations

You also need to take into account all the possible meanings for the term you are defining. To do this, you need to consider both the **denotation**, the literal meaning of the word, and its **connotations**, all the associations that also come with the word.

For example, a common meaning of *artful* is its literal meaning, "skillful and clever." But it also holds other shades of meaning, many with negative connotations, including "devious," "sly," and "deceitful." To describe a supervisor at work as artful is to leave your reader with a question: is the supervisor highly skilled or carefully dishonest? As you develop your definition essay, be sure to consider both the denotation and connotations of the words you choose, making sure your reader always knows what you mean.

Appropriate Personal Interpretations or Experiences

With some topics, especially abstract ones, including a personal interpretation or experience may help you heighten reader interest and bring the subject into greater focus. If you were writing about fear, you would certainly want to discuss the physical effects it can create. You could then buttress this discussion by referring to a time when you had to deal with fear:

Last year, I was behind the counter of the convenience store when a kid pointed a gun at me and told me to give him all the money in the register. I had never experienced fear like that. I remember how enormous that gun looked and how cold the store suddenly seemed. I felt detached from my body, as if I wasn't really involved in the scene at all, and the whole situation seemed to be happening in slow motion.

This kind of example clearly shows the physical effects of fear, thus supporting the main point.

A Definition Essay Checklist

Once you complete a draft of a definition essay, use the following **Definition Essay Checklist** to evaluate it. Then ask an objective reader to do the same.

9

DEFINITION ESSAY CHECKLIST

❏ Does the introduction kindle the reader's interest and clearly iden-tify the term to be defined in the body?

❏ Is there sufficient transition throughout the essay to keep the reader on track?

❏ Has a combination of limited and extended definitions been employed?

❏ Does the essay incorporate and build upon the elements of an effective dictionary definition?

❏ Have synonyms, negation, and etymology been used to expand or enhance the definition?

❏ Have both the denotation and connotations of the term been considered?

❏ Are personal interpretations or experiences included when appropriate?

Use the answers to these questions help you revise your essay and create an effective final draft.

Analysis: Examining an Annotated Definition Essay

The Geek Staring Back at You

The introduction features a united definition of a geek, offering the primary characteristics and preparing the reader for the discussion to follow in the body of the essay.

Among the more common stereotypes on television or in the movies is the geek. As seen on the screen, a geek is captivated by some esoteric or highly technical subject and out of touch with the mainstream, dressed oddly, and socially inept. Like most stereotypes, this one is largely myth, but that doesn't mean that there is no such thing as a geek. After all, who doesn't have an intense interest in a subject that many people don't necessarily care about or understand? Who doesn't have the desire to share it with people with the same interest? Whose fashion sense isn't sometimes questionable and

The thesis prepares the reader for the discussion in the body that will discuss the characteristics of this definition in fuller detail.

who isn't occasionally awkward or ill at ease in the company of others? You might as well face it: all you need to do to find a geek is to look in a mirror.

The stereotype holds that the typical geek is interested in matters requiring serious brainpower, things like applied mathematics, astrophysics, and computer science chief among them. But what's complicated and

The first body paragraph begins the extended definition of a geek. It discusses one aspect of the stereotypical portrait of a geek—the deep, all-consuming interest in arcane subjects.

complex for one person is second nature for another. Consider your own background and experiences. Chances are good that you know a great deal about at least one subject that lots of people, perhaps most people, don't. For example, are you an expert on exotic cars, able to explain body types and lines, specifications, and options for multiple models? Or have you practiced and studied up to learn shortcuts to help you to slash through *Guitar Hero* or some other computer game? Are you able to repeat the plot and whole passages of dialogue from multiple episodes of shows like *The Family Guy, The Simpsons*, and *South Park*? This kind of knowledge probably seems normal to you. The person who has the same level of information about black holes or the latest microchip no doubt sees that information as normal, too. If extensive knowledge of a subject qualifies the astronomer or computer enthusiast as a geek, then your knowledge of your specialty makes you a geek as well.

> These additional **specific examples,** in the form of a series of questions, help to expand and support the point that most people have a great deal of knowledge about a subject that others would find unusual.

9

The examples strengthen the reiteration of this characteristic of the **expanded definition** as well as the point that everyone is a geek to some degree.

The stereotype also suggests that a geek always seeks out the company of other geeks who share the same interests. At national and regional *Star Wars* or *Star Trek* conventions, for instance, many fans are so obsessed with the plots and characters that they dress in costume and get together

Note how this use of **transition** guides the reader from the first characteristic of the **expanded definition** to the second characteristic.

This **specific example** illustrates the idea that geeks choose the company of fellow geeks.

to discuss minute details of the lives and behaviors of these fictional characters. This behavior may seem pretty geeky to you, but think for a minute about your own interests.

hese examples fer support for e idea that not st stereotypical ards seek out e company of ke-minded folks d engage in d behaviors.

Maybe you know all kinds of details about Hollywood figures and log onto message boards and blogs to discuss the latest rumors. Perhaps you have the entire roster of your favorite NFL team, including the backup players and specialty coaches, memorized. On game day, you may wear a jersey with a player's name on it. Maybe you even paint your face, wave a special towel, or wear a plastic cheese hat while you watch the game with other people doing the same thing. That

The examples strengthen the reiteration of this characteristic of the **expanded definition** as well as the point that everyone is a geek to some degree.

9

ote the use of **synonym** to arify this part the **expanded** finition.

seems to be about as geeky, or to use a common synonym, *nerdy*, as those fans in Darth Vader or Mr. Spock costumes.

ote how this se of **transition** ides the reader om the second aracteristic of e **extended** finition to the al examples.

In addition, the stereotypical portrait of a geek often features a person in ill-fitting or mismatched clothes, with a strange hairstyle and clunky glasses, mumbling or grinning inappropriately when interacting with others. Nobody would accuse a geek of being stylishly dressed or at ease at parties or in other social situations. But before you distance yourself from this part of the description, denying it has anything to do with you, you should open a photo album and take a

These **specific examples** illustrate two additional qualities often associated with being a geek: poor fashion sense and weak social skills.

The examples strengthen the reiteration of this characteristic of the **expanded definition** as well as the point that everyone is a geek to some degree.

Note how this use of **transition** directs the reader from the first of the final two characteristics of the **expanded definition** to the second.

9

This use of **transition** creates flow between the body of the essay and the conclusion. Note the use of **etymology** to clarify the overall definition of a geek.

look at your clothes and hair from five years ago. Perhaps you thought you looked fine then, maybe even fashionable, but what do you think now? If that isn't bad enough, imagine what you will think when you look back at your appearance five years from now. Furthermore, you are an unusual person indeed if you haven't found yourself completely out of place at some social gathering, either tongue-tied or babbling mindlessly while trying to ignore the stares of others. The stereotypical portrait may be of a geek, but that geek should seem quite familiar to you.

At one time the word *geek* was used to describe a circus or sideshow freak who performed outrageous acts like biting off the heads of live chickens. These kinds of geeks were pretty rare. But the real geek behind the stereotype of a brainy, goofy, socially clumsy individual is far more common. In fact, you can find a geek anytime you want, as long as you can see your own reflection.

These examples remind the reader that what is stylish in fashion or hairstyles is highly subjective, which supports this aspect of the **expanded definition**.

This example underscores the point that occasional social awkwardness is common, which supports this aspect of the **expanded definition**.

The conclusion offers another variation of the **limited definition** provided in the introduction while also reminding the reader that we are all geeks to some degree.

1. The introduction features four rhetorical questions in a row, one for each of the characteristics making up the extended definition in the body of the essay. In your view, would the introduction have been better or worse if the writer had chosen another approach to introduce the subject to the reader? Why?

2. How would you describe the tone in this essay? What in the essay leads you to this conclusion? Do you think it is appropriate for the subject matter presented? Explain your reasoning.
3. The writer's thesis suggests that, in general, all people are geeks in one way or another. Do the examples and details provided convince you that this premise is correct? Why or why not?

WRITING A DEFINITION ESSAY A

This essay suggests that many people, perhaps most people, have a geek side—in other words, that being geeky is far more common than generally acknowledged. But the polar opposite of geekiness—*coolness*—is an altogether different thing. For this assignment, think of what it means to be cool and then create an expanded definition that explores and explains this rare quality. As you write, consider various aspects of definition, including denotation and connotation; use of etymology, synonyms, and negation; and appropriate personal interpretations or experiences.

WRITING A DEFINITION ESSAY B

A geek, as paragraph 4 of this essay indicates, has little style in fashion and personal appearance. But what does a term like *style* even mean? Use the power of definition to write an essay of about 500 words in which you spell out the characteristics of this highly subjective term. Think in terms of the elements of an effective definition as well as denotation and connotation. Include any personal interpretations or experiences, as well as synonyms, etymology, or negation, that will help communicate your meaning to your reader.

9

Illustration: Considering a Definition Essay

YELLOW SKIES, BLUE TREES
Joe Rogers

Chief among the things that sighted people take for granted about vision is that the colors in the world match their names and the expectations generally held about them—the blue of the ocean, the green of the grass, the orange of, well, oranges. But as anyone who has ever taken a basic art course or simply closely examined places and things knows, any single color involves a whole range of shades. Still, when the majority of people look at the yellow of a daffodil or the red of a Valentine heart, they perceive the same basic hue. For a sizable minority, however—by some counts around 12 percent of males of European descent—the pink of a rose or the purple of an eggplant is quite different from what the majority see. In the following essay, which originally appeared as a "My Turn" piece in Newsweek, *journalist Joe Rogers offers an extended definition of colorblindness that takes his reader into a world that is far from colorless.*

In a world full of vibrant colors, what does it mean to be colorblind?

A fellow fourth grader broke the news to me after she saw my effort on a class assignment involving scissors and construction paper. "You cut out a purple bluebird," she said. There was no reproach in her voice, just a certain puzzlement. Her observation opened my eyes—not that my eyes particularly help—to the fact that I am colorblind. In the 36 years since, I've been trying to understand what that means. I'm still not sure I do.

My research hasn't been overly scientific. I know colorblindness is almost always a genetic condition, affecting males far more often than females. It has to do with color receptors, called cones, in the retina. There's some question as to whether the problem exists in the cones themselves, or the brain's ability to process the signals the cones send.

That debate I leave to others. I'm more concerned with the practical effects, such as: how can I tell when the hamburgers I'm grilling are done? Some of my past dinner guests can attest to the difficulty I've had making that determination.

On the positive side, there's a certain conversational value in the condition. When I confess my colorblindness (it often has a way of coming up), people at first assume my world resembles a Mathew Brady photograph or a 1930s movie, pre–Ted Turner. I explain to them the failing of the word itself. Total colorblindness is exceedingly rare. People who suffer from it usually have a host of other problems as well, including extreme sensitivity to light and poor visual acuity. Those of us with a simple color-vision deficiency face much more mundane problems: If I wear this shirt with these pants, will people stare? Or, worse, laugh?

Early on, I learned the hazards of shopping alone for clothes, when I bought a blue shirt that turned out to be—yes—purple. Even dressing myself is hazardous. I've mistaken green shirts for gray, brown pants for green. And I'm hopeless with ties. I never wear one unless it's been cleared for use by someone I trust.

Fortunately, some clothing makers include the color of their garments on price tags. Unfortunately, those colors tend to be listed in terms such as raisin, sesame, citron, salmon, shrimp, celery, saffron, wheat and maize. It doesn't help to tell me my clothes are the color of a fruit, grain, seasoning or water creature when I don't know what color any of them is, either.

Because the most common form of colorblindness involves distinguishing red and green, people logically assume it involves only those two hues. That is the type I have, but the problem is not as simple as it sounds. Sometimes I can tell red from green. Sometimes I can't. It depends on how intense the colors are, how much light is available, how far away I am from the objects in question.

I can always tell a red traffic signal from a green one, for instance. I can't tell a lone red signal from a yellow one. At night, from a distance, I can't tell a green signal from the glow of a street light. My confusion can make for some adventurous driving.

Other nonassertive colors can be troublesome, too. When I bought my house a few years back, I assumed the living-room walls were some variation of a neutral white tone. A visitor told me they were, in fact, quite pink—that I was more or less living inside a bottle of Pepto-Bismol. I called a painter who recommended something he called eggshell. I took his advice.

That sort of thing is a source of great amusement for my color-visioned friends. When they learn my world is not completely black and white, they get a kick out of pointing to various items and asking what color I think they are. When I say I don't know, they almost invariably ask: "Well, what color does it look like?"

It's hard to explain that the color they see simply isn't on my list of options. They seem to prefer to think that I see all the right colors but in the wrong places. That life for me, and those similarly afflicted, is a psychedelic planet of yellow skies, blue trees and orange oceans. I admit, I sometimes wonder myself whether other people see a completely different world.

Usually my problem is of little consequence. Like not knowing whether I've picked up a spearmint or cinnamon gum ball until I put it into my mouth. Or having to ask a store clerk what, precisely, is meant by a tag that says a jacket is "bark."

Of course, my career options have been limited by my condition. Fashion designer or interior decorator were never on the list. And in the case of war, where it might be of real importance to differentiate the people in green uniforms from those in brown or gray, I would not be your man.

There have been certain drawbacks in my job as newspaper reporter. When it comes to painting a picture in words, my palette is limited. There are no comparative allusions to sunsets in my work, no evocations of azure or magenta. No one has ever described my writing as colorful.

At least two purported cures exist. One involves a red-orange contact lens, worn only on one eye. A Japanese clinic claims results with treatments involving electrodes at specific points—a sort of electric acupuncture. I haven't personally investigated either, partly because I'm not sure my brain could handle a world without color confusion. Besides, I wonder how much real need there is to be able to perceive jute or ocher.

Over the years I've considered petitioning the federal government to include colorblindness among the legally recognized disabilities, but I suspect we lack collective political clout. I've also made some passing effort to form an association—a League for the Color-Vision Impaired, say. Unlike left-handers, however, we seem disinclined to rally round our deviation from the norm. Thus there's no ready source of information about how many presidents, or military heroes, or rock singers have been colorblind.

Based on the law of averages, though, there must have been some. We are everywhere, trying to cope, trying to blend in. Usually we succeed. Until someone spots our purple bluebirds. Then the jig is up.

9

MASTERY EXERCISE 2 Considering Significance and Meaning

1. According to Rogers, what is the biggest misconception most people have about colorblindness?
2. Most of Rogers's examples concern mundane matters—mismatched clothes, shopping issues, decorating concerns, and so on. By concentrating on these kinds of examples, what is Rogers suggesting about being colorblind?
3. In his final two paragraphs, Rogers suggests and then discards the idea of political action to bring attention to colorblindness. In doing so, what point is he reemphasizing about being colorblind?

MASTERY EXERCISE 3 **Analyzing Method and Technique**

1. Rogers offers a limited definition of colorblindness in the second paragraph. How does this brief definition help move the extended definition forward?
2. In both the fourth and seventh paragraphs, Rogers includes negation. How does this use of negation help him develop his definition?
3. In your view, which of Rogers's many examples of colorblindness does the best job of developing or supporting his extended definition? What about this example makes it stand out?

WRITING A DEFINITION ESSAY C

Certainly, Rogers's primary focus is to explain colorblindness to, in his words, the "color-visioned." At the same time, however, his essay concerns *perception* and *sensitivity*. For this assignment, choose one of these two terms and write an essay of about 500 words in which you use definition to communicate the meaning of this general, abstract term in clear and complete detail to your reader.

WRITING A DEFINITION ESSAY D

As a colorblind person, Rogers is different from the majority of people, an outsider of sorts. But what does it actually mean to be an outsider, someone on the fringe of some part of the mainstream? In Rogers's case, it is being colorblind in a world of color-sighted people. For others, it is being left-handed; having a musical, artistic, or athletic gift; being overly sensitive; having a great or a poor memory; and so on. For this assignment, consider an element of your own combination of talents and characteristics—or the combination possessed by someone you know—that indicates outsider status. Then write an essay of about 500 words in which you turn to definition to spell out what it means to be different from most people.

Summary Exercise

1. Prewrite on one of the following topics, identifying the specific characteristics that distinguish it:

   - An optimist
   - Proper etiquette, 21st-century style
   - The perfect date

2. Create a draft essay of about 500 words in which you use definition to delineate in full detail the unique elements and qualities of your subject so that your reader understands it as you do.

3. Using the Definition Essay Checklist, page 130, as a guide, revise your draft. Make sure your introduction indicates the idea or concept to be defined and that you have built upon the elements of an effective dictionary definition. At the same time, check to see that you have included both a limited and an expanded definition; synonyms, etymology, and negation when appropriate; and personal interpretation or experiences. Finally, be sure that you have considered denotation and connotation and provided sufficient transition throughout. Remember to seek the assistance of an objective reader to evaluate your essay relative to these points.

4. Addressing any problems you and your reader have identified, create a final draft of your definition essay.

9

10

Comparison and Contrast

Understanding Comparison and Contrast

Whenever your goal is to make your reader understand the commonalities or distinctions between subjects, the organizing strategy to turn to is **comparison and contrast**. *Comparison* means examining similarities, and *contrast* means examining differences. Through this organizing mode, you can explain how subjects—people, objects, phenomena, and so on—are alike or how they are different and then draw some conclusions from your findings.

In other college courses, you'll likely turn to comparison and contrast to deal with essay questions, research papers, and other analytical writing tasks, for instance, examining competing theories on economic development or dominant approaches to treat anxiety. In a writing course, comparison and contrast would enable you to evaluate such subjects as e-book technology versus traditional printed texts. Both as a student and as a professional beyond the classroom, you will often be called on to evaluate alternatives, so the mode of comparison and contrast is an important technique to master.

The Elements of an Effective Comparison and Contrast Essay

To make your comparison and contrast essay effective, be sure to include the elements described on this and the following pages.

Sufficient Transition

The following transitional expressions will be valuable when you write a comparison and contrast paragraph. With similarities, consider the words and phrases listed for "Comparison," and with differences, refer to the ones listed for "Contrast."

TRANSITIONAL EXPRESSIONS FOR COMPARISON AND CONTRAST WRITING

Comparison		Contrast	
also	just as	although	however
both, neither	like	but	on the other hand
in the same way	similarly	in contrast	unlike

Clear Subjects and Focus

10

No matter what you are writing about, your reader depends on you to provide a clear direction about what your essay will discuss. With a comparison and contrast essay, you provide this clear direction by identifying your subjects and specifying your focus, either comparison or contrast, in your introduction.

The ideal spot to make these points is your thesis. Consider the following thesis for an essay contrasting computer game systems:

But the biggest reason to choose Sony's PlayStation over Microsoft's Xbox 360 is that the PlayStation has features, including a Blu-ray player and Wi-Fi capability, that the Xbox doesn't.

This thesis indicates that the subjects are Sony's PlayStation and Microsoft's Xbox 360, and that the focus is on contrast. It also prepares the reader for the discussion to follow, which will spell out in full detail why PlayStation is preferable to the Xbox.

Keep in mind that it may take more than a single sentence to provide a specific direction. In such cases, just make sure that you've made your point clear by the end of your introduction.

A Clear Basis for Comparison or Contrast

Whenever you use comparison and contrast, you need to establish your **basis for comparison**. In other words, once you have chosen your subjects and your focus, you must specify the characteristics or elements you are going to examine.

If you were going to write an essay contrasting two movements in art—Neoclassicism and Romanticism, for example—you might examine issues related to the two movements like *the purpose art should serve, the way nature should be viewed, the roles form and structure should play*, and *the relative position and significance humans should occupy*.

Once you have established this basis of comparison, the next step is to discuss each of these issues for each of the movements. To be sure you include comparable information for both movements on every point, you may find it helpful to construct a planning chart like this one:

	Neoclassicism	Romanticism
The purpose art should serve		
The way nature should be viewed		
The roles form and structure should play		
The position and significance humans should occupy		

10

Keep this point in mind: it is certainly possible to write a comparison and contrast essay that examines three or more subjects relative to each other. However, you'll likely find that an examination of two alternatives with common ground is more manageable for you and easier for your reader to follow.

A Thorough and Specific Presentation

With a comparison and contrast essay, just as with any other essay, you need to examine the subjects fully. Of course, no rule specifies the number of points of comparison you should establish, but common sense indicates that subjects striking you as similar or dissimilar do so because of more than one or two aspects. Therefore, as you work through the writing process, shoot for a basis of comparison that contains at least three points and then add any additional points that you develop as you write.

For example, imagine you were going to write a paper contrasting downhill skiing with snowboarding. Certainly, these two winter sports are different in terms of equipment required (skis, boots, poles, and so on, for downhill skiing versus a snowboard for snowboarding) and terrain preferred (steep mountain slopes for downhill versus half-pipes, tables, and jumps for snowboarding). An essay covering only these points would provide an incomplete, ineffective analysis of the two winter activities. But add discussions of common injuries suffered (ankle and knee injuries in downhill—especially torn ligaments and cartilage from sharp turns—versus wrist, face, and tailbone injuries for snowboarders falling with feet locked into their boards), and the picture of the differences between these sports is far clearer for your reader.

An Effective Arrangement for Your Comparison or Contrast

How you present the information in an essay is always important because an effective arrangement makes it easier for your reader to follow your line of reasoning. In a comparison and contrast essay, organization is especially important because the focus is on an examination of more than one subject.

With an essay comparing or contrasting two subjects, you have three possible methods of arrangement: the **block method**, the **alternating method**, and the **mixed method.** Imagine, for example, you were writing about two supervisors for whom you've worked, and you had established this basis of comparison: knowledge of the job, leadership, patience with workers, and basic fairness.

With the block method, as this informal outline shows, after the introduction you would first discuss these qualities for supervisor 1—paragraph by paragraph—and then discuss the same criteria in the same order for supervisor 2, followed by a conclusion:

Block Method

Introduction

Supervisor 1

    Knowledge of job

    Leadership

    Patience with workers

    Basic fairness

Supervisor 2

    Knowledge of job

    Leadership

    Patience with workers

    Basic fairness

Conclusion

With the alternating method, after the introduction you would first discuss knowledge of the job for supervisor 1 and then for supervisor 2. Next, you would discuss leadership for supervisor 1 and then for supervisor 2, and so on, until the conclusion, as this informal outline shows:

Alternating Method

Introduction

Knowledge of Job

    Supervisor 1

    Supervisor 2

Leadership

    Supervisor 1

    Supervisor 2

Patience with Workers

    Supervisor 1

    Supervisor 2

Basic Fairness

    Supervisor 1

    Supervisor 2

Conclusion

10

With the mixed method, as the name suggests, you use a combination of techniques in order to emphasize some point. In the essay contrasting your two supervisors, you might follow the block format for the first three points and then switch to the alternating format for the final point to underscore how important it is that a supervisor consistently treat employees with basic fairness.

A Comparison and Contrast Essay Checklist

Once you complete a draft of a comparison and contrast essay, use the following **Comparison and Contrast Essay Checklist** to evaluate it. Then ask an objective reader to do the same.

COMPARISON AND CONTRAST ESSAY CHECKLIST

❏ Does the introduction specify the essay's focus and the subjects to be compared or contrasted?

❏ Is there sufficient transition to make it easy for the reader to make sense of the different aspects of comparison or contrast?

❏ Is a clear basis for comparison or contrast established and closely followed?

❏ Has a thorough and specific presentation involving at least three points of discussion been provided?

❑ Are the points arranged effectively, following the method—block, alternating, or mixed—that most effectively communicates the point about the subjects?

Use the answers to these questions to help you revise your essay and create an effective final draft.

Analysis: Examining an Annotated Comparison and Contrast Essay

Turning the Pages: Print Books versus E-Books

This introduction identifies the **two subjects**—e-books and traditional, printed books. The final sentence serves as the **thesis**, indicating a **focus** of contrast—that traditional books are superior to e-books.

Here is the first of the three points of contrast comprising the **thorough and specific presentation**. Note the many precise examples and illustrations concerning costs associated with both e-books and print books.

For hundreds of years, when people picked up a book, they could count on one thing. The book would look pretty much like books have looked since the development of the printing press. But consumers now have a new choice: e-books. Today, companies like Barnes and Noble and Amazon.com sell specialized e-book readers that are wirelessly connected to their bookstores. They hope that this digital technology will transform everyone's reading habits, but I won't be one of the converts. When it comes to cost, ease of lending, and functionality, you can't beat an old-fashioned printed book.

One important consideration when it comes to e-books is cost. It's true that a number of e-books are available for free, and even new e-books downloaded wirelessly to a reader generally cost only around $10. The issue isn't the price of the books but the cost of the e-book

Note the **clear basis of comparison** between the two kinds of books: **cost, ease of lending,** and **functionality** of e-books versus print books.

10

reader. Both Amazon's Kindle and Barnes and Noble's Nook retail for over $200, which is a hefty investment just to read a book. In contrast, when it comes to traditional books, even a hardcover best seller costs under $30. Paperbacks and discounted hardcover books cost far less, with perfectly good used books costing only a fraction of the original price. Furthermore, with a traditional book, nothing else is needed. All you have to do is open the cover and turn the pages.

> The essay follows the **alternating method**, discussing e-books first and then print books. The **transitional expression** *In contrast* indicates the movement from the first to the second subject.

Another issue to consider is ease of lending your books to others. Right now, if you purchase and download an e-book to a Kindle, the only way you can share that book with someone else is also to share your Kindle, which would leave you without a reading device. If you purchase an e-book on a Nook, you can share it with someone else, but the other person also has to have a Nook, and the book can be shared for only 14 days. On the other hand, with a traditional book, once you purchase it, you can do what you want with it. You can read your book, and lend it to a friend for as long as you'd like. Then, when it is returned, you can lend it to someone else and repeat the process as often as you'd like. You can even give your book away—or, if you wish, throw it away. It doesn't get more flexible than that.

> Here is the second of the **three points of contrast** comprising the **thorough and specific presentation**. Note the many precise examples and illustrations related to lending the two different types of books.

> The essay follows the **alternating method**, and the **transitional expression** *On the other hand* indicates that the discussion is moving from e-books to print books.

Maybe the biggest issue to consider with e-books is basic practicality. It is not that e-readers like the Kindle and Nook make reading difficult

Here is the third of the **three points of contrast** comprising the **thorough and specific presentation**. Note the many precise examples and illustrations related to the practicality involved in using the two different types of books.

because they certainly don't. In fact, both readers use E-ink technology, which makes the electronic page look very much like the printed page. Furthermore, the devices make negotiating through the text and performing simple steps like bookmarking sections and highlighting passages easy. But an e-reader is still a sensitive electronic device. If you drop it or spill water on it, it could be severely damaged, perhaps even beyond repair, and you would certainly need to think twice before taking one to the beach. An e-book reader is just not practical enough for that. You don't have any of

The essay follows the **alternating method**, and the **transitional expression** *however* indicates the switch from a discussion of e-books to a discussion of print books.

these concerns with a traditional book, however. What could be easier and more convenient? If you drop it, you just pick it up, dust it off, and resume reading. If you spill something on it, just wipe off the pages. When you want to note a section or passage, you can use an actual bookmark or highlighter. If you want to read at the beach or in the bathtub, go right ahead. It's just that simple.

10

In today's world, technology continues to play an increasingly large role. In most cases, it makes our lives better or easier. But when it comes to reading, I don't think the digital version of a printed text is necessarily an improvement over what already exists. In terms of cost, ease of lending, and practicality, a traditional printed book remains a better choice than an e-book any day, at least for me.

This conclusion restates the significance of the thesis and the supporting paragraphs: that relative to cost, ease of lending, and practicality, a traditional book is superior to its electronic counterpart.

MASTERY EXERCISE 1 **Responding to the Annotated Essay**

1. From the introduction through the entire essay, e-books are discussed before print books. Why do you think the writer chose to discuss the subjects in this order? Do you agree with this strategy? Why do you feel this way?

2. The essay is arranged according to the alternating method. How do you think the overall effectiveness of the essay would be altered if the examples had been set up in the block method? Explain your reasoning.

3. Of the supporting examples and details about the two types of books, which do you think does the most to support the main idea? Why do you feel that this example is superior to the others?

10

WRITING A COMPARISON AND CONTRAST ESSAY A

This essay concerns a contrast between two forms of the same thing, one older, more traditional, and long established and the other newer, more modern, and innovative. In some ways, it also serves as a commentary on the past versus the present. For this assignment, think of two forms of the same thing, one older and one newer—for example, vinyl records versus CDs or other digital forms of music, a classic car versus a similar contemporary vehicle, a vintage blockbuster movie versus a recent blockbuster production, and so on—and write an essay of about 500 words. As this annotated essay does, be sure to identify your focus and subjects and establish a clear basis for comparison. At the same time, be sure to provide at least three points of discussion and to choose an effective method of arrangement, either the block, alternating, or mixed method, with appropriate transition.

WRITING A COMPARISON AND CONTRAST ESSAY B

The annotated essay discusses two competing e-book readers, Amazon's Kindle and Barnes and Noble's Nook. For this assignment, write an essay of about 500 words in which you use comparison and contrast to examine two versions of the same type of device or technology—competing brands of cell phones, BlackBerry devices, MP3 players, laptop computers, computer game systems, and so on. Use the annotated essay as a guide, making sure to specify your subjects and focus and establish a clear basis of comparison with at least three points of discussion. Decide on the best method of arrangement—block, alternating, or mixed—and provide transitions to make it easy for your reader to follow your presentation.

Illustration: Considering a Comparison and Contrast Essay

HOLIDAYS HELP REMIND US OF ALL THAT HAS CHANGED
Margery Eagan

Among the indisputable truths of life is that time marches on, bringing with it unavoidable changes, good and bad. Here, Boston Herald *columnist Margery Eagan deals with this issue relative to holiday traditions within her extended family. As a featured columnist, Eagan writes on a wide variety of subjects from parenting to politics. Her career has also included stints for* Boston Magazine *and several other newspapers. In addition to her duties as a* Boston Herald *columnist, she currently co-hosts a morning drive-time talk show in Boston. In this essay, Eagan pits memories of family Thanksgivings from her youth against contemporary celebrations, an examination that she labels "bittersweet."*

Do the differences that occur because of the passing of time mean that newer celebrations or traditions will always fall short in comparison to celebrations or traditions of the past?

10

Life is a series of adjustments, my mother used to say. Holidays remind us of that.

My own Thanksgivings began in formal days when father knew best. He wore a thin tie and wingtips and lit up a Winston for the short ride to our cousins' in a smoky Chevrolet. We girls wore black patent leathers and smocked dresses with crinolines. Mothers' handbags matched their suits.

Certain other details are well-remembered: the grown-ups' table set with damask linen and Aunt Anna's family china: ivory colored with pink roses and green leaves not just painted on but slightly raised, like rosebuds in relief. Franciscan Desert Rose was its name.

The teen-age cousins' table offered nothing memorable, nor the little cousins'. But we did play press-the-fork-into-the-peas, thus squishing them open and into gravy-soaked mashed potatoes. Then we played hide and seek among 20 or so winter coats piled onto couches in the den by my parents, Aunt Anna and Uncle Bill, Rita and Philip, Mary and Frank, some neighbors and too many children to name. These were ancient times: not even *The Wizard of Oz* on TV for the kids.

After those years, things got complicated. If you went away to college, Thanksgiving became the time to come home and compare roads taken with high school friends at the Thanksgiving football game. It became the time to criticize, often obnoxiously and out loud, everything that suddenly seemed embarrassing, parochial and oh-so-unsophisticated about grandparents, siblings, the mother and father who'd known best just months before.

Once married, you were forced every other year to abandon the cousins for the in-laws' foreign rituals. Their stuffing tasted fishy. They blasted the football game from a TV just inches from a table adorned not with linen and rosebud china but with a paper tablecloth and gallon-sized Pepsi bottles. At least by then we had Thanksgiving TV specials to gather round: *E.T. the Extra-Terrestrial* had landed.

Things became more complicated still when half the cousins divorced. Somebody's children were always missing, spending Thanksgiving with the ex and his new wife's family. A cousin far too old to be dating at all showed up with a new young girlfriend and two sullen teens pining for their presplit family.

This is the time when Thanksgiving turns bittersweet, when it's much about who isn't there: children of divorce, parents and grandparents who've died. This is when there's a change in venue from the childhood home, sold to strangers now, to the home of a little cousin all grown up. Typically that's a daughter, a 30 something or middle-age orphan who steps up to produce the annual feast, to keep traditions going; to fret over thawing times and serving spoons without advice and counsel from the previous producer, her mother. She'd captained her kitchen seamlessly, with such authority. But she took her secrets with her.

Last week I visited the cousin who inherited Aunt Anna's Desert Rose china. It was there in the kitchen cabinet, ready for another holiday season, its rosebuds and pale greens as shiny and pristine as ever. The Desert Rose has not aged. Yet Aunt Anna's been dead five years on Saturday, my own mother eight years yesterday; the dapper fathers who mixed the holiday Manhattans? Two decades ago.

This year most of those sitting before the Desert Rose can't even imagine a world in which good fathers blew smoke rings to enchant their little girls. But then life is a series of adjustments, my mother used to say. Holidays remind us of that.

10

MASTERY EXERCISE 2   Considering Significance and Meaning

1. According to Margery Eagan, what were the Thanksgivings of the past like for the adults in her family? What were they like for her and her cousins?
2. As Eagan and the people in her family grew older, what experiences, events, and transitions became "complicated"?
3. Through all the changes in Eagan's family's holiday traditions over the years, what item links the past and present?

MASTERY EXERCISE 3 Analyzing Method and Technique

1. Throughout the essay, Margery Eagan provides lots of details and examples to illustrate the Thanksgivings of her youth and the various stages of her adulthood. In your view, which general period does she capture more effectively? Which detail or example does the most to help illustrate this particular era? What about it leads you to this conclusion?

2. Eagan employs the mixed order to arrange her essay, first discussing her childhood memories of family Thanksgiving celebrations and then memories of family Thanksgiving celebrations during different periods of adulthood. In what ways does this method of arrangement contribute to the effectiveness of her essay?

3. In general, a conclusion should capture the significance of the main point and the ideas, examples, illustrations, and details that explain or support it. Consider Eagan's conclusion: in your view, does it fulfill this requirement? Why do you feel this way?

10

Writing a Comparison and Contrast Essay C

In her essay, Margery Eagan recalls family Thanksgivings over the years, largely focusing on differences that have resulted from the passing of time and the changing of circumstances. How about your own family holiday festivities? For this assignment, use comparison and contrast to write an essay of about 500 words in which you discuss one of your own regular family gatherings. You might, as Margery Eagan does, examine how this celebration has changed over the years. Or, if you'd prefer, you might explore the ways that a particular annual get-together has remained constant. Regardless of your approach, be sure to clarify your subjects and focus, establish a clear basis for comparison or contrast, and deal with the points of discussion in detail. At the same time, choose a method of arrangement—block, alternating, or mixed, with appropriate transition—that most effectively communicates your point to your reader.

Writing a Comparison and Contrast Essay D

In the beginning of her essay, Margery Eagan discusses elements and details from her childhood, a time of "formal days when father knew best," a world far different from today's. In what specific ways has the world changed since your own childhood? For this assignment, write an essay of about 500 words in which you examine significant ways that today's world differs from the one you experienced as a child. As you do, indicate your subjects and focus, establish a clear basis for comparison or contrast, and cover your points of discussion in detail. Consider the pros and cons of the block method, alternating method, and mixed method, and choose the most appropriate order of arrangement along with suitable transition to make sure your ideas flow smoothly.

Summary Exercise

1. Prewrite on one of the following topics, focusing on similarities or differences that come to mind:

   - Two similar sports, for example, ultimate fighting and boxing, football and soccer, or lacrosse and hockey
   - Two teaching or communication styles
   - Two related academic or professional fields, for instance, psychology and sociology, oceanography and marine biology, or justice studies and forensic science

2. Create a draft essay of about 500 words in which you use comparison and contrast to examine one of the subjects in relation to the other and communicate your findings to your reader.

3. Using the Comparison and Contrast Essay Checklist, pages 146–147, as a guide, revise your draft. Make sure that you include an effective introduction that identifies your subjects and your focus. In addition, provide a clear basis for comparison or contrast and explain and fully support your points of discussion. Finally, ensure that you have chosen the most appropriate method of organization—the block method, the alternating method, or the mixed method—and included sufficient transitions throughout. Have an objective reader evaluate your essay in terms of these points as well.

4. Addressing any problems you and your reader have identified, create a final draft of your comparison and contrast essay.

10

11

Cause and Effect

Understanding Cause and Effect

When you write, the mode that allows you to establish what led to an event, condition, or situation, or what resulted from it, is known as **cause and effect**. Cause is *why* something happened, and effect is the *outcome* or *consequence* of an incidence. This organizing strategy enables you to analyze and explore the significance of a subject, considering the reasons that it occurred or the outcomes—or consequences—because it occurred.

An essay about how cybercrimes have affected personal privacy would call for cause and effect. This writing technique would also be the natural choice for an essay about why an auto accident occurred. Because it enables you to examine the often-complex relationships between an event or experience and what led up to it or resulted from it, the mode of cause and effect is important to master.

The Elements of an Effective Cause and Effect Essay

To make your cause and effect essay effective, be sure to include the elements described on the following pages.

Sufficient Transition

The following transitional expressions will be especially useful when you write a cause and effect essay. If your focus is on what leads to something, refer to the words listed under "Cause," and if your focus is on what happens as a result, consider the words listed under "Effect".

Cause		Effect	
because	since	as a result	if
cause	so that	consequently	therefore
reason	unless	effect	thus

An Appropriate Focus

Because of its power to untangle the web of relationships inherent in complex subjects, the organizational strategy of cause and effect has enormous value to you as a writer. The exact focus will of course depend on the scope of your writing task, your aim, and your audience's needs.

Sometimes, you'll find an examination of both cause and effect necessary to help your reader gain a full understanding of the significance of the subject of your essay, as this thesis illustrates:

> But genuine education reform involves the identification of
> *causes*   *effects*
> policies that led to the system-wide failure to achieve and meaningful policies to ensure that the same mistakes aren't made again.

With other essays, you'll concentrate exclusively on cause, as this thesis demonstrates:

> The truth is that a person can develop a phobia for many
>   *causes*
> different reasons.

Other times, you'll write an essay that focuses on effect alone, as this thesis shows:

> Just one experience of forgetting my lines during a play in the
>   *effects*
> second grade has had a lot of unexpected consequences.

Remember that your reader always depends on you to provide a clear direction. As these examples illustrate, one sure way to provide this direction in a cause and effect essay is to specify your focus in your thesis.

Direct and Related Causes and Effects

All events and situations have *direct* causes and effects and *related* causes and effects. It's important to distinguish between them to ensure that you don't inadvertently misstate any of the relationships you discuss.

Consider what happened to the U.S. Midwest during the 1930s, a phenomenon that became known as the "Dust Bowl." After several years of drought, the topsoil became so parched that it literally turned to dust and blew away.

Clearly, the *direct* cause of this disaster was the weather. But *related* causes included the farmers' ignorance about such farming techniques as proper crop rotation, fertilization, and irrigation and the marketplace's demands, which encouraged farmers to grow the same crops year after year, even though doing so eventually strips soil of its vitality.

The *direct* effect of the calamity was widespread crop failure. Two *related* effects were the permanent displacement of thousands of families, whose heavily mortgaged farms were taken by the banks, and an increase in the population of migrant workers in agriculturally rich California.

Be sure not to confuse cause and effect relationships with *coincidence*—events, ideas, or experiences that occur at the same time or in sequence but purely by accident. That you bought a new computer before your doorbell stopped working doesn't mean that one event caused the other.

Finally, to ensure that you don't overstate your case, use appropriate *qualifying language,* words that allow for another option or outcome. These words—*might be, seems, appears, rarely, often, sometimes, maybe, perhaps, probably, seldom,* and so on—will help you avoid making a claim that you can't support. When you write, "Kaisha's decision to run the first mile of the 5K race a little more slowly than her normal pace *might be* the reason that she was able to pass five other runners in the last 400 yards," you allow for the possibility that she finished strongly for some other reason.

Awareness of Multiple Cause and Effect Situations

Once you have determined that you are dealing with a legitimate causal relationship, you need to present the relationship in its full complexity. Most situations and conditions have multiple causes and multiple effects. Furthermore, a single cause may have more than one effect, and one effect may have several causes.

For example, your decision a few years ago to pursue guitar lessons had a number of outcomes—increased confidence, new friends, involvement in a band, and so on. The failure of a restaurant happened because of a number of factors, including a lack of advertising, limited parking, higher-than-average prices, a poorly trained waitstaff, and an unimaginative menu. Therefore, be sure that you thoroughly examine your subject to avoid oversimplifying what led up to it or what has happened or will happen as a result of it.

An Effective Arrangement

In order to present all cause and effect relationships as clearly and convincingly as possible, you must select an *effective arrangement*. For example, chronological order would be a good choice to explain the gradual and cumulative effects of acid rain, spelling out how particulates from expended fossil fuels rise into the atmosphere and eventually return to earth in the form of acidic precipitation, which gradually erodes limestone, marble, and mortar and damages the surfaces of structures and vehicles.

If you were writing about the impact that volunteerism can have on a community, you might focus on the transformation of a neglected city park after you and your campus club cleaned and rehabilitated it. In this case, spatial order would enable you to walk your reader through the park in a logical fashion—in this case, front to back. You might start near the now spotless parking lot, move on to the new equipment in the children's playground behind it, and then shift to the rear of the park and the basketball courts, with new backboards and nets and freshly marked lines, plus the newly painted comfort station to the right of the court.

With many topics, however, especially complex subjects involving multiple cause or effect relationships, you will likely find emphatic order the best method of arrangement. Consider a subject like childhood obesity. Health care specialists frequently use words like *crisis* and *epidemic* to describe this issue, and they have identified a number of causes, including socioeconomic status, lack of exercise, genetics and family history, and poor eating habits. Certainly, all these points contribute to childhood obesity, but in your view, two of them—poor eating habits and lack of exercise—are the biggest problems. Emphatic order would enable you to structure your essay so that you move from a significant cause to more significant causes, saving the most significant causes for last, as this informal outline shows:

Introduction Childhood obesity is a national crisis with a number of identifiable—and largely controllable—causes.

- socioeconomic status
- genetics and family history
- poor eating habits
- lack of exercise

Conclusion An unhealthy future awaits obese children, so the time to make changes is now.

A Cause and Effect Essay Checklist

Once you complete a draft of a cause and effect essay, use the following **Cause and Effect Essay Checklist** to evaluate it. Then ask an objective reader to do the same.

11

CAUSE AND EFFECT ESSAY CHECKLIST

❑ Does the introduction identify the subject and indicate the specific focus on cause or effect?

❑ Is there sufficient transition throughout to guide the reader through the cause and effect relationships?

❑ Does the essay distinguish between direct causes and effects and related causes and effects and between actual cause and effect relationships and simple coincidence?

❑ Has appropriate qualifying language (*might be, seems, appears, could, may*) been used to avoid overstating any relationship?

❑ Does the essay effectively illustrate multiple cause and effect relationships, with enough examples and details to avoid oversimplification?

❑ Is the order of arrangement—chronological, spatial, or emphatic—appropriate to make all cause and effect relationships clear for the reader?

Use the answers to these questions to help you revise your essay and create an effective final draft.

Analysis: Examining an Annotated Cause and Effect Essay

Not Just One of Those Things

e opening —•
ntences of the
roduction
aw the reader
by playing on
e common
citement most
ung people
el at the
ospect of
tting their
ver's license.

For as long as I can remember, all I wanted to do was get my driver's license. As soon as I turned sixteen, I began counting down the days until I could take my driver's education classes, get my learner's permit, and finally get behind the wheel. On the day I turned sixteen and a half and was eligible for a license, I took my driver's test and passed. When the woman at the Department of Motor Vehicles snapped my picture and then handed me my license, I was on top of the world. Three weeks later, my feelings were quite different when I had my first accident. The police determined that the accident wasn't my fault, and that was a good thing as far as my insurance rates are concerned. The truth is that a number of factors contributed to the accident that shook my driving confidence and left two cars heavily damaged.

•—The thesis
indicates the
subject—an
automobile
accident—and
the **focus**, in this
case, on the
causes of the
accident.

ur **direct**
uses of the
cident are
sented,
icating that —•
e cause and
ect situation is
mplex.

For one thing, the accident occurred at a spot that has been identified as the third most dangerous intersection in the entire state because of the heavy foliage that reduces visibility. I had seen more than one accident there over the years, so I was being cautious, but the other driver was from out of state. She just barely stopped at the stop sign and then accelerated without noticing that I was already in the intersection. When I saw her, I immediately jammed on my brakes, but her car skidded into the front quarter of my mother's car. Her lack of familiarity with the area was probably a contributing factor. If she had known more about the area, maybe she would have taken a second look before stepping on the gas.

Of course, the weather on the day of the accident didn't help either of us. It was a rainy mid-November afternoon, and the street was covered with wet leaves. When I saw the car heading towards me and hit the brakes, I felt the car skid a little, even though I was barely moving at the time. The other driver was traveling faster than I was, so when she braked, her car actually seemed to pick up speed for a couple of seconds as it slid on wet leaves before slamming into my car.

Another contributing factor is that the other driver might not have been paying full attention to her driving. As her car hit me, I thought I saw her holding something in her hand. A witness later said that it was her phone, and that she appeared to be texting. When the

---

*Notice the inclusion of **a related example**—the other driver's lack of knowledge about the area—and the **qualifying words** probably and maybe.*

11

*Here is the third of the four **direct causes**—the other driver's apparent inattention. The arrangement of the examples in **emphatic order** accentuates the point that this factor contributed even more than the reasons previously presented.*

*The causes are arranged in **emphatic order** The first **direct cause**—that the intersection was an acknowledged dangerous area—was certainly an important factor*

*The supporting ideas are presented in **emphatic order** stressing that the second of the four **direct causes**—slippery road conditions—contributed even more than the particular intersection and other driver's lack of familiarity with the area.*

police officer asked her about it, she denied that she was talking on her phone or sending a text message, but her phone was open and on the floor of her car. In any case, the officer cited her for reckless operation of a motor vehicle, a pretty good indication that he thought she had been paying more attention to her phone than to the road in front of her.

Note the inclusion of the **qualifying words** *might not, I thought*, and *appeared to be.*

Here is the fourth **direct cause**—inexperience on the part of both drivers. The examples are presented in **emphatic order**, so the point is that of all the causes presented, overall lack of experience is the most significant factor of all.

But maybe the biggest problem was overall inexperience. I had been a licensed driver for only three weeks, and I had never driven under such weather conditions, with wet debris in the roadway. Even though the other driver was almost a year older than I was, she had gotten her license the same week I had gotten mine, so she had never driven under those kinds of conditions, either. If I had had more experience as a driver, maybe I wouldn't have just jammed on my brakes when I saw her car heading towards me and instead managed to swerve out of the way. If the other driver had been more experienced, she might have paid more attention to the heavy foliage, recognizing it as an indication that she needed to be extra cautious.

11

Note the use of **qualifying words** like *maybe, If,* and *might have.*

Even though the emphasis in this essay is on cause, note the inclusion of some **effects**—the amount of damage to the car and the anxiety about driving following the accident.

My mother's car sustained almost $6,000 of damage, but fortunately I escaped without a scratch. My parents were really supportive, making sure that I started to drive again right away, even though I was a little scared at first.

The **conclusion** recaps the main point, that an auto accident is a complex event, likely the result of several factors.

"It was just an accident," my mother said, "just one of those things." But the truth is that my first accident wasn't one of those things at all. Instead, it was several things.

MASTERY EXERCISE 1 Responding to the Annotated Essay

1. The essay presents four causes that led to an auto accident. In your view, which of these examples is developed most fully and captures the true complexity involved? What about this example makes it superior to the others?

2. As the annotations accompanying this essay indicate, the causes are arranged on the basis of emphatic order. Imagine that the writer has asked you to evaluate this order. Do you agree with how the causes are currently presented, or would you suggest changing the order of one or more of the supporting paragraphs? Why do you feel this way?

3. At several spots in this essay, qualifying language has been used. Choose two of these qualifying words or expressions and explain how they affect the meaning of the passages in which they appear.

11

WRITING A CAUSE AND EFFECT ESSAY A

In our modern, highly mobile society, it's the rare person indeed who hasn't been involved in or witnessed an auto accident. For this assignment, focus on an accident that you experienced as a driver or passenger or on an accident that you witnessed, either in person or through video (television, YouTube, etc.). Then, in an essay of about 500 words, use cause and effect to examine the event, identifying the various elements that led to the event or detailing what specifically happened as a result.

WRITING A CAUSE AND EFFECT ESSAY B

Another contributing factor in auto accidents is driver fatigue. People push on along roads and highways long after they've become tired and simply fall asleep at the wheel. As hard as they try, they can't stop sleep from overtaking them because their minds and bodies need the rest. But this kind of fatigue is nothing like *sleep deprivation*, a level of exhaustion that can have some serious mental and physical consequences. For this assignment, do some research on the subject of sleep deprivation. Then write an essay of about 500 words in which you employ cause and effect to discuss in full detail how people become sleep deprived or what can happen to them when they reach that stage.

Illustration: Considering a Cause and Effect Essay
THE SWEET, FRESH SMELL OF MORNING
Stanley Aronson

What happens if we choose the wrong brand of clothing to wear, the wrong neighborhood in which to live, the wrong type of car to buy: what will people think? Sadly, many of us are far more concerned than we should be about the opinions of others. Our fears can be even more severe with issues over which we have precious little control—things like skin texture, baldness, blushing—that others may judge as socially inferior or offensive. But how did these things come to be viewed as socially unacceptable in the first place? What are the causes? In the following essay, Stanley Aronson, Dean Emeritus of the Brown University School of Medicine, considers this question relative to one such social no-no: bad breath. Through a thorough cause and effect analysis, Aronson traces how bad breath was transformed from a simple condition to a horrible social offense.

Why did people become convinced that a harmless, naturally occurring phenomenon is instead something that calls for immediate and regular intervention and treatment?

In a tormented world burdened with all manner of human affliction, it is bizarre, if not outrageous, to go out of one's way to create a new disease. Were this to happen today, it might properly be construed as an act of bioterrorism. In fact, such a happening did take place in 1921; it was the brainchild not of some malevolent enemy, but of a paid publicist.

11

1921 was a year of renewed hope, progress and recovery. American troops had recently returned from this nation's first major conflict conducted on European soil. And the American people, both civilian and military, were recuperating from a devastating influenza pandemic that had killed more people than the trench warfare of the recently concluded Great War. Warren Harding from Ohio was president and this nation was soberly functioning with a constitutional amendment prohibiting the manufacture and sale of alcoholic beverages. The peacetime economy, no longer based upon armaments, was seeking alternative products and newly innovative ways of using previously established products. The American economy, increasingly, relied upon advertising as its medium for converting skeptics to consumers.

The pharmacies of the 1920s provided many products for mouth care. Over a score of toothpastes were available, differing only in the composition of their flavoring agent. And in a saturated market, there was little, beyond rank hyperbole, that these oral-hygiene products could possibly offer to the public. Unless, of course, a new threat to human health could be identified—or devised.

One of these oral-hygiene companies offered an astringent mouthwash to supplement the twice-daily use of toothbrushing. It was called Listerine to exploit the 19th Century accomplishments of the great British surgeon Lord Joseph Lister, who had revolutionized surgery by converting the operating room into an aseptic chamber, thereby reducing postoperative mortality caused by infection.

The original formulation for Listerine was devised by Dr. J.J. Lawrence in the early 1880s and was then sold to the Lambert Drug Co. of St. Louis. Other companies eventually duplicated the formula, and by 1921 Listerine was no longer unique. Its makers then asked the obvious question: Since all mouthwashes were essentially of the same composition, what claim might be made in behalf of Listerine to make it again indispensible to the general public? And in some smoke-filled room, a group of eager young publicists sought an answer.

All of the mouthwashes extolled the bacteria-killing attributes of their product. But the public, in the absence of some immediate threat to themselves, continued to remain indifferent. However, if some palpable hazard could be ascribed to these oral bacteria, it was argued, the public passivity might abate.

It was known that oral bacteria somehow caused bad breath. But bad breath was not life-threatening nor had medicine listed it as a definable disease. The first step, then, was to provide bad breath with the aura of clinical disease. And thus, in 1921, was created a new hybrid word, halitosis (from the Latin, *halitus*, meaning breath) and the Greek suffix *-osis* (meaning an excess of, or disease of). The accusation was then spelled out: If you have bad breath you suffer from a defined social disease called halitosis and you are therefore at grave risk of being isolated by a public offended by fetid breath.

A great advertising campaign was then initiated, carrying whispered hints of job loss, marital discord and social quarantine unless one's bad breath was instantly neutralized. The full extent of this campaign can still be measured over eight decades later.

Offensive breath did not originate in the Roaring Twenties. Physicians, particularly those examining the mouth, were certainly aware of it; it is likely that even the breaths of ancient cave dwellers were less than aesthetic; but given their more compelling problems, they probably didn't get terribly excited about it.

11

If, then, bad breath accompanied man through the millennia, what the admen of 1921 had intentionally created was not a new disease, but rather a profound fear of the possibility of bad breath, a social condition now called halitophobia.

Once halitosis had been ingrained in the public consciousness as a major social lapse (comparable in stature, perhaps, to embezzlement) it then easily aroused latent fears and defensive behaviors such as talking with a hand covering one's mouth or avoiding close contact with other persons.

The specter of halitosis was made somewhat more complex by two opposing realities: First, that in truth halitosis was quite common (an estimated 31 percent of Americans are identified by spouses or close friends as having offensive breath); and second, that dental research has now clearly identified its causes and cures.

11 Bad breath may be a sign of certain systemic diseases such as diabetes; or it may be generated by smoking or by ingesting substances such as garlic. But in the overwhelming majority of instances halitosis is caused by colonies of bacteria, on the back of the tongue, metabolizing sulfur-containing proteins originating in post-nasal secretions or in saliva-yielding aromatic organic substances. These oral bacteria, usually anaerobic, proliferate in the small crypts on the back of the tongue. Offensive breath may then be reduced by bacteriocidal lavage or by regularly brushing the back of one's tongue.

Our credulous children, learning the fundamentals of life from 30-second television advertisements, have come to believe that mortal failings such as premature baldness, body odor, dandruff and bad breath are major impediments to social acceptance and the good life. But those who have created unrest by bluntly disclosing these human shortcomings are not without compassion. They also offer solutions. And providentially these solutions are readily available as over-the-counter products in our neighborhood pharmacies.

Last year, Americans invested almost $4 billion on oral-hygiene products alone, a sum exceeding the national budgets of some Third World nations.

Halitosis yields readily to simple interventions, but the cure of obsessive halitophobia, on the other hand, will require a more substantial tolerance of one's body image, receding hairline and even one's occasional bad breath.

MASTERY EXERCISE 2 Considering Significance and Meaning

1. During 1921, what changes were occurring in the economy of the United States?
2. How did the newly created word *halitosis* contribute to the idea that bad breath is a terrible social failing?
3. In his final three paragraphs, what is Aronson saying about the relationship between advertising and social attitudes?

11

MASTERY EXERCISE 3 Analyzing Method and Technique

1. For the most part, Aronson's article focuses on both causes and effects. In what ways would the effectiveness of his article be altered had he chosen to focus on causes *only* or on effects *only*?
2. How does Aronson's approach to cause and effect arouse and maintain the interest of his readers in bad breath's improbable journey from a simple fact of living to a condition that could ruin one's life?
3. Aronson waits until near the end of the article—paragraph 13—to explain in specific terms the likely biological or medical causes of bad breath. Why do you think he saved this information for the end of the document rather than present it at the beginning? Do you agree with his strategy? Explain your reasoning.

Writing a Cause and Effect Essay C

Aronson is certainly correct about how easily people can be convinced that baldness, sweaty palms, dandruff, body odors, and so on, are "mortal failings" or somehow the result of some action on the part of ourselves or our families. But what are the actual causes and effects related to one of these common physical characteristics or conditions or some other not listed? For this assignment, select a condition above, do some research, and then write an essay of about 500 words in which you use the organizing strategy of cause and effect to explore it thoroughly, explaining the truth behind the myths or old wives' tales.

Writing a Cause and Effect Essay D

When was the last time you felt genuinely embarrassed? For this assignment, write an essay of about 500 words in which you use cause and effect to examine why this particular incident had such an impact on how you behaved, reacted, or reasoned as a result. Or you might consider what caused the embarrassing incident or the ways this incident has influenced your thinking or behavior. Regardless of your focus, be sure to discuss all cause and effect relationships thoroughly, in their full complexity.

11 Summary Exercise

1. Prewrite on one of the following topics, concentrating on some inherent cause and effect relationship:
   - Poor morale at the workplace
   - Anxieties related to traveling
   - The unexpected serious injury to or death of someone important to you

2. Create a draft essay of about 500 words in which you explore and then explain to your reader what led to an event or situation or what happened as a result.

3. Using the Cause and Effect Essay Checklist, page 160, as a guide, revise your draft. Make sure that you identify your subject and focus in the introduction. At the same time, spell out all cause and effect relationships in full detail and in full complexity, choosing the method of arrangement—chronological, spatial, or emphatic—that most effectively communicates your supporting information. Finally, remember to provide transition so that your reader is able to understand the cause and effect relationships you have identified and presented. Be sure to have an objective reader evaluate your essay in terms of these points as well.

4. Addressing any problems you and your reader have identified, create a final draft of your cause and effect essay.

12

Division and Classification

Understanding Division and Classification

When you want to simplify complex subjects in order to communicate their full meaning to your reader, the organizing strategy to turn to is **division and classification**. Actually, division and classification are separate processes of *analysis*—examining the parts that make up the whole. *Division* involves breaking up a subject into its component parts, and *classification* involves arranging component parts into groups on the basis of some principle or characteristic.

This mode would be an excellent choice for an essay about social networking activities. It would also be the ideal approach for an essay about managing the demands a college student faces. Much of the writing you will do for school and beyond the classroom will entail highly complex subjects. Because division and classification allows you to simplify complex subjects, this organizing strategy is important to master.

The Elements of an Effective Division and Classification Essay

To make your division and classification essay effective, be sure to include the elements described on this and the following pages.

Sufficient Transition

When you write a division and classification essay, the following transitional words and expressions will help you emphasize the elements or groups that make up your subject:

TRANSITIONAL EXPRESSIONS FOR DIVISION AND CLASSIFICATION WRITING

can be categorized (classified)	the first type (kind), second type, etc.
can be divided	the last category

A Logical Method of Analysis

Regardless of your subject, you need to specify your **focus**—on division or classification—and establish a **logical basis of analysis**. Most subjects can be presented in a variety of ways. You need to choose portions or categories that will make it possible for your reader to view the subject piece by piece. As a result, the whole issue or concept becomes easier to understand.

12

If you decided to write about the local hospital where you work, division would be an appropriate focus, enabling you to explain the hospital's role as a full health care center. You could discuss its emergency department, its inpatient treatment area, its diagnostic testing center, and its rehabilitation clinic. But you could also explain the hospital's role as a business, focusing on its administrative division, customer service area, treasurer's department, fund-raising center, and other functions.

If you were writing about mobile communications options, classification would be the obvious choice. You could discuss touchscreen phones, BlackBerry devices, personal digital assistants (PDAs), and Backflip phones on the basis of *purchase prics, coverage area, calling plans*, and *ease of operation*. But you could also examine these devices based on *support services, special features, available applications, memory*, and so on.

A Clear and Consistent Presentation

With division and classification writing, you also need to create a *clear* and *consistent* presentation of the component parts or classes you establish. A presentation is clear when your reader can easily identify the elements of division and classification, and it is consistent when you provide the same general degree of coverage for each category or class, with no unrelated categories.

The presentation in a critical paper about child abuse would be clear as long as particular subcategories—for example, *physical abuse, emotional abuse, verbal abuse,* and *sexual abuse*—are included. The presentation would be consistent when a similar degree of attention and detail is supplied for each type of abuse.

Imagine you were writing an essay about managing expenses. You would be likely to discuss such items as *rent, food, clothing, savings,* and *entertainment,* because each is an example of a common expenditure. You wouldn't discuss an upcoming raise or an expected tax return, because these two items are unrelated to your subject. They are not expenses but sources of income.

Distinct and Complete Elements

As you develop a division and classification essay, you also need to use *distinct and complete elements.* When a segment is *distinct,* it is clearly distinguished from other segments, with little or no overlap or blending. When it is *complete,* it is expressed in full detail.

Imagine that you were writing an essay about professional sports shown on television. If you discussed MLB baseball, NFL football, and NBA basketball, your groupings would be distinct. These sports are certainly different from each other. But such a discussion would be far from complete because it ignores many other professional sports available to fans in the form of network, cable, and Internet broadcasts.

To make sure your essay is complete, you need to change your focus. You might discuss in great detail a narrower set of groupings, for instance, the professional sports that attract the largest television audiences (football, baseball, basketball, soccer). Or you might discuss more sports by putting them in groups: *traditional professional team sports* (MLB baseball, NFL football, NBA basketball, NHL hockey); *traditional individual professional sports* (PGA golf, USTA tennis, PSA figure skating, PBA bowling); and *nontraditional professional sports* (NASCAR racing, UFC mixed martial arts, professional skateboarding, snowboarding).

Remember—a subject can be analyzed and presented in more than one way. Regardless of the focus you choose, however, be sure to keep the elements you examine distinct and complete.

12

An Appropriate Method of Arrangement

Once you have established your method of division and classification, you must choose an arrangement to present it to your reader. You must decide which category to introduce first and which last—and, most important, *why*. The order you choose should best serve the purpose of your document.

For example, when you need your reader to understand the physical layout of an object or place, *spatial order* would make the most sense. If you were writing about a massive cruise ship, discussing it as a kind of small city at sea, you might discuss it deck by deck, indicating the locations of various shops, restaurants, theaters, nightclubs, gyms, and so on.

With an essay about stages in adolescent growth, your purpose involves making your reader understand a process or series of events. Therefore, the best choice would be *chronological order* to discuss the characteristics of each of the stages. Because the stages occur as part of the natural progression of age and because each stage builds on the previous one, it would make sense to present them from earliest to latest:

- Early adolescence (middle school age, approximately 11 to 13)
- Late adolescence (high school age, approximately 14 to 18)
- Early adulthood (college age, approximately 19 to 25)

12

However, if your intent is to persuade or inform, *emphatic order*—moving from strong or significant to stronger or more significant to strongest or most significant—ranks as the ideal strategy. If you were writing about the pollution that threatens our waterways, you might begin by discussing such sources of contamination as untreated sewage and agricultural runoff, both serious concerns because they change the nutrient balance in the water. You might then move to a discussion of the destruction caused by oil spills and radioactive waste, which, because of their long-term effects on the environment, is even more serious. Finally, you might discuss a type of contamination that most people don't even notice: thermal pollution that results from the discharge of heated water from a power plant or some industrial facility. This threat is especially serious because a change of a degree or two in water temperature changes the oxygen content in the water and also inhibits the ability of fish and other organisms to reproduce, a consequence that can affect our entire ecosystem. Presented in this way, these classes form a persuasive case that pollution in our rivers, streams, lakes, and oceans puts our very survival at risk.

A Division and Classification Essay Checklist

Once you complete a draft of a division and classification essay, use the following **Division and Classification Essay Checklist** to evaluate it. Then ask an objective reader to do the same.

DIVISION AND CLASSIFICATION ESSAY CHECKLIST

- ❏ Does the introduction specify the focus—either division *or* classification—and establish a logical basis of analysis?
- ❏ Is there sufficient transition throughout to guide the reader through the elements or groupings presented?
- ❏ Is the presentation clear—readily apparent to the reader—and consistent—featuring balanced coverage with no unrelated categories?
- ❏ Are all elements distinct and complete?
- ❏ Has the most effective arrangement to communicate your divisions or classifications to your reader been employed?

12

Use the answers to these questions to help you revise your essay and create an effective final draft.

Analysis: Examining an Annotated Division and Classification Essay

The Best Lessons about College That
I *Never* **Heard**

The introduction indicates the focus and logical basis of analysis—classification of college challenges.

As I was waiting to begin my first semester in college, I felt ready for the challenges awaiting me. After all, my parents had been talking about them for as long as I could remember, and my teachers had spent the previous four years pushing me in the

The clear and consistent presentation is outlined here, with all categories actual college challenges.

classroom. But two weeks on campus have demonstrated that I am clearly not as prepared for the changes that college represents. To my surprise, I have struggled more than I ever thought I would with things like time management matters, everyday personal tasks, interpersonal concerns, and financial issues. I wish I had considered these aspects of college life more thoroughly because they all have the potential to affect my performance and therefore my level of success.

The categories—**time management matters, common personal tasks, interpersonal concerns**, and **financial issues**—are definitely distinct.

In high school, time management was a nonissue for me because my teachers managed it for me. Most of my classes were rigid and predictable, so whether it was a quiz, exam, paper, or presentation, I always knew what was expected. But my schedule at college is completely different. For example, on Mondays I have classes and labs from 8 a.m. to 4 p.m., but on Tuesdays I have just one class during the day and a first-year-student seminar at 7 p.m. I'm finding it hard to get into the kind of rhythm I'm used to.

The four classes are presented in **emphatic order**, beginning with this strong category: time management. The specific details make the example **complete**.

12

The increase in personal responsibilities I have encountered as a college student has been even more surprising to me. Before college, I didn't have to do any planning when it came to everyday personal tasks like planning meals, getting supplies, or doing

In keeping with **emphatic order**, the second **distinct category**—increased everyday tasks—is identified as "more surprising" than the previous category.

1ese specific ——• laundry. For the most part, my mother took
2tails about care of these issues. But now I am in charge,
xpectations and I am having trouble managing it all. I
2rsus reality thought that once I was in college, I would be
1sure that this able to spend my spare time enjoying myself,
2tegory is socializing, or going to the gym. A Friday
2mplete. night spent doing my laundry as I did last
week wasn't part of my plans.

keeping with ——•   Dealing with other people and sharing
nphatic order, space with them is something else that has
e third **distinct** put even more pressure on me. When I lived
2tegory— at home, I had a room to myself and I didn't
terpersonal have to adapt to anyone else's habits or to
sues—is adjust my own to suit anyone else's needs. If
2ntified as I wanted to play my stereo or leave papers or
ut[ting] even clothes spread all over, I could do so. Right
ore pressure now, three of us are living in a 15-square-foot
me." room. I'm doing my best not to get on their
nerves while trying to get used to their styles
of living, but the truth is that I have found
this adjustment really difficult.

12

These specific details about the difficulties of adjusting to living with others make this example **complete**.

keeping with ——•   Of all the challenges, financial issues
nphatic order, related to college have been particularly hard
e final **distinct** for me. I am fortunate because I received a
2tegory— merit-based scholarship from the college to
ancial cover half of my tuition. I also received a Pell
sues—is Grant and a $1,000 annual scholarship from the
2ntified as company where my father works, which took
articularly care of the rest of my tuition. I used the money
ard."

from my summer job and took out a student loan of $7,000 to cover fees, living expenses, and books. I figured I had everything all set.

These examples of incidental expenses help make this category **complete**.

Once classes began, I found out that I hadn't given enough thought to incidental expenses that pop up from day to day. Just taking a walk off campus for a cup of coffee and a snack with friends or splitting the cost of a pizza leaves me broke for the rest of the week. Right now, I'm worried about whether I'll have enough spending money for the rest of the semester.

12

Even worse, the college administration has notified students that the state legislature has just cut the college's operating budget by several million dollars, the first time the college has faced such a cut after classes have begun. Unless the legislature reverses its decision, tuition and fees will increase retroactive to the opening of the semester. For me, that adds up to almost $1,300 I don't have. Finding a part-time job now won't be easy, so I'll probably have to take out another loan, making the amount due when I graduate even larger. It's a worry I never expected to face.

These additional specific details about costs assigned after the beginning of the semester make it clear that this category clearly represents the biggest challenge of all.

The conclusion recaps the four categories and restates the significance expressed in the introduction and body: that there is more to being a successful college student than dealing with academics.

These first weeks of classes have taught me that college is more than just reading, studying, and attending classes. It's also about managing time, taking on more personal responsibilities, getting along with others, and dealing with finances. Incoming college students would be better off if parents and teachers emphasized that academic challenges won't be the only ones they will face in college.

MASTERY EXERCISE 1 Responding to the Annotated Essay

1. The organizing strategy of division and classification—with emphasis on classification—dominates in this essay. As usually happens when you write, however, other modes play supporting roles, especially, in this case, comparison and contrast. Take another look at this essay and then explain how the use of comparison and contrast affects the overall impact of the piece.

2. As the annotations indicate, this essay is arranged on the basis of emphatic order. From your own experiences as a college student, do you agree with how the categories have been ranked or would you have arranged them in some other way? Explain your reasoning.

3. The final paragraph in the discussion of the fourth category— financial concerns—addresses an expense levied by the school after classes had begun. In what way does this material support the overall point of the essay?

12

WRITING A DIVISION AND CLASSIFICATION ESSAY A

As a college student yourself, you are certainly familiar with at least some of the challenges discussed in this essay. But your role as a college student is just one of many aspects or dimensions of your life, each of which involves specific challenges. What impediments or complications must you deal with to stay in good physical shape, for example, or to maintain a long-standing friendship or other important relationship? For this assignment, consider one of the other dimensions of your life and identify the different forces that you must deal with in order to be successful with it. Then write an essay of about 500 words in which you use division and classification to explain these challenges.

WRITING A DIVISION AND CLASSIFICATION ESSAY B

The most pressing matters outlined in this essay about college challenges are financial concerns. How about you—what financial issues do you face on a weekly or monthly basis? Considering your own budget (or the budget that you think the average person your age might have), break it up on the basis of financial obligations. For instance, which grouping contains obligations, goods, services, and so on, that simply must be met—no exceptions? Which grouping features items that are worth paying for because of the pleasure or contentment they provide? Which grouping includes things that could—and probably should—be eliminated because they are overly expensive, frivolous, or unnecessary? Then use division and classification to write an essay of about 500 words in which you explain the budget and justify the money spent.

Illustration: Considering a Division and Classification Essay

WHAT'S IN YOUR TOOTHPASTE
David Bodanis

12

Consider the many things you ingest or are exposed to every day. Do you know what ingredients make up all these items? Even drinking water isn't necessarily what people think, generally containing multiple chemicals, some naturally occurring and some added to disinfect the water and make it safe for drinking. And the alternative that many people choose—pure bottled water—is sometimes anything but pure, with contaminants ranging from bacteria to chemicals used to manufacture plastic. So it should probably come as no surprise that a lot more goes into another common, regularly used item—toothpaste—than most of us probably want to know. In the following excerpt from The Secret House, *David Bodanis employs division and classification, with a focus on division, to make the point that toothpaste, like many other products we use every day, consists of both very basic and very strange elements.*

Should we really be surprised that some of the things we use every day are actually anything but common and ordinary?

Into the bathroom goes our male resident, and after the most pressing need is satisfied it's time to brush the teeth. The tube of toothpaste is squeezed, its pinched metal seams are splayed, pressure waves are generated inside, and the paste begins to flow. But what's in this toothpaste, so carefully being extruded out?

Water mostly, 30 to 45 percent in most brands: ordinary, everyday simple tap water. It's there because people like to have a big gob of toothpaste to spread on the brush, and water is the cheapest stuff there is when it comes to making big gobs. Dripping a bit from the tap onto your brush would cost virtually nothing; whipped in with the rest of the toothpaste the manufacturers can sell it at a neat and accountant-pleasing $2 per pound equivalent. Toothpaste manufacture is a very lucrative occupation.

Second to water in quantity is chalk: exactly the same material that schoolteachers use to write on blackboards. It is collected from the crushed remains of long-dead ocean creatures. In the Cretaceous seas chalk particles served as part of the wickedly sharp outer skeleton that these creatures had to wrap around themselves to keep from getting chomped by all the slightly larger other ocean creatures they met. Their massed graves are our present chalk deposits.

12

The individual chalk particles—the size of the smallest mud particles in your garden—have kept their toughness over the aeons, and now on the toothbrush they'll need it. The enamel outer coating of the tooth they'll have to face is the hardest substance in the body—tougher than skull, or bone, or nail. Only the chalk particles in toothpaste can successfully grind into the teeth during brushing, ripping off the surface layers like an abrading wheel grinding down a boulder in a quarry.

The craters, slashes, and channels that the chalk tears into the teeth will also remove a certain amount of built-up yellow in the carnage, and it is for that polishing function that it's there. A certain amount of unduly enlarged extra-abrasive chalk fragments tear such cavernous pits into the teeth that future decay bacteria will be able to bunker down there and thrive; the quality control people find it almost impossible to screen out these errant super-chalk pieces, and government regulations allow them to stay in.

In case even the gouging doesn't get all the yellow off, another substance is worked into the toothpaste cream. This is titanium dioxide. It comes in tiny spheres, and it's the stuff bobbing around in white wall paint to make it come out white. Splashed around onto your teeth during the brushing it coats much of the yellow that remains. Being water soluble it leaks off in the next few hours and is swallowed, but at least for the quick glance up in the mirror after finishing it will make the user think his teeth are truly white. Some manufacturers add optical whitening dyes—the stuff more commonly found in washing machine bleach—to make extra sure that that glance in the mirror shows reassuring white.

These ingredients alone would not make a very attractive concoction. They would stick in the tube like a sloppy white plastic lump, hard to squeeze out as well as revolting to the touch. Few consumers would savor rubbing in a mixture of water, ground-up blackboard chalk, and the whitener from latex paint first thing in the morning. To get around that finicky distaste the manufacturers have mixed in a host of other goodies.

To keep the glop from drying out, a mixture including glycerine glycol—related to the most common car antifreeze ingredient—is whipped in with the chalk and water, and to give *that* concoction a bit of substance (all we really have so far is wet colored chalk) a large helping is added of gummy molecules from the seaweed *Chondrus Crispus.* This seaweed ooze spreads in among the chalk, paint, and antifreeze, then stretches itself in all directions to hold the whole mass together. A bit of paraffin oil (the fuel that flickers in camping lamps) is pumped in with it to help the moss ooze keep the whole substance smooth.

With the glycol, ooze, and paraffin we're almost there. Only two major chemicals are left to make the refreshing, cleansing substance we know as toothpaste. The ingredients so far are fine for cleaning, but they wouldn't make much of the satisfying foam we have come to expect in the morning brushing.

To remedy that every toothpaste on the market has a big dollop of detergent added too. You've seen the suds detergent will make in a washing machine. The same substance added here will duplicate that inside the mouth. It's not particularly necessary, but it sells.

The only problem is that by itself this ingredient tastes, well, too like detergent. It's horribly bitter and harsh. The chalk put in toothpaste is pretty foul-tasting too for that matter. It's to get around that gustatory discomfort that the manufacturers put in the ingredient they tout perhaps the most of all. This is the flavoring, and it has to be strong. Double rectified peppermint oil is used—a flavorer so powerful that chemists know better than to sniff it in the raw state in the laboratory. Menthol crystals and saccharin or other sugar simulators are added to complete the camouflage operation.

Is that it? Chalk, water, paint, seaweed, antifreeze, paraffin oil, detergent, and peppermint? Not quite. A mix like that would be irresistible to the hundreds of thousands of individual bacteria lying on the surface of even an immaculately cleaned bathroom sink. They would get in, float in the water bubbles, ingest the ooze and paraffin, maybe even spray out enzymes to break down the chalk. The result would be an uninviting mess. The way manufacturers avoid that final obstacle is by putting something in to kill the bacteria. Something good and strong is needed, something that will zap any accidentally intrudant bacteria into oblivion. And that something is formaldehyde—the disinfectant used in anatomy labs.

So it's chalk, water, paint, seaweed, antifreeze, paraffin oil, detergent, peppermint, formaldehyde, and fluoride (which can go some way towards preserving children's teeth)—that's the usual mixture raised to the mouth on the toothbrush for a fresh morning's clean. If it sounds too unfortunate, take heart. Studies show that thorough brushing with just plain water will often do as good a job.

MASTERY EXERCISE 2 Considering Significance and Meaning

1. If the dominant ingredient of toothpaste—in some cases close to half of the volume—is simply water, why are manufacturers able to charge as much as they do for this product?
2. Another main component of toothpaste is chalk. What purpose does its inclusion serve? In what way does this ingredient negatively affect the user?
3. The list of ingredients in toothpaste is surprising—and quite unappetizing. How do manufacturers ensure that their product doesn't have an unpalatable taste?

CHAPTER 12 Division and Classification

185

MASTERY EXERCISE 3 Analyzing Method and Technique

1. How would you describe the overall tone that Bodanis adopts in this excerpt? In your view, how does this tone affect the overall impact of the piece?
2. In this writing, Bodanis provides a clear and consistent presentation, thoroughly breaking down toothpaste to its ultimate components. Of those components, which do you think is most completely and effectively discussed? What makes this section superior to the others?
3. In the last paragraph of the body of this excerpt, Bodanis identifies one final ingredient: formaldehyde. Why do you think he saves the discussion of this element until the end? Do you agree with his strategy? Explain your reasoning.

WRITING A DIVISION AND CLASSIFICATION ESSAY C

David Bodanis explains that the chalk particles in toothpaste are the remains of "wickedly sharp outer skeleton[s] that these [ocean] creatures had to wrap around themselves" to remain safe. They are not alone in this regard. We humans also work hard to protect ourselves from danger, including threats to psychological and emotional well-being—things like sadness, unpleasant situations, ideas or facts we don't want to hear, and so on. For this assignment, write an essay of about 500 words in which you explore at least four types or categories of behavior that people engage in to shield themselves from things they would rather avoid.

WRITING A DIVISION AND CLASSIFICATION ESSAY D

Toothpaste has this in common with thousands of other products: when you purchase a tube, you usually have to remove it from a box, packaging that is clearly unnecessary and wasteful. For this assignment, identify four different products, services, situations, activities, and so on, that involve some degree of incongruous waste. Then write an essay of about 500 words in which you use division and classification to explain the subjects—and the waste involved—to your reader.

Summary Exercise

1. Prewrite on one of the following topics, focusing on sections or groupings of the subject that you have chosen.

   • Categories of e-commerce
   • Vacation options
   • Spectators at a concert, sporting event, or amusement park

2. Create a draft essay of 500 words in which you use division and classification to make the subject easier for your reader to understand.

3. Using the Division and Classification Essay Checklist, page 175, as a guide, revise your draft. Evaluate your introduction, ensuring that it specifies your focus—either division or classification—and establishes a logical basis of analysis. At the same time, check that you have maintained a consistent presentation and used distinct and complete elements or groupings. Finally, make sure your use of transition and your order of arrangement are effective so that your division or classification analysis comes across clearly. Have an objective reader evaluate your essay using these criteria, too.

4. Addressing any problems you and your reader have identified, create a final draft essay.

12

13

Argument

Understanding the Aim of Argument

Think of **argument** as the mode that isn't.

Unlike narration, description, definition, and the rest of the organizing strategies presented in the previous eight chapters, argument is not a mode but an aim or purpose. With argument, you use a variety of modes to persuade your reader to accept a point of view.

Some people draw a distinction between *argument* and *persuasion,* with argument referring to writings that rationally and dispassionately attempt to convince the reader of the validity of a position, and persuasion referring to writings that rely on additional appeals, including appeals to emotion, to sway the reader. For the most part, though, you need not be concerned about this distinction, since supporting a stand on an issue will likely involve both approaches.

An essay asserting that the popular vote and not the Electoral College should decide U.S. presidential elections would be argument. So would an essay maintaining that informal roadside memorials for accident victims should not be allowed. As a college student, as a professional beyond the classroom, and as a citizen concerned about local and national issues, you will often be called on to present and support your stance on some issue. Therefore, it's important that you master the principles of argument.

The Elements of an Effective Argument Essay

To make your argument essay effective, be sure to include the elements described on this and the following pages.

Sufficient Transition

Transitional words and phrases can help guide your readers through your line of reasoning and highlight your essay's emphatic order. You'll likely find the following expressions especially helpful as you develop your argument essay:

TRANSITIONAL EXPRESSIONS FOR ARGUMENT

To Establish Reasons	To Answer the Opposition	To Conclude
first (second, third, etc.)	some may say	therefore
most important	on the other hand	thus

An Explicit Stance

With an argument paper, you must clarify where you stand on an issue to prepare your reader for the line of reasoning constituting your argument. In other words, you need to state explicitly at some point in your introduction whether you are in favor of or against the issue you are discussing.

Imagine that you are writing an essay about school uniforms in public schools. If you are in favor of such a proposal, you might write a thesis like this:

In Favor of: If public school officials are serious about exercising better control and improving the learning environment in today's classrooms, then they should require all students to wear uniforms.

But if you are against the policy, your thesis might look like this:

Against: A policy that requires public school students to wear uniforms would be a bad idea for a number of reasons.

With an explicitly stated thesis in place in your introduction, your reader knows exactly where you stand and therefore prepared for the line of reasoning to follow in the body of the essay.

The Appropriate Combination of Modes

With an argument paper, your goal is to convince your reader to agree with your point of view, or at least to accept your point of view as worthy of consideration. To accomplish this goal, you will need to use several modes in combination.

Imagine, for example, that you are writing an essay about some parents' practice of involving their children, sometimes as young as two or three, in intensive academic tutoring or high-pressured training in athletics, dance, or music. You are opposed to this concept, so your purpose is to persuade your reader that no matter how well intentioned these parents may be, saturating very young children in a focused activity can have serious consequences.

To fulfill this aim, you'd employ several modes, including classification to spell out the wide variety of intensive programs available and definition to clarify the kinds of pressure and stress children may experience. You might also to turn to example to illustrate the kinds of unstructured activities lost out on as well as cause and effect to discuss the physical effects like chronic headaches and depression seen in some overscheduled youngsters. The point to remember is that the organizing strategies that best help you make your case and convince your reader are always the best ones to use.

13

Sufficient, Valid Support

When it comes to supporting your stance, you need to make sure that the evidence you include is both **sufficient** and **valid**. There is no specific minimum—or maximum—amount of information needed. Consider some controversial subject: how much support for a position related to this subject would you need to see before you found it worthy of consideration? Chances are that you would require several solid supporting details and examples. Your reader demands the same of you. As a general rule, include at least three reasons, or points, to support your stance.

Valid evidence is accurate and truthful. Keep in mind the relationship between **facts**—verifiable truths—and **opinions**—reasonings based on fact. That icy roads can be dangerous for drivers is a fact. There is no room for discussion. An opinion, however, is a belief founded on impressions, experiences, or knowledge base. When you state that city officials' delay in treating icy roads during a recent storm means that they don't care about people's safety, that's an opinion. The validity of an opinion depends on how well it is supported by facts, so be sure to incorporate facts as often as possible to buttress your opinions. Finally, remember that *personal feelings* and *attitudes* generally offer little in the way of valid support. That you dislike winter because of the frequent cold and icy conditions won't do much to strengthen any argument.

To help develop your argument, make two lists, one of information that supports your position and the other of information expressing an opposing point of view. The value of the first list is obvious: these ideas will form the framework for your presentation. But the second list also serves a useful purpose. If you can refute or adapt any of these opposing points, you can turn them to your advantage, making your argument even stronger.

Imagine that you are writing an essay in which you express your objection to a proposal that English be established as the official national language of the United States. Here are two lists of ideas you've generated about the subject, one against the proposal and one supporting it.

Against the Proposal

- The United States was founded so that all could enjoy freedom, regardless of background.
- When we force people to reject their heritage, we all lose.
- The proposal discriminates against immigrants—it's prejudice.
- Learning a new language is too difficult for many old people.
- English-language classes aren't readily available, especially for working people.
- If we become an English-language-only country, some people won't be able to work—adding to welfare lists.

In Favor of the Proposal

- It saves money on things like bilingual education and government forms that now have to be printed in several languages.
- If people want to live here, they should learn to speak English.
- The majority rules.
- Some advertised jobs are only for people who can speak a language besides English. Native speakers shouldn't lose out on jobs because they can't speak another language.

The points you've developed to oppose the proposal are valid, so you could feel comfortable including any of them in your writing.

13

In addition, you could also contest and rebut some of the points favoring the proposal and include them to strengthen your argument against making English the national language:

- It's true that printing government forms in multiple languages and providing bilingual education cost taxpayers money, but a prosperous nation like the United States should put people's needs ahead of dollar signs.

- People who become permanent residents of the United States should learn English, but not because a law mandates it. Clearly, knowing the primary language of the United States opens up economic doors, making life easier overall. Rather than punishing people for not knowing English, our government should more aggressively educate newcomers concerning how speaking English will benefit them.

Certainly, ideas from the list opposing the proposal would dominate in the essay. But the addition of details adapted from the ideas favoring the proposal would make the draft that much stronger and more effective.

13

Support from Experts

Because the focus of an argument essay will often be controversial—and likely complicated—you may want to include expert opinion to buttress your argument. As Chapter 14, "Research and Documentation Activities: A Brief Guide" (pages 214–230), makes clear, the process has two facets: (1) identifying and including information that offers valid support for the point you are making and (2) correctly acknowledging and documenting that information.

Consider again the essay about subjecting young children to rigorous academic, music, arts, or athletic preparation. Perhaps you attended a class presentation by a child psychologist, heard a podcast, or read an online or print article that supports your argument. As Chapter 14 illustrates in greater detail (pages 220–222), you can incorporate and acknowledge this information in your essay in the form of a *direct quotation*, a *paraphrase*, or a *summary*. A direct quotation is a word-for-word excerpt from a document, enclosed in quotation marks; a paraphrase is a restatement, in your own words, of a passage; and a summary is a greatly reduced version of an original text, also expressed in your own words.

Here are examples of how this kind of expert opinion would appear in your essay:

- a **direct quotation**:

    A 2007 *Wall Street Journal* article, "Helping Overbooked Kids Back Off," makes the same point: "But the trend has gone too far, the American Academy of Pediatrics said in January in the journal *Pediatrics*; kids need more time for free play and family togetherness" (Shellenbarger).

- a **paraphrase:**

    A podcast of a 2002 NPR series on children made the point that overscheduled children often miss out on other, less-structured possibilities for learning while also dealing with increased pressure from parents to perform (Stamberg).

- a **summary:**

    In a recent guest lecture here on campus, a child psychologist who has worked for years with preschool children emphasized that he is convinced that the harm in terms of stress and frustration that very young children experience from intensive study and practice is far greater than any benefit they could gain (Kyd).

Note that regardless of the type of expert information, you need to acknowledge the source in your essay. Here, in accordance with MLA guidelines for nonprint documents or information, you include the author's last name in parentheses. With paginated texts, you also include the page number. (See Chapter 14 for a more detailed explanation of in-text documentation.)

Of course, whenever you incorporate expert opinion into your paper, make sure to give the complete citations at the end of your essay in a section entitled *Words Cited*:

Works Cited

Kyd, Peter. Guest Lecture. PSY 52.04—Child Psychology. B-213.

Brayton Hills College, Springfield, MT. 25 Oct. 2010.

Shellenbarger, Sue. "Helping Overbooked Kids Cut Back." *The Wall*

Street Journal Online. May 2007: D1. Wall Street Journal, Web.

11 Nov. 2010.

<http://online.wsj.com/article/SB117936376700505665>.

Stamberg, Susan. "Overscheduled Kids." *Morning Edition.* Nat. Public

Radio. 3 Sept. 2002. Web. 11 Nov. 2010. Podcast.

<http://www.npr.org/templates/story/story.php?storyId=1149374>.

The Different Approaches of Persuasion

13

The ancient Greeks identified three types of approaches or *appeals* used to persuade someone to accept a line of reasoning: *ethos, pathos,* and *logos.* Writers still embrace these concepts, which today are referred to as appeals on the basis of *reputation, emotion,* and *logic.*

It's important to recognize that, as with the modes, these appeals generally do—and should—appear in combination. An essay with an argument based just on a person's endorsement or just on appeals to emotion or just on appeals to logic would have some serious weaknesses.

An example of an appeal to emotion alone would be a statement advocating the immediate imprisonment of leaders of hate groups because their speeches are treatises on prejudice. Such a paper would no doubt inspire cheers, but it would be flawed. Freedom of speech and expression is the bedrock of the U.S. Constitution. As personally upsetting as it can be sometimes, preserving this freedom for all of us means allowing people to express attitudes offensive to the majority.

A better approach for this paper would be to adjust the presentation by incorporating appeals to logic and reputation:

> The ACLU and the U.S. Supreme Court agree that people can't be imprisoned merely for holding detestable beliefs. When their words or actions cross the line and become hate speech, however, they should be prosecuted, and, if convicted, face the maximum penalty allowed under the law.

The references to the American Civil Liberties Union and the U.S. Supreme Court, top legal authorities, add an appeal to reputation, and the suggestion of vigorously prosecuting group leaders the instant their words or actions exceed the threshold of protected expression, a reasonable and legal approach, adds an appeal to logic. The result is a strong, effective point.

A Reasonable and Convincing Tone

13

Another aspect that will affect how your point of view is accepted is its *tone*, the attitude expressed about the subject. If your tone is haughty, patronizing, or sarcastic, you may alienate a reader whom you might otherwise persuade to agree with your point of view. But if your tone is respectful, sincere, and concerned, you'll increase the chance that your reader will favorably received your point of view.

Imagine an essay asserting that school officials must step up their efforts to eliminate the problem of bullying, including cyberbullying. This behavior has become increasingly—and alarmingly—more common and has led to tragic violence, including suicide. With such an emotionally charged subject, it's easy to understand how a passage such as the following might appear in an early draft:

> A person would have to be stupid not to realize that bullying in our schools is not just a harmless little dispute between students. Rather, it is an extremely serious problem responsible for violent attacks and suicides of students who could no longer handle the actual and virtual harassment.

The message in this passage is valid, but the tone is insulting. Now consider this version of the passage:

Many people seem unaware that bullying in our schools is not just a harmless little dispute between students. Rather, it's an extremely serious problem responsible for violent attacks and suicides of students who could no longer handle the actual and virtual harassment.

The message is essentially unchanged, but the tone is clearly more neutral. It no longer suggests that a person who hasn't arrived at this conclusion is somehow deficient. As a result, a reader who hadn't really considered how serious a problem bullying has become may be more receptive to this point.

One way to adjust the tone of your writing is to avoid using **absolute terms**. For instance, stating that people *rarely* stay alive more than a few minutes in the frigid winter waters of the North Atlantic is better than stating that they *never* do because *rarely* allows for that extremely unusual, unexplainable survival. Here is a list of more moderate terms that you can substitute for absolute language:

Absolute Word	Moderate Substitute
all	most
always	frequently
every	many
never	rarely

Common Errors in Logic to Avoid

To persuade a reader, an argument essay must have a logical line of reasoning that leads to a valid conclusion. You establish this line of reasoning by engaging in one of two primary ways of thinking: **induction** and **deduction.** Although the goal of the two reasoning processes is the same, they involve approaching a subject from opposite directions.

Induction refers to reasoning from a series of specific matters to a general conclusion. Physicians employ inductive reasoning when they conclude that a particular skin rash is a form of eczema, because every other rash they've examined like this one has proven to be eczema. An answer reached in this way involves an *inductive leap,* which means that even though such a diagnosis is a reasonable conclusion, it isn't necessarily the only possible valid explanation. While the rash might closely resemble the one resulting from eczema, it might actually be the result of another, less common condition.

Deduction entails reasoning from a series of general statements to a specific conclusion. For example, flat, low-lying, inland areas are especially susceptible to tornadoes. If your aunt lives in a flat, low-lying, inland area, then it is accurate to say that her neighborhood faces a strong possibility of being hit by a tornado.

Regardless of whether you use induction, deduction, or some combination of the two to make your point, be sure to avoid the following common errors in logic, often referred to as *logical fallacies,* which are listed here with examples:

Fallacy	Examples of Faulty Logic	Instead, Use Sound Logic
Argument *ad hominem* (Latin for "argument to the man")		
Attacking the person	*Why pay attention to environmental advocate Sierra Larges, who wants everyone to carpool and drive smaller cars to lessen our dependence on fossil fuels but who just lives off her family trust fund and doesn't even have a real job?*	Respond to the opposing positions.
Bandwagon approach		
Urging acceptance because "everybody does it"	*Demolishing that historic building is the right thing to do because everybody thinks it's ugly and out of step with other neighborhood buildings.*	Cite objective, qualified authorities or statistics.
Begging the question		
Assuming as fact what must be proven	*Accountable Accountants, which does nothing but misrepresent the assets it handles, should be banned from bidding on financial management accounts in this state.*	Provide relevant, documented evidence.
Circular reasoning		
Merely repeating your opinion and calling it a valid point	*That car is the best choice because, compared to the competition, it is superior.*	Give real reasons.

13

Fallacy	Examples of Faulty Logic	Instead, Use Sound Logic
Creating a red herring Diverting attention to an unimportant point	*The mayor's failure to submit his budget on time cost the city $1 million, but how about the school committee members who didn't attend Employee Appreciation Day?*	Provide compelling evidence.
Either/or reasoning Suggesting only two alternatives when many possibilities exist	*Unless we completely change the way we teach mathematics, our children will never attain acceptable test scores.*	Explore all relevant possibilities.
Hasty generalization Making an assumption based on insufficient evidence	*I've been taking that vitamin supplement for almost two weeks and I don't feel any more energetic, so it obviously doesn't work.*	Base conclusions on many objective facts.
***Non sequitur* (Latin for "it does not follow")** Coming to an incorrect conclusion in relation to the evidence	*Homeless people don't have permanent places to live, so it's obvious that they have no pride.*	Think through relationships using logic.
Oversimplification Wrongfully reducing a complex subject	*Using solar energy will eliminate all our energy problems.*	State all important aspects; admit inconsistencies.
***Post hoc, ergo propter hoc* (Latin for "after this, therefore because of this")** Assuming a cause-effect relationship between two things that occurred by coincidence	*The killer had just eaten at a fast-food restaurant, so something in the food must have triggered his aggression.*	Check your thinking for irrational statements.

13

Find the logical fallacy in the following passage about Transportation Security Administration (TSA) regulations for air travelers:

Since 2001, the TSA has increased the amount of screening that airline passengers must endure before being allowed to fly. First, we had to face long lines followed by personal screening and metal detectors. Then we had to deal with time-consuming examination of all baggage, including carry-on bags Next, following the failed attempts by the so-called "Shoe Bomber," we all had to remove our footwear, so that it, too, can be examined. None of these steps has ever been conclusively shown to increase safety, but that hasn't stopped the TSA. Now people in some major airports have to step through a machine that performs a virtual strip search, flashing an image of their near naked bodies to TSA officials. If we don't find a way to stop the TSA, it won't be long before all our rights disappear for good.

As you probably noted, the weakness in logic appears in the final sentence: "If we don't find a way to stop the TSA, it won't be long before all our rights disappear for good." True, the required screening since the 9/11 attacks can be both annoying and time consuming, and true, there has been no demonstrable proof that any of these steps increases the safety of air travelers. But including another level of screening will not automatically lead to an elimination of all rights. This statement is a case of both *oversimplification* and *either/or reasoning*. Many other outcomes are possible, including the discontinuation of this latest level of screening if it proves to be an unnecessary impediment to air travel.

An Effective Arrangement

Although it's not the only suitable way to arrange an argument paper, emphatic order is often the best choice. The idea is to use the initial points to spark your reader's interest and then the subsequent examples to feed that interest, thus cultivating acceptance of your point of view.

Consider the order of the supporting points in the following informal outline for an essay whose writer is opposed to keeping animals in captivity and forcing them to perform for humans:

Thesis: We humans don't have the right to capture animals and force them to perform for our pleasure in circuses, zoos, or aquatic parks.

Point 1: Creatures such as elephants, great apes and other primates, and dolphins are highly social and accustomed to living in large groups. But most animals in captivity live in far smaller groups, which deprives them of the wider interaction they would enjoy in the wild.

Point 2: Because they enjoy regular meals in settings free from predators, these animals stop relying on their natural impulses and instincts. As a result, the prospect of their survival if they should ever be released into their natural habitat is not promising.

Point 3: Even under the best of circumstances, the physical environments in which animals like killer whales, polar bears, lions, and tigers live in captivity are shamefully inadequate. They are a mere fraction of the hundreds of miles these creatures would recognize as their territory in the wild.

Point 4: When we force animals to perform for us, we fail to respect their native intelligence, grace, and dignity. Instead, we allow orangutans, elephants, and dolphins to be subjected to long hours of training to make them behave in ways that are simply not normal for these highly intelligent animals.

As you can see, the supporting examples follow emphatic order. The initial reason—the isolation that these creatures often experience in captivity—is strong. Depriving naturally social animals of the comfort of others is simply cruel. The second point—the altered natural behavior that occurs as a result of free meals and protection from predators—is even stronger. Ironically, this kind of intervention increases the dependence these animals have on humans and makes them generally unsuitable for release back into the wild. The third point—that the environments in zoos, circuses, and aquatic parks are vastly less expansive than the animals' natural habitats—is stronger still. The images of huge animals like polar bears or killer whales held captive in a compound that is miniscule in comparison to what they would experience in nature is compelling. But the final point—training animals to make them behave in ways that they don't in nature—is strongest of all. Forcing animals to perform in this fashion goes against their nature, and we are allowing their behaviors to be twisted for our own selfish pleasure.

Because it fosters a movement in reasoning from a significant reason to a more significant reason and so on, emphatic order stirs and sustains the reader's interest. As a result, it increases the chances that the reader will see the entire presentation as reasonable, valid, and convincing.

An Argument Essay Checklist

Once you complete a draft of an argument essay, use the following **Argument Essay Checklist** to evaluate it. Then ask an objective reader to do the same.

13

ARGUMENT ESSAY CHECKLIST

❑ Does the introduction explicitly state the stance on the subject?

❑ Is there sufficient transition throughout the essay so that the reader can follow along from one supporting example to the next?

❑ Has an appropriate combination of modes to persuade the reader been employed?

❑ Are there sufficient examples and details to support the stance expressed?

❑ When appropriate, has expert opinion been included and properly acknowledged?

❑ Is the tone reasonable, sincere, and serious, with moderate language in place of any inappropriate, absolute terms?

❑ Have any logical fallacies been identified and eliminated?

❑ Has emphatic order been used to capture and hold the reader's attention and to foster support for the reasoning within the document?

Use the answers to these questions to help you revise your essay and create an effective final draft.

Analysis: Examining an Annotated Argument Essay

The Side of the Road Is No Place for a Memorial

About 50 yards before the highway exit I take to go to school, there is a small pile of flowers, all brown and decaying, surrounding a hand-lettered sign. Some of the lettering has washed or faded away, so all that is left is "R.I.P. Peter Santi." This memorial apparently was put together the night after a car accident several months ago. It's hard to pinpoint when the practice of marking accident sites started, but this roadside display is only one of many on the streets and highways around the city right now, and they are all in pretty bad shape. It's time for the city to pass and enforce an ordinance against these kinds of unauthorized roadside memorials. As well intentioned as the people who create these displays may be, these memorials just don't belong on our streets and highways.

For one thing, these kinds of informal roadside memorials force everyone to deal with the tragedy, including those who didn't know the victim or the circumstances of the accident. In some cases, this factor is likely one of the motivations for assembling a display.

The introduction **xplicitly states** ₁e stance—that **informal** ₂adside ₃emorials **hould be** ₄rbidden.

₁ote the **tone,** ₂hich is **espectful** of ₃eople who have ₄uffered a loss.

₁ere is the first ₂f the **four ₃pecific ₄xamples,** ₅esented in **mphatic order ₆ support the ₇oint of view,** ₈elping to ₉trengthen the ₁rgument.

13

The **modes of example** and **cause and effect** help persuade the reader.

For example, the highway display near the exit for the college marks the site of an accident caused by a drunk driver. Another display in the south end of the city identifies the point of a fatal accident that resulted from illegal street racing. But people living in the city probably already know the circumstances, so the display simply makes a sad situation even more depressing and turns what should be a private matter into a public spectacle. Meanwhile, visitors unfamiliar with the city will have little idea about the intended lesson behind the display.

Note the use of the **moderate terms** *likely* and *probably.*

13

More significant, however, the displays themselves usually become shabby-looking before too long. The flowers that were initially beautiful and colorful quickly wilt. If they have been wrapped in any way, the paper or plastic eventually fades, shreds, or disintegrates because of the constant exposure to sun, rain, and wind. Ribbons and bows get increasingly dirty and shopworn, and notes and cards fade or simply blow around. The result is just an eyesore that ultimately seems disrespectful to the victim's memory.

In keeping with **emphatic order,** the **transitional phrase** *More significant* signals that this second supporting example is more serious than the first.

The **modes** of description, **cause and effect,** and **division and classification** help to persuade the reader.

Even more significant, it's not appropriate—and it shouldn't be legal—to turn public streets and highways into personal memorials. Municipal and state roadways belong to everyone. When people turn the

In keeping with **emphatic order,** the **transitional phrase** *Even more significant* indicates that this third supporting example is more important than the preceding ones.

median strip of a busy street or the guardrail of
a state highway into a memorial for a private
citizen, they are overstepping their bounds.
Although it is easy to understand why grief-
stricken family and friends would want to
acknowledge the death of their loved ones, the
fitting place to do that is a cemetery or mausoleum, where this loss can be noted with the
solemnity and dignity it deserves.

But most important of all, these memorials marking the locations of fatal traffic accidents are potential traffic hazards themselves.
From unpredictable auto and pedestrian traffic
to street markers to safety signs to advertising
billboards, today's drivers already face enough
distractions as they travel from place to place.
These makeshift memorials are set up precisely
to attract the attention of people driving by.
When drivers turn their gaze on such a memorial, they are no longer concentrating on the
road in front of them, increasing the possibility
of a driving error, especially on a dangerous
roadway.

The pain that follows the sudden accidental death of a family member or friend is
unimaginable, so the urge to acknowledge the
loss by marking the site of the accident is certainly understandable. But for a number of reasons, the kinds of informal roadside memorials

13

The conclusion restates the —→ **stance** while emphasizing the **supporting ideas** presented in the body of the essay.

that are often set up following fatal accidents are just not appropriate. Streets and highways don't belong to any one person or group. City officials need to pass an ordinance banning unauthorized memorials and should remove them as soon as they appear.

MASTERY EXERCISE 1 Responding to the Annotated Essay

1. The introduction to this essay features a specific detail—a roadside memorial that the writer passes while traveling to school. How does the description of this site help set the stage for the specific stance and the supporting paragraphs that follow?

2. As the annotations accompanying the essay indicate, the supporting ideas are presented in emphatic order. Imagine that the writer has asked you to respond to the arrangement of the supporting material. Do you agree with the order in which the paragraphs currently appear, or would you recommend moving one or more of them? Why?

3. No doubt about it: this subject is certainly controversial and emotionally charged, especially for anyone who has lost a loved one in an accident. Do you think the presentation is sensitive enough relative to the delicate feelings of such readers, or would you suggest additional adjustments in tone? Be sure to explain your reasoning thoroughly, referring to specific points in the essay.

13

WRITING AN ARGUMENT ESSAY A

Public spaces present a dizzying array of challenges for cities and towns, including finding the money to maintain them properly. One controversial solution involves accepting funds from private entities—either companies or individuals—to maintain parks or other town or municipal facilities (school buildings and buses, city meeting halls, and so on) in exchange for allowing the posting of advertising or the awarding of naming rights. For example, an area retailer pays a fee or otherwise provides maintenance and is then permitted to put up advertising banners throughout city parks. Or a local philanthropist provides money to replace the sound system in a middle school auditorium, and in return the school renames the auditorium after the contributor. Consider your feelings on this issue—these efforts ensure that the facilities are maintained, but should public assets be up for sale in this fashion? For this assignment, first consider the pros and cons and decide where you stand. Then write an essay of about 500 words in which you express and support your point of view with the goal of persuading your reader to see the issue as you do.

WRITING AN ARGUMENT ESSAY B

One point raised about outlawing makeshift roadside memorials is that after a relatively short period of time, they become eyesores. While at first glance the resulting messiness may seem like a trivial matter, the truth is that people make judgments about a place and the people who live there based on appearances. This idea, some-times called the Broken Window Theory of Crime, suggests that blight leads to greater blight. It also suggests that the opposite is true—that eliminating blight leads to a greater sense of safety and civic pride. For this assignment, consider your community, your neighborhood, perhaps even your college campus: What changes would you propose to clean up or improve the atmosphere or environment? Then, in an essay of about 500 words, explain what specific modifications or adjustments you believe should be made and why such alterations would make your chosen area a better place.

13

Illustration: Considering an Argument Essay

WHATEVER HAPPENED TO ENERGY CONSERVATION
Michael Schirber

Simpler is better.

It's a common maxim, and like many aphorisms or adages, it's often true. The evidence that science writer Michael Schirber provides here indicates that this sentiment is certainly accurate regarding energy conservation. Schirber has a Ph.D. in astrophysics and an M.A. in journalism as well as undergraduate degrees in math and philosophy. His work has appeared in such venues as Scientific American.com, Science, *and* Physics World. *This essay was published in* LiveScience, *a Web site devoted to science, technology, and health issues. Its media partners, which regularly feature LiveScience articles and video presentations, include MSNBC.com, Yahoo, and AOL. Drawing on the work of a variety of energy experts, Schirber makes a compelling argument that the easiest and most effective way to reduce energy consumption and greenhouse gas emissions is perhaps the most basic approach of all: consuming less energy through efficiency.*

Is it actually possible to cut energy consumption to a significant degree simply by being more efficient in energy use?

The most talked-about solutions for global warming involve alternative energies, but the straightest line to reduced greenhouse gas emissions is using less energy, period. "The cheapest, cleanest energy is the energy you don't use," said Jenny Powers of the Natural Resources Defense Council (NRDC).

The idea was once called energy conservation, but that gave the impression of sitting at home in the dark wearing three sweaters to stay warm. The more favorable term is "efficiency," which implies doing more with less.

A report issued earlier this year by McKinsey & Company, a global management consulting firm, found that adopting certain efficiency measures could cut the increase in the world's energy demand by more than half, without sacrificing economic growth.

"It doesn't seem as sexy as solar and wind, but efficiency is the cornerstone of reducing our environmental impact," Powers told *Livescience.*

Waste not

The world consumed 422 quads of energy in 2003 (a quad is a quadrillion BTUs, or the energy in 180 million barrels of oil). The

United States alone used 92 quads in the same year, making it the largest single energy consumer.

The report, "Curbing Global Energy Demand Growth," predicts that global consumption will increase by 2.2 percent annually, reaching 613 quads in 2020. However, by becoming more efficient, the world could slow its growing appetite, so that only 478 quads are needed in 2020.

These cuts don't have to hurt. In fact, many of the report's energy-conserving proposals would pay for themselves in a few years, but the problem is that most people and organizations don't realize how they are being wasteful.

To raise awareness in the industrial sector, the Department of Energy has a program called Save Energy Now, which provides free energy assessments to the biggest energy-consuming plants in the nation. So far, assessors have visited more than 300 plants and identified more than $600 million in possible energy reductions, corresponding to 5.1 million tons of prevented CO_2 emissions.

"This is why we are focusing on the largest consumers," said program manager Bob Gemmer. "The cost saving is a number you can get your arms around."

The assessments target fire-heating equipment and steam systems, which together account for almost 70 percent of industrial energy use. The DOE has recommended a range of efficiency improvements from adding proper insulation to installing a heat and power system that uses wasted heat to make electricity.

Companies are not obligated to make these changes, but Gemmer told *LiveScience* that many of the plants could cut their energy bill by almost 10 percent.

"There's a mindset out there that the best way to make money is to make more stuff," Gemmer said. But some companies could increase their profits by 50 percent just by reducing the cost of powering their plants.

Want not

Although industry accounts for 46 percent of energy consumption, more and more of the globe's energy is being used for homes, workplaces and transportation, especially in wealthier nations.

"Consumers are increasingly the driving force of energy consumption as the world economy has shifted away from industry and toward less energy-intensive service industries," according to the McKinsey report.

China alone could account for a third of the total growth in energy demand, thanks in large part to its burgeoning middle class and folks' desires for cars and appliances.

The report found the global residential sector had the greatest opportunity to reduce its energy demand by implementing better insulation, compact fluorescent lighting and high efficiency water-heating.

But surprisingly one of the biggest inefficiencies in the home is standby power: the little lights and displays that stay on when you turn something off. Standby power consumes between 20 to 60 watts, which may not seem like much, but over the course of a day it accounts for 4 to 10 percent of a house's energy consumption.

"The biggest standby culprits are your home computer and cable box," Powers said.

Why not

There is technology currently available that reduces standby power to 1 watt. In fact, most energy efficiency ideas—such as Energy Star appliances and sustainable architecture—exist right now, as opposed to some alternative energies, such as affordable solar panels that are still years away.

"Everything [in this report] is within the reach of today's technologies," said NRDC President Frances Beinecke. "Nothing needs to be invented. There are no magic wands. Americans will not be asked to live in trees or mud huts."

So what is holding us back? Part of the trouble is that efficiency does not have the big profile of a wind mill or a fuel-cell vehicle, Powers said. "You can't see it, touch it, taste it."

To increase perception, the report recommends that utility companies provide an itemized bill that lets consumers see how much each appliance is costing them and how much they could save by installing something more efficient.

13

MASTERY EXERCISE 2 **Considering Significance and Meaning**

1. According to the report by management consulting firm McKinsey & Company, what would result in terms of world energy consumption if people made efficiency a major priority?
2. In 2003, where did the United States rank worldwide in terms of energy consumption?
3. As Schirber explains, efficiency is a simple and effective way to reduce energy consumption. So why doesn't energy efficiency attract the attention that the evidence suggests it deserves?

MASTERY EXERCISE 3 **Analyzing Method and Technique**

1. How does Michael Schirber's introduction prepare the reader for the points he makes in the body of his essay?
2. Many of the supporting ideas that Schirber supplies contain specific figures and statistics. What effect does this factual information have on the overall impact of his argument?
3. How would you describe Schirber's tone? What details or examples in the essay lead you to this conclusion?

WRITING AN ARGUMENT ESSAY C

In his essay, Michael Schirber makes a compelling case that basic energy efficiency can greatly reduce energy consumption worldwide. But no amount of efficiency will eliminate the need for sources of energy. Here in the United States, we continue to struggle for energy independence, with more than half of the oil we use still coming from other countries. Not everyone agrees on the best way to solve the problem. Some people advocate a wholesale movement to alternative energy—wind, geothermal, solar, tidal, and so on. Others assert that it's time to concentrate on the natural resources right here in the United States. We have huge deposits of coal along with the potential of shale oil and offshore and Alaskan deposits of natural gas and oil. Proponents of this approach argue that the money that would have to be expended on alternative energy would be better spent on technology that would make these traditional fuels cleaner. For this assignment, consider how you feel about this issue. If you haven't yet decided where you stand, do some research. Then write an essay of about 500 words in which you express and support your point of view regarding the best way for the United States to develop greater energy independence without contributing further to the deterioration of the environment. Remember to acknowledge any expert opinion you include as support.

WRITING AN ARGUMENT ESSAY D

If the United States is going to maintain its prominence—and its citizens the lifestyle that accompanies it—the country must continue to be a leader in science and technology. But when it comes to producing high school and college graduates in these vital areas, many experts are concerned that the United States is lagging behind where it needs to be. One suggestion to address this issue is to increase the amount of science and math that students at all levels must study, even it means a reduction in other areas, for example, the arts, history, physical education, and so on. But others argue that these latter kinds of courses are vital to the intellectual and creative development of students, and that imagination plays as important a role in solving problems as knowledge does. For this assignment, consider where you stand on this issue, perhaps examining the opinions of experts who have examined these kinds of dilemmas. Then write an argument essay of about 500 words in which you state your point of view and offer plenty of supporting ideas and examples to help persuade your reader.

Summary Exercise

1. After considering the following topics, prewrite on the one with which you most strongly agree or disagree.

   - All college students should be required to complete 50 hours of documented community service during each academic year.
   - For everyone's safety, government officials should have the right to monitor the activity on the Internet—including tracing visits to Web sites and screening e-mail and social networking communication—of people it suspects may represent some kind of threat.
   - Campers, hikers, mountain climbers, extreme skiers, and so on, who require rescue, as a result of getting last or becoming injured, should be responsible for the expenses involved in the recovery efforts.

2. Create a draft essay of about 500 words in which you support your stance on the subject you have chosen.

3. Using the Argument Essay Checklist, page 200, as a guide, revise your draft. Make sure that your stance on the subject is explicitly stated and that you have provided sufficient, valid support for your point of view, with an appropriate combination of modes and plenty of transition to guide your reader. If you have included expert opinion, check that you have correctly documented its use. At the same time, evaluate your

13

essay's logic, tone, and arrangement to ensure that your point of view comes across clearly and effectively to your reader. Have an objective reader evaluate your essay in terms of these points as well.

4. Addressing any problems you and your reader have identified, create a final draft of your argument essay.

13

PART III

Specific Applications: Issues of Research and Documentation

CHAPTER 14 Research and
Documentation Activities:
A Brief Guide

14

Research and Documentation Activities: A Brief Guide

OVERVIEW

Understanding the Research and Documentation Process

Among the most potentially confusing and intimidating writing assignments that students face is a research paper or project of some kind. With one of these assignments, your job is usually to fulfill one of two main aims: *informative*—providing background on a subject—or *persuasive*—presenting and supporting a position on some subject. Regardless of your topic and purpose, however, you follow the same process. You identify a sufficiently limited subject; uncover, evaluate, and integrate information from a variety of traditional and electronic sources; and then document those sources both in the text and at the end of your paper.

Identifying and Narrowing Your Topic

In a way, a general topic is like a diamond with multiple facets, each worthy of exploration. It's not reasonable to expect to be able to deal with all the aspects in a single document. Instead, you need to choose one portion of a broad subject and then develop a specific focus on which to concentrate.

A topic like alternative energy is a good example. Although it is certainly a rich area for examination or analysis, alternative energy is too large and complex to cover in a single research paper. You could, however, deal with a single aspect of this wide-ranging subject—for instance, solar energy.

With a more manageable topic identified, the next step is to identify a specific focus—the issue about the narrowed topic that you will investigate. For a research paper of five to ten pages, the promise that today's solar energy technology holds would be a manageable topic. You may find it necessary to adjust your topic a bit as you learn more about the subject, but at least now you have a starting point.

Exploring Sources

No matter what your subject is, completing a research paper will involve a close study of information. Some of the information will be *primary-source* material—original, firsthand explorations, things like interviews, surveys, questionnaires, experiments, and so on.

Much of the information you examine, however, will likely be *secondary-source* material—the reports or results of others who have studied your topic. These resources exist in a variety of forms. Traditional print information includes

- books
- periodicals
- reference texts—indexes, bibliographies, abstracts, and so on

The ever-broadening array of electronic information, much of it available on the Internet, includes

- Web sites
- bibliographic and full-text databases
- e-books and electronic articles
- online journals and magazines
- podcasts and blogs
- wikis and online forums
- social networking sites and other online communities

Assessing the Validity of Potential Sources

A remarkable—and, in some cases, almost unimaginable—amount of print and electronic information is available on most subjects. The problem you face is figuring out if the material you are considering is *valid*—sound, believable, authentic, and reliable.

The validity of some information is easy to assess. It is supported by figures, statistics, other factual evidence, and the work of numerous established experts over many years. But you may find

14

other material that contradicts this information, offering different details, examples, explanations, and so on. And other material will offer insights that you had not previously seen or considered.

Unfortunately, no single, simple way exists to assess the validity of the information you discover during your research. Still, a couple of general guidelines can help you evaluate the sources you are considering:

1. Traditional print sources like books and periodicals are more likely to have been vetted for inconsistencies or factual errors. Publishers are always concerned about their reputations for accuracy—and about their wallets, since errors or misstatements can lead to litigation.
2. The Internet belongs to nobody, which means that no authority manages it or evaluates the accuracy of the information posted on the Web.

But don't be fooled. These statements aren't absolute truths. Just because a document is in print, that doesn't automatically make it valid. Stories abound about reporters who make up news stories; about writers who manufacture events, facts, or statistics in books; about publishers who produce and market dubious texts based on false or outmoded information.

Equally important, just because information is on the Web, that doesn't mean it is automatically suspect. Legitimate writers and publishers—in many cases, the same writers and publishers of print material—regularly use the Web to distribute material. It is true that the same kinds of evaluative filters that many print sources go through don't exist on the Web, but that doesn't mean the material isn't true or hasn't been fact-checked and verified. In other words, the information that you find on the Web is not necessarily inaccurate simply because it appears in a different venue.

To help you assess the validity of a source:

- Check if the information can be confirmed in another source—if the information is valid, it has likely been published in more than one place.
- Consider the writer's reputation or credentials, including publishing history, related academic or professional experience, and overt political or social stances.
- Take into account the publisher's reputation and association with special-interest business, religious, or political organizations.
- Note the suffix of any Web page address, which indicates the general focus of—and any possible bias associated with—a site, for instance, *.com* (commercial enterprise), *.edu* (educational institution or concern), or *.org* (nonprofit organization).

14

As you conduct your research, you may be tempted to draw information from one of the most frequent stops on the information superhighway, the online encyclopedia Wikipedia. Like all wikis, Wikipedia is a collaborative Web site allowing users to add to, delete, revise, and correct information, and this fluid nature represents a problem. Because it is relatively easy to change or adapt entries in Wikipedia, you have no guarantee that the information you find there is consistently accurate.

But even more important in terms of your research activities, Wikipedia, like traditional print and online encyclopedias (*Encyclopedia Britannica, Encyclopedia American, The World Book Encyclopedia,* etc.), is a repository of *general* information. It is a good starting point to develop a working knowledge of your subject, giving you enough background to understand the more complete, more complex documents you will come across. But don't plan on using entries from Wikipedia or any other encyclopedia in your research paper. Your job is to supply specific—not general—supporting information, and that's simply not the role of an encyclopedia.

Base Camp for Research Activities: Your College Library

Modern technology has made it possible for you to do some of your research from home. A few keystrokes and mouse clicks in combination with a search engine will locate many of the virtual texts you are seeking.

But visiting your college library—both in person and online—remains a crucial step in your research journey. For one thing, your college library will likely have many of the hard-copy sources you need or will be able to obtain them through interlibrary loans or exchanges. Your college library also provides access to a number of electronic sources that you can't get through your own Internet service, such as the library's catalog of holdings as well as specialized databases in a wide variety of academic areas and professional fields containing bibliographic information and full-text collections.

Developing a Working Bibliography

Your research will bring you into contact with many documents related to your subject. You'll thus need to examine each potential source to identify the ones that seem, at this point in the writing process, to offer the strongest support for your main point.

14

But as with any writing task, you won't know exactly what you are going to write until you start composing your draft. Therefore, it makes sense to develop and maintain a *working bibliography* that includes those documents that you might be able to use. Record the information that you need to prepare your **Works Cited** section. (See "How to Document Your Sources," pages 223–230). Then download the electronic sources you are considering and photocopy possible print sources, making sure they are properly labeled and carefully organized. A little extra attention now will save you valuable time as you develop your initial and final drafts.

Using the Writing Process to Develop a Draft

To complete a draft of your research paper, you will follow the same steps you do with any other extended writing. That means working through the stages of the writing process—prewriting, composing, and revising. And because the process is recursive, you'll move back and forth through the stages as you find source material and integrate it into your writing.

Just as you do with any extended writing, you need to plan and structure your research paper carefully, presenting your study in the same basic divisions of *introduction, body,* and *conclusion.*

The introduction of a research paper contains the thesis and lays out the structure. By identifying your specific topic and focus, the thesis makes sure that the introduction provides a clear direction for your reader. A thesis such as "Life in the future promises to be filled with alternative energy sources, and technological advances ensure that solar power will play a major role" lets the reader know what to expect in the body of the paper.

The body should contain multiple paragraphs that feature the supporting information you have uncovered and push your ideas forward. With a research paper on the promises of solar energy, a good strategy would be to discuss briefly the history of solar energy, move on to current applications, and then cover designs and hopes for the future. The actual number of paragraphs in the body of the paper will depend on the amount and strength of the supporting information you discovered as well as the scope of the assignment.

The conclusion should restate the significance of the main idea and the supporting information. With a research paper on solar energy, the conclusion would sum up what solar power can already accomplish and reinforce the role it will no doubt play in the future.

14

Avoiding Plagiarism

When you include ideas or details from some other source in your work, you need to tell your reader where you found this information. Otherwise, you are guilty of **plagiarism**—taking someone else's work and passing it off as your own. Plagiarism is literary theft, and the penalty can range from a failing grade for the document to failing the class to being dismissed from school. It doesn't make any difference whether the act is accidental or intentional. When you fail to acknowledge your source for any reason and in any subject area, you are guilty of plagiarism.

Fortunately, the solution is fairly simple. Whenever you include information from another document, indicate in two places in your paper where you found the information. The first spot is in the actual text of the paper, immediately after the information. The second place is at the end of the paper, in a formal list of all the sources you used. In both spots, you adhere to the guidelines of proper documentation, which involves providing essential information about the source of the material—information that would enable a reader to find the original document from which you took the material. (See "Understanding the Process of Documentation," pages 222–226.)

Incorporating Source Information into Your Writing: The Basic Strategy

Regardless of your aim, subject, and focus, you follow one basic strategy to integrate information from a source into your writing. Consider the following figure:

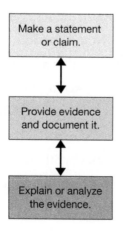

14

As this figure shows, you first make a *statement* or *claim* about your subject. You offer *evidence* from a source that supports or illustrates the statement or claim, and then you document it properly. Finally, you *explain* or *analyze* the evidence, emphasizing its significance and connection to the point you are making.

You can expect to repeat this process multiple times in your paper. Think of yourself as a lawyer presenting a case. The more evidence you provide, the more often you will repeat the process. Every time you repeat this strategy, you make your case that much stronger.

Deciding How Best to Present Evidence

You have three ways to present the supporting evidence you decide to include in your paper: **direct quotation, paraphrase,** and **summary.**

Direct Quotation

A direct quotation is a passage taken word for word from the original work and presented within quotation marks. In general, you should use a direct quotation when the words in the passage have special significance or are so ideally phrased that expressing them in your own words wouldn't capture the full meaning. Here's a direct quotation from Jim Ostroff's "Eight Innovations that Will Change Your Future," which appeared December 9, 2009, on the *Kiplinger* Web site:

"University and private labs in the U.S., Australia, Switzerland and Canada are developing cost-effective plastic coatings containing microscopic particles of copper, indium, gallium and titanium. Painted on building rooftops and exteriors, they'll absorb sunlight and produce electricity just as bulky solar panels do now. One big plus: The cell coatings could generate power even on cloudy days, making this solar catcher up to three times more efficient than today's solar modules. That'll give them the potential to cut a company's electricity purchases by 50% to 75% and even offer some companies the chance to sell power to utilities when their own needs ebb."

14

Direct quotation is a good choice whenever your goal is to highlight or emphasize the special quality of a writer's phrasing or the particular meaning of an author's words, as would be the case when examining a work of literature.

Incidentally, if you wish to leave out part of a direct quotation that will not alter the meaning of the passage, signify the omission by using an **ellipsis**—three spaced periods—in place of the words you've left out, as this version of the passage shows:

"University and private labs in the U.S., Australia, Switzerland and Canada are developing cost-effective plastic coatings containing microscopic particles of copper, indium, gallium and titanium. . . . The cell coatings could generate power even on cloudy days, making this solar catcher up to three times more efficient than today's solar modules. That'll give them the potential to cut a company's electricity purchases by 50% to 75% and even offer some companies the chance to sell power to utilities when their own needs ebb."

Remember, though, that your responsibility is to present the expert's information in a way that reflects the original thinking. Therefore, make sure that you use an ellipsis only when it won't change that original meaning.

Paraphrase

A paraphrase is a passage that contains the meaning of the original but is expressed in your own words. Sometimes you'll feel that the original words are not distinctive, striking, or clear enough to include word for word. In this case, you should prepare a paraphrase by writing what the passage says and what it means.

Here is a paraphrase of the same passage about solar energy technology from Jim Ostroff's December 9, 2009, article:

Researchers in several countries, including the United States, Switzerland, and Australia, are working on an affordable special coating that can be applied to surfaces like roofs and walls to produce

14

solar energy. Tiny particles of titanium and copper embedded in the material will enable it to function as more traditional solar panels do, converting sunlight into energy. This newer material will generate energy even when the sun is not shining brightly, increasing efficiency and dramatically reducing costs. Once it is readily available, this innovation could help to spark interest in widespread use of solar energy.

As this example shows, a paraphrase is not enclosed in quotation marks because the phrasing is different from that in the original.

Summary

A summary is a greatly reduced version of the original, expressed in your own words. Sometimes a writer's point is impressive or useful, but you feel it can be expressed in a greatly reduced form and still make sense. In such a situation, summary is your answer. Here is a summary of the passage from Jim Ostroff's Web article:

Scientists in several countries are at work on a solar energy innovation that involves applying a specially prepared plastic coating to rooftops and other large surfaces. Elements embedded in the coating react to the sun, even on cloudy days, to produce solar energy that is more cost-efficient than traditional solar panels.

As you can see, this summary preserves the main idea but reduces the passage by half, from 103 words to 51 words. As with a paraphrase, don't enclose a summary within quotation marks.

Understanding the Process of Documentation

Documentation is a system of textual recognition that identifies the specific moments in your writing when you are integrating the words or ideas of others. It also provides readers with the information they need should they desire to access the information you've integrated.

14

Why You Must Provide Documentation

Documentation enables you to

- acknowledge and honor the work of those who have come before you
- build off the strengths and weaknesses of those who have come before you
- help an audience trace your train of thought and understand why you have drawn the conclusions you have
- ensure that you avoid plagiarism. Writing is intellectual property, something for which writers deserve credit.

When You Must Provide Documentation

Anytime you take information from another source, you must acknowledge it. The exception is information classified as *common knowledge*—ideas, principles, examples, concepts, and so on, that have appeared in print or been broadcast so often that they are part of the general public consciousness. That U.S. presidents may serve only two four-year terms and that rejection remains a threat in organ transplantation are examples of common knowledge. The problem is that it's often hard to tell whether something is indeed common knowledge. Therefore, if you are at all in doubt, document the information.

How to Document Your Sources

Regardless of how you choose to present the information from another source, you must acknowledge your source in two locations in your document following a standard method of documentation. In Writing and English courses, as well as other Humanities courses, the Modern Language Association (MLA) system is the method to use.

MLA guidelines call for you to first acknowledge your source immediately following the material. After providing some transition to prepare your reader for the material, you present the material and then provide a set of parentheses that contains the author's last name and page number, as these examples show:

MLA Parenthetical Documentation

rect quotation m a book

clude JTHOR'S LAST AME and PAGE JMBER in ARENTHESES. ——•

As people who work the sea every day know, the power of ocean waves is extraordinary. "On a steel boat the windows implode, the hatches fail, and the boat starts to downflood" •— (Junger 173). Sometimes in a matter of mere

Because the included material is a DIRECT QUOTATION, provide QUOTATION MARKS to enclose the quotation.

14

minutes, a ship can sink beneath the waves, taking some or all of the crew with it.

Paraphrase from a book

As people who work the sea every day know, the power of ocean waves is extraordinary. Once a truly massive wave hits, it causes catastrophic damage to a boat, including doors and windows that burst inward, leading to massive flooding (Junger 173). Sometimes in a matter of mere minutes, a ship can sink beneath the waves, taking some or all of the crew with it.

Because the included material is a PARAPHRASE, NO QUOTATION MARKS are needed.

Include AUTHOR'S LAST NAME and PAGE NUMBER in PARENTHESES.

If the information you are including comes from a Web page or other electronic format that doesn't include page numbers, simply list the author's last name—or, if no author is given, the first main word of the title—in parentheses.

The second place that you must acknowledge your source is at the end of your paper, in a section called *Works Cited*. (If you have taken information from one source only, entitle the section *Work Cited*.) Regardless of the types of documents from which the material has come, list sources in alphabetical order on the basis of the author's last name:

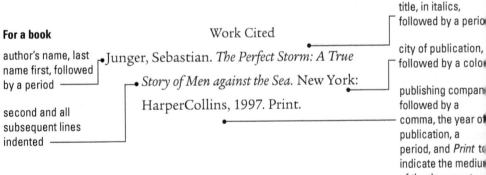

For a book

Work Cited

Junger, Sebastian. *The Perfect Storm: A True Story of Men against the Sea.* New York: HarperCollins, 1997. Print.

author's name, last name first, followed by a period

second and all subsequent lines indented

title, in italics, followed by a period

city of publication, followed by a colon

publishing company followed by a comma, the year of publication, a period, and *Print* to indicate the medium of the document

14

Here is how to arrange the notations of some common types of documents according to the MLA style of documentation:

Book, Two or Three Authors

Le Couteur, Penny, and Jay Burreson. *Napoleon's Buttons: How 17 Molecules Changed History.* New York: Penguin Putnam, 2003. Print.

Book, Four or More Authors

Fowler, Martin, et al. *Patterns of Enterprise Application Architecture.* Boston: Addison-Wesley, 2003. Print.

Book with Editor(s)

Graydon, Don, and Kurt Hanson, eds. *Mountaineering: The Freedom of the Hills.* Seattle: The Mountaineers, 1997. Print.

Work in Anthology or Collection; Book Chapter

Carver, Raymond. "Fat." *What Are You Looking At? The First Fat Fiction Anthology.* Ed. Donna Jarrell and Ira Sukrungruang. Orlando: Harcourt, 2003. 259-64. Print.

Article in Newspaper, Magazine, or Journal
(identified by date)

Warschauer, Mark. "Demystifying the Digital Divide." *Scientific American* Aug. 2003: 42-47. Print.

(identified by volume)

Stross, Brian. "The Hybrid Metaphor: From Biology to Culture." *Journal of American Folklore* 112 (1999): 254-67. Print.

(identified by volume and issue numbers)

Freeman, Mara. "A Celtic Mandala." *Parabola* 28.3 (2003): 29-34. Print.

Personal Interview or Conversation

Wright, Jacqueline M. Telephone interview. 2 Sept. 2010.

14

Lecture or Presentation

Lewis, Sara E. "Trans-mutations: *Boys Don't Cry*, Transgenderism, and Mass Market Trauma Narratives." Modern Language Association. New Orleans. 4 Oct. 1999. Lecture.

Film or Television Program

Shakespeare in Love. Dir. John Madden. Perf. Gwyneth Paltrow, Joseph Fiennes, Geoffrey Rush, Colin Firth, Ben Affleck, and Judi Dench. Universal Studios, 1998. Film.

Personal Letter or E-mail

Bazinet, Norman. "Plans for League Play." Message to Ken Fitzgerald. 29 May 2011. E-mail.

Web Site

The Gnostic Theater. A Casa Actors' Theater, n.d. Wed. 20 Feb. 2010. <http://www.acasaweb.com>.

You'll find complete explanations and thorough illustrations of the MLA system in the reference section of your college library and in writing handbooks as well as online.

Examining Some Annotated Pages from a Research Paper

Take a look at the following pages from a research paper on solar energy. The annotations highlight key features to consider.

14

Willette 1

Gary L. Willette

Dr. William J. Kelly

English 101: Composition 1—College Writing

December 1, 2011

Solar Power:
A Small Part of Our Past—
A Big Part of Our Future

The first developments of solar cells and solar power were far from a necessity when they were discovered. There were no shortages of oil, no high gas prices, and, most important of all, very few electrically powered devices. But as time progressed, so did technology. Over time, solar cells became more efficient, more powerful, and more useful. Today's high prices for traditional energy sources have driven many homeowners and business owners to embrace solar power. Life in the future promises to be filled with alternative energy sources, and technological advances ensure that solar power will play a major role.

The first discovery of electric energy created by sunlight belongs to French physicist Antoine-César Becquerel. Becquerel observed the first *photovoltaic effect*, the basic physical process through which a solar cell converts sunlight into electricity, while experimenting in 1839 (Bellis). His rudimentary work did not involve an actual solar cell but rather a "solid electrode in an electrolyte system." Still, his study showed that it was possible to use the power of the sun to generate energy.

14

Willette 4

Note that these body paragraphs from the middle of the paper, in accordance with the plan for this research paper, discuss the current state of solar energy.

Single-crystal cells are the most commonly found solar cells today. The wafers, or collectors, in these cells are cut from single-crystal cylindrical ingots of grown silicon. In many modern solar panels, the wafers are cut to a thickness of 200 microns (Seale). One micron is equivalent to one-millionth of a meter. Because the wafers are sliced from cylindrical ingots, they are disks, so there is a significant amount of space between them on a typical solar panel. This space is one of the reasons these solar panels don't have a much higher efficiency. Cells of this type have reached efficiencies of 24 percent in research labs, and 15 percent in commercial products. This is the most efficient type of solar cell but also the most expensive (Neville 77).

Note the parenthetical reference acknowledging the original source of the information—a Web page. The full citation is in the **Works Cited** list at the end of the paper.

Note the parenthetical reference acknowledging the original source of the information—a book. The full citation is in the **Works Cited** list at the end of the paper.

Multicrystalline solar cells are made from cast square ingots of multicrystalline silicon. It is called multicrystalline because it is composed of many different single-crystal structures. This composition means that the cells have a "metal flake" texture as opposed to single-crystal cells. The square shape of these cells allows only a small amount of wasted space on the solar panel. In general, this feature would account for a greater efficiency rating, but due to their composition, the rating of each individual cell is less. These cells have impurities other than silicon, which makes them less efficient than pure single-crystal cells (Castaner and Markvart 123).

Note the parenthetical reference acknowledging the original source of the information—a book. The full citation is in the **Works Cited** list at the end of the paper.

Note the parenthetical reference acknowledging the original source of the information—a book. The full citation is in the **Works Cited** list at the end of the paper.

Integrated thin-film modules are significantly thinner than any other types. Thin-film modules are currently the most efficient complete modules, with a rating of around 11 percent. Rather than single- or multi-crystal silicon, these modules use amorphous silicon as their semiconductor, and are the only type thin enough to be used for solar-powered watches, calculators, and garden lights (Hamakawa 54).

14

Willette 7

Note that these body paragraphs from the final part of the paper, in accordance with the plan for this research paper, discuss the future of solar energy.

As Jim Ostroff notes, considerable research is currently ongoing to find even simpler, less expensive applications of solar energy, including innovative surface coatings:

Note the repeated running head.

MLA guidelines indicate that with direct quotations running more than four lines, the entire passage should be indented.

> University and private labs in the U.S.,
> Australia, Switzerland and Canada are
> developing cost-effective plastic coatings
> containing microscopic particles of copper,
> indium, gallium and titanium. Painted on
> building rooftops and exteriors, they'll ab-
> sorb sunlight and produce electricity just as
> bulky solar panels do now. One big plus:
> The cell coatings could generate power even
> on cloudy days, making this solar catcher
> up to three times more efficient than today's
> solar modules.

The author of this article from a Web site has been identified earlier in this research paper, so no notation is needed at the end of the passage.

This kind of innovative approach will make it even easier for both businesses and homeowners to commit to solar energy, significantly reducing our dependence on carbon-based fuels.

The conclusion of a research paper should restate the importance of the information presented in the introduction and the body.

Solar power has come a long way in less than two centuries and even farther in the past two decades. Worldwide collaborations are making the fastest advancements ever in solar energy. Solar cells have doubled in efficiency in the last 75 years or so, and developments are now better than ever. Once durable, inexpensive solar cells with an efficiency rating of 50 percent are developed and widely available, the solar revolution will have officially arrived.

14

Willette 8

Works Cited

Aldous, Scott, and Jessika Toothman. "How Solar
    Cells Work." *HowStuffWorks.com*,
    1 Apr. 2000. Web. 16 Oct. 2010.

Bellis, Mary. "Definition of a Solar Cell—History
    of Solar Cells." *About.com*, n.d. Web.
    4 Dec. 2010.

Castaner, Luis, and Tom Markvart. *Solar Cells:
    Materials, Manufacture and Operation.*
    Great Britain: Elsevier, 2005. Print.

Hamakawa, Yoshihiro. *Thin-Film Solar Cells:
    Next Generation Photovoltaics and Its
    Applications.* New York: Springer-Verlag,
    2004. Print.

McClintock, Meredith, and Elizabeth Flammini.
    *Learn About Solar Energy and Solar Panel
    Installation.* Video. *Google Tech Talks.*
    Google, 12 Sept. 2008. Web. 16 Oct. 2010.

Neville, Richard C. *Solar Energy Conversion: The
    Solar Cell.* 2nd ed. Amsterdam: Elsevier,
    1995. Print.

Ostroff, Jim. "Eight Innovations that Will Change
    Your Future." *Kiplinger.* 9 Dec. 2009. Web.
    17 Oct. 2010.

Seale, Eric. "Solar Cells." 11 July 2003. Web.
    16 Oct. 2008.

14

PART IV

Dealing with Matters of Form

15

Parts of Speech and Parts and Types of Sentences

OVERVIEW

Parts of Speech and Parts and Types of Sentences Defined

Specialists in any field need to have a common language to ensure that they can communicate and discuss their work with their colleagues. For writers, this common language includes such elements as the parts of speech—**nouns, pronouns, adjectives, adverbs, conjunctions, prepositions, interjections**, and **verbs**. It also involves the essentials of the basic unit of writing, the sentence, and its primary parts, the **subject** and **verb**. In addition, it entails the different types of sentences—**declarative, interrogative, imperative**, and **exclamatory**—and different classifications of sentences—**simple, compound, complex**, and **compound-complex**. This information is the foundation you need to express your good ideas in a simple, clear, and correct form.

Understanding the Parts of Speech

Six of the parts of speech can be grouped on the basis of their *function*: the **namers**, nouns and pronouns; the **modifiers**, adjectives and adverbs; and the **connectors**, conjunctions and prepositions.

The Namers—Nouns and Pronouns

15

Nouns name persons, places, things, and ideas, and pronouns take the place of nouns and other pronouns. If a word names something that exists in fact or fiction, even if what it is naming can't be held, touched, or pointed out, the word is either a noun or a pronoun.

Consider this sentence:

Farmers throughout Iowa, Wisconsin, and Nebraska have faced frustration because of the ongoing drought.

Here, nouns name persons, *Farmers*; places, *Iowa, Wisconsin,* and *Nebraska*; a thing, *drought*; and an idea, *frustration.*

Proper nouns, which begin with a capital letter, name specific persons (*Laura*), places (*India*), things (*Cooperative Education*), and ideas (*Utopia*); and **common** nouns name the rest (*woman, country, educational approach,* and *happiness*).

Nouns function in six ways in a sentence: **subject, predicate nominative, direct object, indirect object, object of a preposition**, and **appositive**.

- a **subject**:

EXAMPLE: **Psychology** remains a popular choice of study for many college students.

- a **predicate nominative**, the word that answers "Who or What?" after a linking verb:

EXAMPLE: My neighbor is an outstanding **runner**.

- a **direct object**, the word that answers "Whom or What?" after an action verb:

EXAMPLE: Lily opened the **envelope** on the table.

- an **indirect object**, the word that answers "To Whom or For Whom?" or "To What or For What?" after an action verb:

EXAMPLE: The professor gave the **class** a study sheet.

- an **object of a preposition**, the word that follows a preposition and completes a prepositional phrase:

EXAMPLE: The book on the **couch** belongs to my cousin.

- an **appositive**, a word that helps to explain or illustrate another noun:

EXAMPLE: The tickets were for the center of the first row, the best **seats** available.

15

Pronouns are like nouns in that they refer to people, places, things, and ideas. The advantage of pronouns is that they are a kind of shorthand allowing you to express your meaning without needless repetition. Also like nouns, pronouns can serve as subject, predicate nominative, direct object, indirect object, object of a preposition, and appositive.

Look at the pronouns in this sentence:

> *Nicole* tried to start **her** *car,* but **it** wouldn't start up, and **anybody who** might have given **her** a ride had already left for work.

In the first half of the sentence, the personal pronoun **her** takes the place of the proper noun *Nicole*, and the personal pronoun **it** takes the place of the common noun *car.* In the second half of the sentence, the indefinite pronoun **anybody** takes the place of the names of a number of people who otherwise would have to be identified. In addition, the relative pronoun **who** refers to **anybody**, and **her** refers back to *Nicole* in the first half of the sentence. Chapter 19 covers the use of pronouns in full detail.

The Modifiers—Adjectives and Adverbs

Adjectives and adverbs describe or *modify* other words, so they are known as modifiers. Adjectives modify nouns (and very occasionally pronouns), and adverbs modify verbs, adjectives, and other adverbs.

Adjectives generally answer the questions, "Which one?", "How many?", and "What kind?" about the words they are modifying, resulting in a more precise representation for the reader. A noun like *desk,* by itself, doesn't create a clear, specific picture. Add some adjectives, however—a dusty, damaged, antique, mahogany roll-top *desk*— and the image is much more exact.

The most common adjectives are the three known as **articles**: *a, an,* and *the.* *A* and *an* are called **indefinite articles** because you use them to modify an unspecified noun: *a* for words beginning with a consonant sound (*a* basketball), and *an* for words beginning with a vowel sound (*an* autograph). *The* is called a **definite article** because you use it to modify a specific noun: *the* basketball, *the* autograph.

Adverbs indicate *when, where, how, why, how much,* or *to what extent* concerning verbs, adjectives, and other adverbs. They describe how someone or something acts, for example, *The kids laughed* **loudly**, or when something occurs, for instance, **Yesterday**, *I took an easy exam.* Adverbs also illustrate degree relative to other modifiers, for example, *The kids laughed* **very** *loudly* or *Yesterday, I took an* **incredibly** *easy exam.*

15

Many adverbs end in *-ly*, and you can often turn an adjective into an adverb by adding *-ly* to it: *loud, loudly.*

But an *-ly* ending doesn't automatically indicate that a word is an adverb. *Early* is an adjective when it modifies a noun, for instance, the *early* bird, but it's an adverb when you use it to describe when something happened, for example, I went to work *early*. Chapter 20 focuses on the proper use of adjectives and adverbs.

The Connectors—Conjunctions and Prepositions

Conjunctions and prepositions enable you to link ideas. A conjunction connects two or more units of the same type—two or more of the same kind of word, two or more phrases, or two or more clauses (**subject–verb units**). A preposition joins the noun or pronoun following it to some other word in the sentence.

There are three types of conjunctions—**coordinating, correlative**, and **subordinating**—each of which creates a slightly different kind of connection:

COORDINATING CONJUNCTIONS

and	nor	so
but	or	yet
for (because)		

(The role of coordinating conjunctions is discussed in fuller detail in Chapter 16.)

CORRELATIVE CONJUNCTIONS

both/and	neither/nor	whether/or
either/or	not only/but also	

(The role of correlative conjunctions is discussed in fuller detail in Chapter 22.)

SUBORDINATING CONJUNCTIONS

after	even though	than	whenever
although	if	though	where
as	in order that	unless	wherever
as if	rather than	until	whether
because	since	when	while
before	so that		

(The role of subordinating conjunctions is discussed in fuller detail in Chapter 16.)

15

Note how the conjunctions join the elements within the following sentences:

EXAMPLES: The children *danced* **and** *sang* all morning.
verb   *verb*

In the park, at the beach, **or** *by the pool,* parents have to keep a close watch on their children.
phrase   *phrase*   *phrase*

We had to stand at the front of the subway car **because**
clause
all the seats in the back were taken.
clause

Remember that the units you link with a conjunction must be the same kind. The exception concerns nouns and pronouns, which you can connect: "*Flo* **and** *somebody* from work went shopping."

A preposition provides a different kind of connection, one between the object of the preposition—the noun or pronoun that follows it—and another word.

Here is a list of commonly used prepositions:

PREPOSITIONS

about	at	but (except)	inside	outside	toward
above	before	by	into	over	under
across	behind	despite	like	past	underneath
after	below	down	near	since	unlike
against	beneath	during	of	than	until
along	beside	except	off	through	up
among	besides	for	on	throughout	upon
around	between	from	onto	till	with
as	beyond	in	out	to	within
					without

In addition to these prepositions, there is another small group called compound prepositions:

COMPOUND PREPOSITIONS

according to	because of	in the place of
along with	in addition to	instead of
as to	in front of	next to
aside from	in spite of	out of

A preposition plus its object is called a **prepositional phrase**, and the resulting unit functions as a modifier. When the prepositional phrase modifies a noun, the prepositional phrase functions as an adjective:

EXAMPLE: The *dog* **in the house** is dangerous.

But when the prepositional phrase modifies a verb, adjective, or adverb, the prepositional phrase functions as an adverb:

EXAMPLES: The dangerous dog *lived* **in the house**.

Its coat was *black* **with red highlights**.

Its barking and snarling would finally end *early* **in the evening**.

Interjections

Words like *hey, wow, oh, well, ah,* and so on, are interjections, which convey excitement or emotion but have no other real connection to a sentence. If the excitement or emotion is particularly strong, an interjection is followed by an exclamation point. As a writer, however, you should use interjections sparingly, only when there is genuine excitement or emotion appropriate to your discussion.

Verbs

Verbs show action or otherwise help to make a statement. Most verbs in English are **action verbs**, whether that action is physical or mental, real or imagined—for example, *examine, laugh, think, speak, eat, worry,* and so on.

EXAMPLE: The workers in the library always **speak** quietly.

Other verbs, called **linking verbs**, indicate a relationship or link between the main idea and some word in the sentence. Most linking verbs are forms of *be,* for example, *is, are, was, were, might be, could have been, was being,* and so on. Verbs like *appear, become, feel, grow, look, remain, smell, seem,* and *taste* can serve as linking verbs if they are used to indicate a relationship rather than an action:

EXAMPLES: My adviser **is** a new faculty member.

Jay **seems** so much more confident. (means Jay *is* confident)

15

Helping or **auxiliary verbs** are forms of *be, do,* and *have* (*will be running, did* play, *has* traveled) that are used with different tenses of other verbs to form additional tenses that express times and conditions in the past, present, and future. The **modals** *may, might, must, can, should,* and *could* also serve as helping verbs. Chapter 18 covers correct verb use in full detail.

Understanding the Essentials of the Sentence

The basic unit of writing is the **sentence**, a group of words expressing a complete thought. A sentence always contains two primary elements, a subject and a verb. In some cases, it also includes a third feature known as a **complement**.

Subjects and Verbs

In a sentence, the verb is a word that shows action or otherwise helps to make a statement. The subject is the word that answers the question, "Who or what is doing the action or being discussed?"

EXAMPLES: Suddenly, the dishes crashed to the floor.

My younger brother was the best tennis player in our high school.

In the first sentence, the verb is *crashed*. Ask, "Who or what *crashed*?", and the answer, and therefore the subject, is *dishes*. In the second sentence, the verb is *was*. The answer to the question, "Who or what *was* the best tennis player in our high school?"—the subject—is *brother*.

With sentences in the **imperative mood**—often called **direct address** or the **command**—the subject is implied, as this example shows:

EXAMPLE: Call 911 for immediate assistance.

The verb is *call*. Ask the question, "Who or what *call* 911 for immediate assistance?", and the answer, even though the word isn't actually in the sentence, is the implied or understood subject *You*.

Complements

In addition to a subject and a verb, some sentences have a **complement**, a word after the verb that *completes* the action or statement. Take a look at this example:

                         subject   *verb*

EXAMPLE: The **quarterback** *threw* the ball over 50 yards.

Now ask the question, "The quarterback *threw* whom or what?" The answer, *ball*, is the complement. An action verb like *threw* transfers the action directly to the complement, so it is called a **direct object**.

Sometimes sentences containing an action verb and a direct object will have an additional complement. Called an **indirect object**, this type of complement appears between the verb and the direct object.

EXAMPLE: On her way to work, **Karen** *mailed* Kevin a **letter**.
subject verb   direct object

The direct object, the word that answers the question, "On her way to work, Karen *mailed* who or what?" and receives the action directly, is **letter**. Another word receives the action indirectly, though. This complement answers the question, "Karen mailed a letter to whom or what, for whom or what?" The answer, *Kevin*, is the indirect object.

Two other types of complements—the **predicate nominative** and the **predicate adjective**—follow linking verbs. A predicate nominative is a noun or pronoun that answers the question, "Who or what?" after a linking verb.

EXAMPLE: My **coworker** for the night *was* an old **friend**.
subject   linking verb   predicate nominative

Ask the question, "My coworker for the night was who or what?" and the answer—the predicate nominative—is **friend**.

A predicate adjective, as the name suggests, is an adjective that answers the question, "Who or what?" after a linking verb.

EXAMPLE: **Lai** *can be* very **persuasive**.
subject linking verb predicate adjective

The word that answers the question, "Lai can be very who or what?" is the adjective **persuasive**, which means it is a predicate adjective.

Phrases

A **phrase** consists of a group of words that functions as a single word. There is more than one type of phrase:

- a **verb phrase**—which consists of a main verb and an auxiliary verb:

EXAMPLE: You **should have** *waited* at the bus stop.

- The auxiliary verb **should have** is combined with *waited* to create a verb phrase. See Chapter 18 for more on verb phrases.

15

- a **prepositional phrase**—which consists of a preposition, the noun or pronoun serving as its object, and any of its modifiers, and acts as either an adjective or an adverb:

EXAMPLES: The coffee **in that pot** is several hours old.

At two o'clock, several stores closed **for inventory**.

In the first example, **in that pot** serves as an adjective modifying *coffee*. In the second example, **At two o'clock** and **for inventory** serve as adverbs modifying the verb *closed*. See Chapter 20 for more on the correct use of modifiers and Chapter 22 for more on the correct use of prepositional phrases.

- **verbal phrases**—which consist of a **verbal** (a form of a verb that acts as another part of speech) plus any modifiers. There are three types of verbals: **participles, gerunds**, and **infinitives**.

    Participles act as adjectives. Present participles end in *–ing*, and past participles end in *–ed* or *–d* for regular verbs:

EXAMPLES: **Pushing spectators away**, the security *guards* kept the pathway open for the players.

Stopped at the door, the lucky *customer* was given a $100 gift certificate.

In the first sentence, the present participial phrase **Pushing spectators away** modifies *guards*, and in the second, the past participial phrase **Stopped at the door** modifies *customer*.

    Gerunds, which also end in *-ing*, act as nouns:

EXAMPLE: **Locating the exits** is one of the first things to do in a theater or nightclub.

Here, the gerund phrase **Locating the exits** answers the question, "Who or what is one of the first things to do?", so it serves as the subject of the sentence.

    Infinitives consist of the basic form of a verb preceded by *to*. An infinitive phrase, which consists of an infinitive plus its modifiers, can act as an adjective, adverb, or noun:

EXAMPLE: Muriel had a *reason* **to complete the rest of the game.**

The infinitive phrase **to complete the rest of the game** is acting as an adjective modifying the noun *reason*.

EXAMPLE: The old man *rushed* **to check on his sick wife.**

The infinitive phrase **to check on his sick wife** is acting as an adverb modifying the verb *rushed*.

EXAMPLE: Joe hopes **to resume all activities soon.**

Here the infinitive phrase **to resume all activities soon** is acting as a noun. It answers the question, "Joe hopes whom or what?", making it the direct object.

Clauses

A **clause** is also a group of words that functions as a single word. Unlike a phrase, however, a clause contains a subject–verb unit. There are two main types of clauses:

- An **independent** or **main** clause can make independent sense.
- A **dependent** or **subordinate** clause relies on a main clause to communicate a full meaning.

Consider this example, which contains both types of clauses:

EXAMPLE: **Laura finally called the police** *after she had waited an hour for a repair truck to arrive.*

The unit **Laura finally called the police** is the main clause because it can stand alone. The second clause, *after she had waited an hour for a repair truck to arrive*, doesn't make independent sense, so it is a subordinate clause.

Subordinate clauses act as three parts of speech:

- **adjective:**

EXAMPLE: The iPod **that Ronnie bought last week** stopped working today.

The subordinate clause **that Ronnie bought last week** modifies the noun *iPod*. (Subordinate clauses like this one, introduced by a relative pronoun like *that, who,* or *which,* are also called **relative clauses.**)

- **adverb:**

EXAMPLE: **When my date spilled an entire cup of coffee all over my new jacket,** the night was ruined.

The subordinate clause **When my date spilled an entire cup of coffee all over my new jacket** modifies the verb phrase *was ruined.*

15

● **noun:**

EXAMPLE: **What the meteorologist predicted** was a week of rain.

● The subordinate clause **What the meteorologist predicted** answers the question, "Who or what was a week of rain?", so it is the subject of the verb *was*.

Understanding the Types and Classes of Sentences

As a writer, you always need to express your ideas in complete sentence form. You have a number of options for doing this, including four different types of sentences and four different classifications.

The Different Types of Sentences

There are four different types of sentences: **declarative, interrogative, imperative**, and **exclamatory**. Each type serves a different purpose.

● Declarative sentences make statements:

EXAMPLE: **My laptop keeps shutting down unexpectedly.**

● Interrogative sentences present direct questions:

EXAMPLE: **When did your laptop start behaving this way?**

● Imperative sentences express commands or requests:

EXAMPLE: **Please disconnect and reconnect the power supply on your laptop.**

Remember—the subject of an imperative sentence, called *you understood*, is implied or understood to be the person who is receiving the command.

● Exclamatory sentences express strong excitement or emotion and are always followed by an exclamation point:

EXAMPLE: **I can't believe that the Better Business Bureau won't investigate that computer retailer!**

The Different Classifications of Sentences

Sentences can also be classified in four different ways. The classes— **simple, compound, complex**, and **compound-complex**—are based on the number and types of clauses a sentence contains.

● Simple sentences consist of a single main clause:

EXAMPLE: **The contributions of early civil-rights marchers deserve more credit.**

- Compound sentences consist of two or more main clauses connected by a coordinating conjunction or a semicolon:

EXAMPLES: The heat is intense, **and** the humidity makes the situation even worse.

The heat is intense; the humidity makes the situation even worse.

- Complex sentences consist of one main clause and one or more subordinate clauses:

EXAMPLES: *Before the rain began,* **the sky turned a dusty gray.**

The attorney *who answered the phone* **refused to answer any questions.**

- Compound-complex sentences consist of two or more main clauses connected by a coordinating conjunction and one or more subordinate clauses:

EXAMPLE: **First, the nightclub** *where we planned to go* **was closed,** and **then the restaurant** *where we stopped* **had a 45-minute wait for a table.**

When it comes to types and classifications of sentences, always use whatever combination helps you communicate your message to your reader.

16

Sentence Errors: Fragments, Comma Splices, and Run-on Sentences

OVERVIEW

Sentence Errors Defined

The three most common—and most serious—sentence errors are the **sentence fragment**, the **comma splice**, and the **run-on sentence**. A sentence fragment is an incomplete sentence, which is a major problem because it keeps your reader from gaining a full understanding of your ideas. A comma splice results from using a comma to connect two sentences. The problem is that *commas can't connect*. A run-on sentence, sometimes called a *fused sentence,* results when two or more sentences don't have a correct mark of punctuation separating them or a semicolon or conjunction connecting them. Comma splices and run-on sentences are also significant concerns because they suggest to your reader that you don't know where one idea ends and the next one begins. This chapter illustrates how to identify and correct fragments, comma splices, and run-on sentences.

Fragments

16

You need to be able to recognize and eliminate several different types of fragments, including

- missing subject fragments
- missing verb fragments
- phrase fragments
- subordinate clause fragments

Correcting Omitted Subject or Verb Fragments

For a group of words to be a sentence, as Chapter 15 explains, it must express a complete thought and contain both a subject and a verb. If either part is omitted, the result is a fragment.

The secret to finding and eliminating this kind of fragment is to focus first on the verb of any unit you set off as a sentence. If you can't find the verb, you have a fragment. If you find the verb, ask, "Who or what?" before it to make sure there is a subject. If no word answers the question, you have a fragment.

Consider the following:

sentence

Faulty: **The park wardens cut down the first diseased tree.**

fragment

But left the second one standing.

The first group of words contains a subject and verb and expresses a complete thought, so it's a sentence. The second group, however, has a verb—*left*—but no subject, so it is a fragment.

The simplest way to correct this fragment is to add a subject, thus turning the fragment into a complete sentence:

Corrected: **The park wardens cut down the first diseased tree. But they left the second one standing.**

You could also eliminate the fragment by adding the missing subject and then combining the sentences by changing the capital *B* in "But" to a lowercase *b* and the period preceding "But" to a comma:

Corrected: **The park wardens cut down the first diseased tree, but they left the second one standing.**

The result is a correct **compound sentence**. (Chapter 15, page 243, discusses compound sentences in greater detail.)

Another variation is to eliminate the period following *tree* and then change the capital *B* in "But" to a lowercase *b*:

Corrected: The park wardens cut down the first diseased tree **but left** the second one standing.

The result is a **simple sentence** with a single subject, *park wardens,* and a compound verb—more than one verb connected by a conjunction: *cut* **but** *left.* (Chapter 15, page 242, discusses simple sentences in greater detail. Chapter 17, pages 258–259, covers verb phrases more fully.)

Correcting Phrase Fragments

As Chapter 15 explains (pages 239–241), a **phrase** consists of two or more words *without* a subject–verb unit that function like a single word. By itself, then, a phrase is always a fragment. Types of phrases that are sometimes mistakenly set off as sentences include **verb phrases, prepositional phrases, verbal phrases**, and **appositive phrases**.

Verb Phrase Fragments   Verb phrases, as Chapter 15, page 239, explains, consist of a main verb plus a helping verb (*is, were, will be,* and so on) or a **modal** (*may, can, must,* and so on). When you set a verb phrase off by itself, it is a fragment:

Verb Phrase Fragment: Will be looking for a new job soon.

To correct this type of fragment, simply add a subject, as this version shows:

Corrected: My aunt will be looking for a new job soon.

Prepositional Phrase Fragments   As Chapter 15 (page 240) spells out, prepositional phrases consist of a preposition and a noun or pronoun that acts as the object of the preposition, plus all the words in between. Here again are the lists of prepositions presented in Chapter 15:

PREPOSITIONS

about	around	beside	down	into	out
above	as	besides	during	like	outside
across	at	between	except	near	over
after	before	beyond	for	of	past
against	behind	but (except)	form	off	since
along	below	by	in	on	than
among	beneath	despite	inside	onto	through

16

throughout	toward	unlike	upon	without
till	under	until	with	
to	underneath	up	within	

COMPOUND PREPOSITIONS

according to	because of	in the place of
along with	in addition to	instead of
as to	in front of	next to
aside from	in spite of	out of

Set off by itself, a prepositional phrase is a fragment because it lacks a subject–verb unit:

Prepositional Phrase Fragment: Throughout her entire apartment.

Additional information is needed to turn this fragment into a complete sentence. Sometimes, this additional information already exists in the form of a sentence that appears before or after the fragment to which the prepositional phrase actually belongs:

Corrected: *Throughout her entire apartment,* **Lily has various paintings and drawings by local artists.**

Other times, you will need to add a subject–verb unit to the prepositional phrase:

Corrected: **Alex had hidden his stuffed animals and toy cars** *throughout her whole apartment.*

Verbal Phrase Fragments   Verbals, as Chapter 15 (pages 240–241) explains, are verb forms that act as other parts of speech rather than as verbs. Present **participles** end in *-ing* and act as adjectives, and **gerunds** end in *-ing* and act as nouns. (**Past participles** end in *-ed*, except with irregular verbs.) **Infinitives** are simple present tense forms of a verb introduced by *to*, and they act as adjectives, adverbs, or nouns. A verbal phrase consists of one of these verbals plus any words accompanying it.

Even though it doesn't act as one, a verbal looks like a verb, so you might think you have written a sentence when you have actually written a fragment. Look at the following:

sentence

Faulty: **The diet center guaranteed that their program**

infinitive phrase fragment

would help clients of any size and age. *To lose weight in a safe way.*

16

sentence

Once the store closed, the staff stocked all the holiday

participial phrase fragment

products. *Including all the new toys.*

In both passages, the initial unit is a complete sentence because it can make independent sense. But the second unit can't because the verbal phrase lacks a subject–verb unit.

You can correct a verbal phrase fragment by adding it to the sentence—before the phrase or after—to which it logically belongs:

Corrected: The diet center guaranteed that their program would help clients of any size and age to lose weight in a safe way.

You can also rephrase the fragment and include a subject–verb unit to create a complete sentence:

Corrected: Once the store closed, the staff stocked all the holiday products. This merchandise included all the new toys.

Appositive Phrase Fragments   An appositive consists of individual words or groups of words that rename or explain a preceding noun or pronoun. Appositives can be very long, and sometimes they can seem to be sentences. But they're not because they can't stand on their own.

Look at this example:

sentence

Faulty: **The convention crowd went wild at the entrance of**

appositive fragment

the candidate. *The person who had worked tirelessly to win the nomination.*

The first group of words is a sentence because it makes sense by itself. But the second group, *The person who had worked tirelessly to win the nomination*, can't stand on its own because it leaves the reader with the question, "What about this person?"

Actually, spotting this type of fragment is easy because appositives generally follow the word they explain or rename. You can eliminate an appositive fragment by adding it to the sentence that contains the word the appositive explains or renames:

Corrected: **The convention crowd went wild at the entrance of the candidate,** *the person who had worked tirelessly to win the nomination.*

Correcting Subordinate Clause Fragments

Probably the most common fragments result from dependent or **subordinate clauses** being set off as sentences. The reason so many writers have trouble with them is that subordinate clauses, unlike phrases, *do* contain subjects and verbs. But as Chapter 15 (pages 241–242) explains, subordinate clauses depend upon main clauses to express their full meaning. Because they can't communicate their message independently, they are fragments.

Subordinate clauses are often introduced by one of the following subordinating conjunctions:

SUBORDINATING CONJUNCTIONS

after	even though	than	whenever
although	if	though	where
as	in order that	unless	wherever
as if	rather than	until	whether
because	since	when	while
before	so that		

Another type of subordinate clause, called a **relative clause**, is introduced by one of the following *relative pronouns:*

RELATIVE PRONOUNS

who	whom	which
whose	that	

Take a look at the following examples:

subordinate clause fragment

Faulty: *Although that LCD television set costs almost $4,000.*
sentence
The picture quality is extraordinary.

sentence   *relative*
My sister scored three three-point shots. *Which made*
clause fragment
all the difference in the game.

With subordinate clause fragments introduced by subordinating conjunctions, the fastest way to correct the fragment is to remove the conjunction and create two sentences:

Corrected: **That LCD television set costs almost $4,000.**
The picture quality is extraordinary.

The problem with eliminating the fragment in this way, though, is that choppy sentences can result. Therefore, a better solution

16

with many subordinate clause fragments is to combine the subordinate clause with the main clause to which it logically belongs, as these corrected versions show:

Corrected: Although that LCD television set costs almost $4,000, the picture quality is extraordinary.

My sister scored three three-point shots, which made all the difference in the game.

Keep in mind that *who, whom, which,* and *whose* can also be used to introduce complete sentences that express a question, called **interrogative sentences**. In these cases, the pronouns are known as *interrogative pronouns*. Consider these examples:

EXAMPLES: **Which** road should I take to avoid the construction project?

Who called the landlord?

The key to knowing whether the pronoun is relative or interrogative is the question mark at the ends of the sentences, which indicates that the pronoun is an interrogative pronoun introducing a question rather than a relative pronoun introducing a subordinate clause. If no question mark follows the unit, you most likely have a fragment to be eliminated rather than a sentence.

Comma Splices and Run-on Sentences

As with finding fragments, the first step to eliminating comma splices and run-on sentences in your writing is to identify all subjects and verbs in the units that you set off as independent ideas. Then, for any sentences containing more than one subject–verb unit, make sure that these units are properly connected. Take a look at the following examples:

Comma Splice: The *warranty* **expired** in March, / *Joni* still **received** service on her broken phone.

Run-on Sentence: Fluorescent *bulbs* **operate** on less energy / many *people* **have eliminated** all incandescent bulbs in their homes.

16

Both examples contain two subject–verb units (separated by a slash), each of which could stand as a simple sentence by itself. In the first example, a comma comes between the subject–verb units. But *commas can't connect*, so the result is a comma splice. In the second example, no connector or separator appears between the subject–verb units. The first unit *runs into* the second, so the result is a run-on sentence.

To eliminate comma splices and run-on sentences, you can use

- a **conjunction** to connect the sentences
- a **semicolon** to connect the sentences
- a **period** or other mark of end punctuation to separate the sentences

Correcting Comma Splices and Run-on Sentences by Adding a Conjunction

Probably the most common method to eliminate comma splices and run-on sentences is to use a conjunction to connect the two sentences. As pages 235–236 of Chapter 15 indicate, there are three kinds of conjunctions: **coordinating conjunctions, correlative conjunctions**, and **subordinating conjunctions.**

Coordinating conjunctions (*and, or, but,* and so on) suggest basic relationships between the elements being connected. For example, *and* acts like the plus sign (+) in mathematics, while *or* indicates an alternative and *but* suggests an exception.

Correlative conjunctions (*either/or, not only/but also, both/and,* and so on) are sets of conjunctions that specify relationships between two units. *Either/or,* for instance, points to only one of two alternatives, but *not only/but also* emphasizes both elements, as does *both/and.*

Subordinating conjunctions (*because, if, when,* and so on) also indicate a conditional relationship between clauses. *Because* indicates the cause of something, *if* suggests a possibility or contingency, and *when* emphasizes time relative to something else.

Take a look at these examples:

Comma Splice: The outside of the house was in terrible shape, the inside was just as bad.

Run-on Sentence: Ami finds time to mentor a young girl in her neighborhood she works all day with children.

In the first example, the comma appears between the end of the first clause and the beginning of the second. But commas can't connect,

16

so this passage is a comma splice. And in the second example, the initial clause *Ami finds time to mentor a young girl in her neighborhood* runs into the next clause, with nothing connecting or separating the clauses. This example is therefore a run-on sentence.

To correct a comma splice using a coordinating conjunction, place the conjunction immediately following the comma that is already between the clauses:

Corrected: The outside of the house was in terrible shape, **and** the inside was just as bad.

The coordinating conjunction **and** now connects the two clauses, indicating an equivalent relationship between them. If it had been a run-on sentence instead of a comma splice, you would also have needed to add a comma between the first clause and the conjunction to provide the necessary pause.

Corrected: Ami finds time to mentor a young girl in her neighborhood **although** she works all day with children.

Here the subordinating conjunction **although** connects the two clauses, emphasizing a contrary or conditional relationship between them.

Notice that when this kind of subordinate clause appears second in the sentence, you don't need a comma before the conjunction. However, if for stylistic purposes you choose to reverse the order so that the subordinate clause appears first, you must put a comma between the clauses to provide the needed pause.

Corrected: **Although** she works all day with children, Ami finds time to mentor a young girl in her neighborhood.

Correcting Comma Splices and Run-on Sentences by Using a Semicolon

Another way to correct a comma splice or run-on sentence is to put a semicolon between the clauses. Think of the semicolon as the Velcro of English—it is the one mark of punctuation that has the power to join clauses. A semicolon is roughly equivalent to *and* preceded by a comma, but the connection is more concentrated, indicating a closer or more significant relationship between the clauses. Essentially, a semicolon says that these two clauses are so closely linked that no word is necessary to show their connection.

16

Look at these examples:

Comma Splice: The Regatta was the worst nightclub I had ever been in, the lighting and sound system were both inadequate.

Run-on Sentence: All I wanted to do was stop for a cup of coffee things didn't work out that way, though.

A semicolon would be a good choice to eliminate these errors. In the initial example, the first clause sets up the reader's expectations by stating that the nightclub was in poor shape, and the second clause fulfills those expectations by giving examples of what was wrong with the place. In the second example, the first clause tells the reader what the plans were, and the second indicates that those plans fell through.

To correct a comma splice with a semicolon, you simply replace the comma between the clauses with the semicolon:

Corrected: The Regatta was the worst nightclub I had ever been in; the lighting and sound system were both inadequate.

With a run-on sentence, place the semicolon at the end of the first clause:

Corrected: All I wanted to do was stop for a cup of coffee; things didn't work out that way, though.

If you want to suggest an additional relationship, you may include one of the following **conjunctive adverbs** immediately after the semicolon:

CONJUNCTIVE ADVERBS

also	however	similarly
besides	instead	still
consequently	meanwhile	then
finally	moreover	therefore
furthermore	nevertheless	thus

Always keep in mind that conjunctive adverbs are adverbs, not conjunctions, so they have no power to connect. Therefore, when you add a conjunctive adverb between clauses, you must use a semicolon to provide the necessary connection, as these examples show:

EXAMPLES: The movie was outstanding; **however,** the people in front of us talked the whole time.

She led the angry patrons to another table; **meanwhile,** the hostess picked up the tray of dirty dishes.

Notice that you also put a comma after the conjunctive adverb to signify the additional pause that follows the adverb.

Using a Period to Correct Comma Splices and Run-on Sentences

Another method that eliminates comma splices and run-on sentences is separating the clauses into individual sentences. With a comma splice, this means changing the comma between independent clauses to a period, and with a run-on sentence, it means putting a period between the independent clauses.

Consider these examples:

Comma Splice: The trip from Chicago to Miami, with a stop in Atlanta, was the longest part of my trip, the flight to Grand Bahama, the second most popular destination in the Bahamas, took less than an hour.

Run-on Sentence: Ali's new job is much easier than her old job at the self-service gas station near the busiest avenue in town now she works in the florist department at a supermarket, making various floral arrangements.

The first example has a comma incorrectly placed between two independent clauses, making the passage a comma splice. The second example features two independent clauses with nothing correctly separating or connecting them, making the passage a run-on sentence.

Now consider these corrected versions:

Corrected: The trip from Chicago to Miami, with a stop in Atlanta, was the longest part of my trip. **The** flight to Grand Bahama, the second most popular destination in the Bahamas, took less than an hour.

> Ali's new job is much easier than her old job at the
> self-service gas station near the busiest avenue in
> town. **Now** she works in the florist department at a
> supermarket, making various floral arrangements.

16

In terms of style, keep this point in mind: Using a period between independent clauses to eliminate a comma splice or run-on sentence makes sense when the independent units are fairly long, as they are with these examples. If you used a conjunction or semicolon to connect the clauses, the resulting sentences would be over 35 words long, which might make them harder for a reader to follow.

But with short independent clauses, using a period to separate them may not be a good stylistic choice because a series of short sentences can make your writing choppy, as this example shows:

Choppy: The goal line stand was dramatic. The defense finally
            sacked the quarterback on the fourth down.

With relatively short sentences like these, connecting the clauses with a conjunction or a semicolon, with or without a conjunctive adverb, would make the writing flow more smoothly:

Improved: The goal line stand was dramatic, **but** the defense
            finally sacked the quarterback on the fourth down.

            The goal line stand was dramatic; **the** defense finally
            sacked the quarterback on the fourth down.

            The goal line stand was dramatic; **however,** the
            defense finally sacked the quarterback on the fourth
            down.

17

Subject–Verb Agreement

Understanding Subject–Verb Agreement

For a group of words to be a complete sentence, as Chapters 15 and 16 make clear, that group must contain a subject and a verb. But meeting these basic requirements isn't enough. For a sentence also to be correct, all subjects and verbs must match up in terms of number—that is, singular verb forms for singular subjects and plural verb forms for plural subjects. In other words, all subjects and verbs must agree, which can sometimes be difficult, particularly when

- the subject follows the verb in a sentence
- phrases or clauses come between the subject and verb
- the subject is compound
- the subject is an indefinite pronoun, collective noun, singular word ending in -s, or noun of measurement, amount, or distance

Errors in subject–verb agreement are serious because they distract your reader from your message, so it's vital to learn how to identify and eliminate these errors.

When the Subject Follows the Verb

Although the subject will come before the verb in the majority of sentences you write, not all your sentences will follow this pattern. In some cases, the subject follows the verb or part of the verb, as with a question, for example:

verb subject   *verb*

EXAMPLE: *Did* **Joanie** really *turn* him down?

Maintaining subject-verb agreement with questions is generally not too difficult. When the plural form *don't* comes before the subject, however, especially in casual conversation, you may find yourself using *don't* incorrectly:

Faulty: *Don't* **Joanie** *understand* how to turn a person down?

To eliminate this faulty subject-verb agreement, use the verb form that matches the singular subject **Joanie**:

Corrected: *Doesn't* **Joanie** *understand* how to turn a person down?

Sentences beginning with the adverbs *there* or *here* often also present problems. Only a noun or pronoun can be a subject, so whenever a sentence begins with *there* or *here*, the subject always comes *after* the verb.

Look at these examples:

Faulty: There *is* several **reasons** for her bizarre behavior.

Here *come* my **brother**.

In the first sentence, the singular verb form *is* is the verb. Ask the question, "Who or what *is* there for her bizarre behavior?", and the answer—the subject—is the plural noun **reasons**, which is a mistake in subject-verb agreement. And in the second sentence, the verb is the plural verb form *come*. The word that answers the question, "Who or what *comes* here?" is the singular noun **brother**, again a mistake in subject-verb agreement.

To correct errors of this kind of subject-verb agreement, simply make the two parts agree by changing one of them:

Corrected: There *are* several **reasons** for her bizarre behavior.

or

There *is* **one main reason** for her bizarre behavior.

17

Corrected: Here *come* my **brothers**.

or

Here *comes* my **brother**.

You might also restate the sentence and eliminate *there* or *here* completely, which is even better from a stylistic standpoint:

Corrected: Several **reasons** have led to her bizarre behavior.

My **brothers** are coming.

When Phrases or Clauses Come between Subjects and Verbs

A greater chance for errors in subject–verb agreement occurs when other words separate subjects and verbs. The most common interrupters are phrases and clauses.

Subjects and Verbs Separated by Phrases

Phrases coming between subjects and verbs often result in errors in subject–verb agreement. Which of the two verbs in the following sentence is correct?

EXAMPLE: The container in the trunk beside the jack and behind my tools (holds/hold) windshield washer fluid.

As is the case with many of the sentences that you write, the words that come between the subject and the verb here are prepositional phrases: *in the trunk, beside the jack,* and *behind my tools.* Prepositional phrases consist of a preposition and a noun or pronoun serving as the preposition's object. (See page 236 for a complete list of prepositions.) But an object can't be a subject, so the object of a prepositional phrase will never be the subject of a sentence.

What complicates things with sentences like this one is that the object of the preposition, *tools,* comes right before the verb. As a result, you might incorrectly select *hold* because it agrees with *tools.* Computerized grammar checkers often suggest this incorrect choice as well. Or you might be misled by the fact that the trunk contains several items—the container, the jack, and various tools—and choose the plural verb. But even though the trunk is filled with many items, only one—the *container*—holds windshield washer fluid.

When a prepositional phrase introduced by a compound preposition like *along with* or *in addition to* comes between the subject and the verb, you might also have difficulty identifying the actual subject. (For a complete list of compound prepositions, see page 236.) For example, which is the correct verb in the following sentence?

EXAMPLE: Attorney Jeremy Wright, along with Dr. Alex Matos and CPA Leo Nadeau, (leases/lease) space in the same building.

Glance at the sentence quickly and you might conclude that because three people are mentioned, the verb should be the plural form *lease*. But *along with* is a compound preposition, and *Dr. Alex Matos* and *CPA Leo Nadeau* are objects of that preposition. An object can't be a subject, so the answer to the question, "Who or what leases/lease space in the same building?"–the actual subject–is the singular proper noun **Attorney Jeremy Wright**. The correct verb is therefore the singular form **leases:**

Corrected: Attorney Jeremy Wright, along with Dr. Alex Matos and CPA Leo Nadeau, **leases** space in the same building.

Subjects and Verbs Separated by Clauses
Sometimes subordinate clauses placed between subjects and verbs can lead to errors in subject–verb agreement. What is the proper verb in this example?

EXAMPLE: **The 50-percent-off sale,** *which includes all laptop computers*, **(starts/start) on Saturday.**

First identify the main clause, the subject–verb unit that can make sense independently. **The 50-percent-off sale (starts/start) on Saturday** makes sense on its own—it's the main clause. But *which includes all laptop computers* does not—it's the subordinate clause.

Now identify the verb in the main clause. In this case, the verb is either **starts** or **start**. Ask the question, "Who or what **starts/start** on Saturday?", and the answer—the singular noun **sale**—is the subject. The correct verb is therefore the singular form **starts.**

But the last word of the subordinate clause—the plural noun **computers**—is a potential problem because it comes right before the verb of the main clause. If you don't take the time to identify

17

the actual subject of the main clause, you might mistakenly make the verb of the main clause agree with the *computers* rather with the actual subject, **sale.** Computerized grammar-checking features often offer this incorrect alternative. The secret to avoiding these kinds of errors is to identify *each* subject-verb unit and make sure the elements agree—disregarding all phrases and clauses that come between the subject and the verb.

When a Sentence Has a Compound Subject

Some compound subjects are singular and some are plural. The difference depends upon the conjunction connecting them.

Subjects connected by *and* are almost always plural, regardless of whether the two subjects being connected are singular—for example, A **book** and a **magazine** *are* available—or plural—for instance, **Books** and **magazines** *are* available. The exception concerns subjects that are commonly thought of as singular, such as *peanut butter and jelly, peace and quiet, ham and eggs, rock and roll,* and so on.

The use of *or* (or either/or) to connect subjects indicates that only one of the alternatives is possible. If both subjects are singular—*Alex or Owen*—the verb must have a singular form: *understands.* If both subjects are plural—*charts or figures*—the verb must have a plural form—*capture.* Although *neither/nor* indicates an absence of something on the part of both subjects, the rules are the same. If both subjects are singular, the verb must have a singular form—*Neither Alex nor Owen* **understands.** If both subjects are plural—*Neither charts nor figures* **capture**—the verb must have a plural form.

When the compound subject consists of both a singular word and a plural word, the verb agrees with the word closest to it:

EXAMPLE: Either the supervisor or the **workers** *deserve* the blame for the decreased level of production.

If you reverse the order of the subjects so that the singular **supervisor** is closer to the verb, the correct verb is the singular form, *deserves:*

EXAMPLE: Either the workers or the **supervisor** *deserves* the blame for the decreased level of production.

When a Subject Is an Indefinite Pronoun, Collective Noun, Singular Noun Ending in -*s*, or a Noun of Measurement, Amount, or Distance

17

As Chapter 15 (page 234) explains, indefinite pronouns refer to general rather than specific persons and things. Some indefinite pronouns like *anybody, everyone, somebody, no one,* and so on, are always singular and call for a singular form of a verb:

EXAMPLE: **Everybody** in my family *remembers* the last New Year's party.

The indefinite pronouns *both, few, many,* and *several* are always plural:

EXAMPLE: **Both** of those cars *cost* over $50,000.

And the indefinite pronouns *all, any, more, most, none,* and *some* are either singular or plural, depending on the words to which they refer:

EXAMPLES: **All** of her **success** *stems* from her hard work.

All of the **songs** *come* from one composer.

In the first example, **All** refers to **success,** a singular noun, so the proper verb choice is *stems.* In the second example, though, **All** refers to **songs,** a plural noun, so the proper verb choice is *come.*

Collective nouns like *audience, class, committee, faculty, flock, herd, jury, swarm,* and *team* are singular words that name groups of items or individuals. Use a singular verb with collective nouns:

EXAMPLES: This season's basketball **team** *has* already won more games than last year's team.

The entire **flock** *was sitting* on the power line.

Some words, including *antelope, deer, fish, sheep,* and *trout,* have the same singular and plural form. Your choice of verb form—singular or plural—depends on whether you mean one or more than one:

EXAMPLES: That **moose** *ran* right across the highway.

Those **moose** in that clearing *look* unhealthy.

17

The first sentence deals with one moose, so the proper verb choice is *ran*. The second sentence deals with several moose, so the proper verb choice is *look*.

Some nouns that end in *-s*, the letter that often signals a plural form, are actually singular. This group of nouns includes *economics, ethics, mathematics, measles, mumps, news, physics,* and *politics*. Use a singular form of a verb with them:

EXAMPLES: **Economics** sometimes *confuses* students in the beginning.

Measles *causes* serious health problems, especially for children.

Finally, nouns signifying amounts of measurement, money, time, weight, and so on, are also singular, so use a singular verb form with them:

EXAMPLES: **Eighty dollars** *represents* serious savings.

Ten miles *seems* like a long distance to a child.

18

Correct Verb Use: Irregular Forms, Tense, and Voice

Understanding Different Aspects of Verb Use

As Chapter 15 spells out, verbs are words that show action—*examine, laugh, think, eat,* and so on—or otherwise help to make a statement—*is, am, was, will be, seem, feel,* and so on. Because of these qualities, verbs might well qualify as the most important part of speech. They might also qualify as the most complex part of speech to use. Some verbs are *regular,* meaning that you create their past and past participle forms by adding *-ed* or *-d.* Other verbs are *irregular,* meaning that you create their past and past participle forms in more random, less predictable ways. Verbs also have multiple *tenses,* different forms that enable writers to represent distinct periods and conditions of time. And verbs have more than one *voice,* or way they express action or condition relative to their subjects. Mastery of these different features of verb use will go a long way in helping you become a successful writer.

18 Using Irregular Verbs Correctly

Regular verbs in English form their past and past participles by adding -ed:

Present	Past	Past Participle
ask	ask**ed**	(has, had, have, or will have) ask**ed**

Or, if the verb already ends in -e, just add -d:

Present	Past	Past Participle
require	require**d**	(has, had, have, or will have) require**d**

But **irregular** verbs form their past and past participles in ways that, at the least, seem arbitrary and unpredictable. Consider the forms of the irregular verbs *know* and *see*:

Present	Past	Past Participle
know	knew	(has, had, have, or will have) known
see	saw	(has, had, have, or will have) seen

You can usually tell whether a verb is regular or irregular by adding -d or -ed to the present tense form and reading aloud the word that results. If it sounds unusual or odd, chances are good that the verb is irregular. And if you're still not sure, look in a dictionary, which lists the principal parts of all irregular verbs.

You'll find the following list helpful as well. It provides the principal parts of the most common irregular verbs (except for the present participles, which you always create by adding -ing to the present tense form):

IRREGULAR VERBS

Present	Past Tense	Past Participle
am, is, are	was, were	been
arise	arose	arisen
awaken	awoke, awaked	awaked, awoke
become	became	become
begin	began	begun
bend	bent	bent
bind	bound	bound
bite	bit	bitten, bit
bleed	bled	bled
blow	blew	blown
break	broke	broken
bring	brought	brought
build	built	built
burn	burned, burnt	burned, burnt
burst	burst	burst

18

buy	bought	bought
catch	caught	caught
choose	chose	chosen
cling	clung	clung
come	came	come
cost	cost	cost
creep	crept	crept
cut	cut	cut
deal	dealt	dealt
dig	dug	dug
dive	dived, dove	dived
do, does	did	done
draw	drew	drawn
dream	dreamed, dreamt	dreamed, dreamt
drink	drank	drunk
drive	drove	driven
eat	ate	eaten
fall	fell	fallen
feed	fed	fed
feel	felt	felt
fight	fought	fought
find	found	found
flee	fled	fled
fling	flung	flung
fly	flew	flown
forbid	forbade, forbad	forbidden, forbid
forget	forgot	forgotten, forgot
freeze	froze	frozen
get	got	got, gotten
give	gave	given
go, goes	went	gone
grind	ground	ground
grow	grew	grown
hang	hung	hung
hang (execute)	hanged	hanged
have, has	had	had
hear	heard	heard
hide	hid	hidden, hid
hold	held	held
hurt	hurt	hurt
keep	kept	kept
kneel	knelt, kneeled	knelt, kneeled

(*continued*)

18

IRREGULAR VERBS (Continued)

Present	Past Tense	Past Participle
knit	knitted, knit	knitted, knit
know	knew	known
lay	laid	laid
lead	led	led
leap	leaped, leapt	leaped, lept
leave	left	left
lend	lent	lent
let	let	let
lie	lay	lain
light	lighted, lit	lighted, lit
lose	lost	lost
make	made	made
mean	meant	meant
meet	met	met
mistake	mistook	mistaken
pay	paid	paid
plead	pleaded, pled	pleaded, pled
prove	proved	proved, proven
put	put	put
quit	quit	quit
raise	raised	raised
read	read	read
ride	rode	ridden
ring	rang	rung
rise	rose	risen
run	ran	run
say	said	said
see	saw	seen
seek	sought	sought
sell	sold	sold
send	sent	sent
set	set	set
sew	sewed	sewn, sewed
shake	shook	shaken
shine	shone, shined	shone, shined
shine (polish)	shined	shined
shoot	shot	shot
show	showed	shown, showed
shrink	shrank, shrunk	shrunk, shrunken
shut	shut	shut

sing	sang	sung
sit	sat	sat
sleep	slept	slept
slide	slid	slid
sling	slung	slung
slink	slunk	slunk
sow	sowed	sown, sowed
speak	spoke	spoken
speed	sped, speeded	sped, speeded
spell	spelled, spelt	spelled, spelt
spend	spent	spent
spit	spit, spat	spit, spat
spring	sprang, sprung	sprung
stand	stood	stood
steal	stole	stolen
stick	stuck	stuck
sting	stung	stung
stink	stank, stunk	stunk
stride	strode	stridden
strike	struck	struck, stricken
string	strung	strung
strive	strived, strove	strived, striven
swear	swore	sworn
sweat	sweat, sweated	sweat, sweated
swell	swelled	swelled, swollen
swim	swam	swum
swing	swung	swung
take	took	taken
teach	taught	taught
tear	tore	torn
tell	told	told
throw	threw	thrown
understand	understood	understood
wake	woke, waked	waked, woken
wear	wore	worn
weave	weaved	weaved
weave (cloth)	wove	woven, wove
weep	wept	wept
win	won	won
wind	wound	wound
wring	wrung	wrung
write	wrote	written

18

Go through this list, identifying and highlighting those verbs that give you trouble. Pay particular attention to the right-hand column of the list. Remember—always use a form of *to have* with the past participle.

Another good strategy is to group irregular verbs on the basis of certain patterns:

- the same form for the present tense, past tense, and past participle:

Present	Past	Past Participle (with *has, had, have,* or *will have*)
burst	burst	burst
cut	cut	cut
let	let	let
read	read	read

- the same form for both the past tense and the past participle:

Present	Past	Past Participle (with *has, had, have,* or *will have*)
bring	brought	brought
feel	felt	felt
mean	meant	meant
teach	taught	taught

- the same change—*i* to *a* to *u*—as the verbs move from the present to the past tense:

Present	Past	Past Participle (with *has, had, have,* or *will have*)
begin	began	begun
drink	drank	drunk
ring	rang	rung
sing	sang	sung

- the past participles formed by adding *-n* to the end of the present tense:

Present	Past	Past Participle (with *has, had, have,* or *will have*)
blow	blew	blown
grow	grew	grown
know	knew	known
throw	threw	thrown

In addition to focusing on these verb groups, you might learn how to deal with a particularly troubling irregular verb by writing a series of practice sentences using the three forms of the verb. For the verbs *forget* and *tear*, for instance, you could write sentences like these:

EXAMPLES: My memory is so bad that I **forget** to check the weather every morning.

Yesterday, I also **forgot** to empty the trash. Often, I **have forgotten** to log off the office computer, too.

When reading the newspaper, she often **tears** the front page. Yesterday, she **tore** the entire first section. The heavy wind **had torn** the other sections to shreds already.

Recognizing Different Verb Tenses

When it comes to writing, **tense** means "time." All verbs have several tenses, each of which allows you to express a different period or aspect of time, as the following examples using the regular verb *clean* and the irregular verb *speak* demonstrate:

The Simple Tenses

The **simple present tense** of a verb shows in one word something that is happening at one time or that happens habitually. For singular subjects, except *I* and *you*, the present tense of a verb ends in *-s*:

EXAMPLES: The custodian usually **cleans** the common room every other day.

That dentist **speaks** at the area's assisted living center once a week.

The **simple past tense** shows in one word what has already occurred. With regular verbs, you form the simple past tense by adding *-ed* or *-d* to the plural present tense form, the form that doesn't end in *-s*. With irregular verbs, how the past tense is formed depends on the verb itself:

EXAMPLES: You **cleaned** out your backpack a week ago.

Suddenly, the lost child **spoke**.

The **simple future tense** shows what will take place in the future. You form the simple future tense for both regular and

18

irregular verbs by adding *will* to the plural present form, the form that doesn't end in *-s*:

EXAMPLES: The attendant **will clean** the room in about an hour.

Steve **will speak** to his insurance agent tomorrow.

The Perfect Tenses

The perfect forms of a verb indicate that something has already been completed relative to some other action or event. You create the perfect tense of a verb by adding a form of *have* to the verb's past participle. With regular verbs, the past participle is the same as the past tense form, the simple form of the verb ending in *-ed* or *-d*. With irregular verbs, the form of the past participle depends on the verb itself.

The **present perfect tense** shows that something has occurred sometime in the past or that something that was begun in the past may still be ongoing. You form it by adding either *has* or *have* to the past participle:

EXAMPLES: The park workers **have cleaned** up the playground.

She **has spoken** to the mother of that child about his behavior on four different occasions.

The **past perfect tense** shows what has already happened in the past *before* something else happened in the past. You form it by adding *had* to the past participle:

EXAMPLES: The administrative assistant **had cleaned** the desk at the start of the day.

The coach **had spoken** to the team before the game.

The **future perfect tense** shows that something will happen by some point in the future. You form the future perfect tense by adding *will have* to the past participle:

EXAMPLES: By closing time, I **will have cleaned** up all the broken glass on the floor.

The loan manager **will have spoken** to you at least two weeks before the initiation of any court action.

The Progressive Tenses

Each verb also has a set of progressive tenses. In this context, progressive indicates that something is going on or was or will be happening. To show this progress, you use the present participle—a verb form ending in -ing—along with a form of the verb *to be: am, is, was, will be,* and so on.

The **present progressive tense** shows something that is currently ongoing. You create it by adding a present tense form of *to be—am, is, are*—to the present participle:

EXAMPLES: I **am cleaning** up your mess now.

You **are speaking** about a controversial subject.

The **past progressive tense** shows that something was ongoing in the past. You form it by adding *was* or *were* to the present participle:

EXAMPLES: The host **was cleaning** up her apartment after the party.

The leader **was speaking** with great emotion during the peace rally.

The **future progressive tense** shows that something will be ongoing into the future. You form it by adding *will be* to the present participle:

EXAMPLES: Those kids **will be cleaning** out that basement for most of the day.

My best friend **will be speaking** to a class of first graders next week.

The Perfect Progressive Tenses

The perfect progressive forms of a verb indicate that an action, event, or situation that began at one point has been continuing or will have been going on in relation to some other action, event, or situation. You create the perfect progressive tense by adding *has been, have been, had been,* or *will have been* to the present participle, the -ing form.

18

The **present perfect progressive tense** shows that something began in the past and is still ongoing. You form it by adding *has been* or *have been* to the present participle:

EXAMPLES: The new worker **has been cleaning** the kitchen for over two hours.

We **have been speaking** about the same issues for two weeks now.

The **past perfect progressive tense** talks about something that had been happening in the past but stopped before the present. You form the past perfect progressive tense by adding *had been* to the present participle:

EXAMPLES: The two of us **had been cleaning** the storeroom for an hour before the black smoke appeared.

The senator **had been speaking** about health care before the vice president entered.

You use the **future perfect progressive tense** to show that something will be ongoing in the future but will conclude before something else begins. You form the future perfect progressive tense by adding *will have been* to the progressive form:

EXAMPLES: That environmental task force **will have been cleaning** the edges of that stream for almost 50 hours by the end of the week.

By the halfway point in her speech, the candidate for school committee treasurer **will have been speaking** for almost an hour.

Modal Auxiliary Verbs

Of course, these different verb tenses aren't the only verb forms available to you. If you use some form of *can, shall, may,* or *will,* known as the **modal auxiliaries**, you'll alter the meaning of a verb in some way because modals add conditions. Look at these additional forms of *clean* and *speak*:

EXAMPLES: I **could have been cleaning** for a month and never found that lost earring.

April **would have cleaned** the kitchen, but her sister stopped by.

> The campus doctor **should be speaking** about infectious diseases at these student health seminars.
>
> My friend **may have been speaking** to the sales clerk just before the holdup.

In the first sentence, **could have been** indicates what might have happened but didn't. In the second, **would have** indicates what was supposed to happen but didn't. In the third, **should be** indicates something desired that isn't happening. And in the fourth, **may have been** indicates a possibility that something occurred.

Maintaining Consistency in Verb Tense

One of the most important considerations related to verb tense is being consistent. If you are discussing an event from a week ago, it makes sense to use a form of the past tense. If you are writing about your attitude about a subject at this moment, it makes sense to use a form of the present tense, and if you are writing about what you plan to do tomorrow, it makes sense to use a form of the future tense.

What won't make sense to your reader, however, is a sudden switch from one tense to another:

Faulty:	*past* When I **pulled** into the entrance of the gas station, *past* *present* my car suddenly **stalled**. The next thing I **know**, the *present* man in the car behind me **gets** out of his car and *present* *past* **begins** yelling at me. As I **rolled** up my window, he *present* *past* **bangs** on the hood of my car and **kicked** my tires.

The problem here is that half of the story is told in the past tense—**pulled, stalled, rolled, kicked**—and the other half is told in the present tense—**know, gets, begins, bangs**. The result is confusion for the reader. Therefore, assess the needs of your reader and the purpose of your document and then make all the verbs either present tense:

EXAMPLE:	When I **pull** into the entrance of the gas station, my car suddenly **stalls**. The next thing I **know**, the man in the car behind me **gets** out of his car and **begins** yelling at me. As I **roll** up my window, he **bangs** on the hood of my car and **kicks** my tires.

18

or past tense:

EXAMPLE: When I **pulled** into the entrance of the gas station, my car suddenly **stalled**. The next thing I **knew**, the man in the car behind me **got** out of his car and **began** yelling at me. As I **rolled** up my window, he **banged** on the hood of my car and **kicked** my tires.

Employing the Proper Verb Voice

Voice—how a verb expresses the action or discussion relative to its subject—is an additional consideration of verb use. If the subject is actually doing the action that a verb names—*Tara answered* the phone—that verb is in the **active voice**. If the subject is being acted upon—The *phone was answered* by Tara—the verb is in the **passive voice**. You present a verb in the passive voice by adding a form of the verb *to be*—*is, were, could have been, might be,* and so on—to the past participle. This section discusses the appropriate uses of active and passive voice.

The Advantages of the Active Voice

Most verbs in English are action verbs, and that's a good thing. Action verbs convey actual or implied action (*run, jump, eat, ponder, intend,* and so on), keeping writing lively and interesting. In the active voice, the subject *does, has done,* or *will do* the action, so employing the active voice accentuates this sense of action.

Look, for example, at these three sets of sentences, each set showing passive and active voice verbs:

Active: The *top American skier* **set** a new record in the giant slalom.
                     subject   verb

Passive: A new *record* in the giant slalom **was set** by the top American skier.
                     subject   verb

Active: *Ian's sister* **ordered** the tent and two sleeping bags from the catalog.
                     subject   verb

Passive: The *tent and two sleeping bags* **were ordered** from the catalog by Ian's sister.
                     subject   verb

subject   verb

Active: The *science department* **has scheduled** the examination for 10 a.m.

subject   verb

Passive: The *examination* **has been scheduled** for 10 a.m. by the science department.

Each pair of sentences features an action verb, *set, order,* and *schedule.* The verb in the first sentence of each pair is in the active voice, and the verb in the second sentence of each pair is in the passive voice.

The active voice makes a sentence more direct. In these active voice sentences, the subjects *perform* the action: *the top American skier* **set** the record, *Ian's sister* **ordered** the tent and two sleeping bags, and *the science department* **scheduled** the exam. An added advantage with active voice verbs is that sentences generally contain fewer words, so they are also more concise—brief but to the point.

With the verb in the passive voice, however, the subjects are *acted upon.* The reader has to wait until the end of the sentence to discover who actually set the record, ordered the camping supplies, and scheduled the exam. The message is less direct and longer—with no improvement in detail or clarity.

The Appropriate Use of the Passive Voice

In a few cases, the use of the passive voice may be appropriate. Sometimes, for example, you don't know who or what has completed an action. And other times, the subject is less important or prominent than the receiver of the action. Consider these pairs of sentences:

subject

Passive: During the night, *the windshield* on my new car

verb

was smashed.

subject   verb

Active: During the night, *someone* **smashed** my windshield.

subject   verb

Passive: *A $50 million coat* **was worn** by the fashion model.

subject   verb

Active: *The fashion model* **wore** a $50 million coat.

With the first pair of sentences, the passive voice version is a good choice because whoever or whatever smashed the windshield is

18

unknown. And with the second pair of sentences, the passive voice version is also more appropriate because the extraordinary price tag of the coat has more impact than the anonymous model wearing it.

Correctness versus Effectiveness: Choosing the Correct Voice

When it comes to dealing with verb voice, remember that you are not making a choice based on correctness. If a sentence contains a subject and a verb and expresses a complete thought, it will be correct regardless of whether the verb is in the active or the passive voice. But active voice verbs are more direct and concise, so they better serve the needs of your reader. Therefore, make the active voice your default choice and stick with it unless you can make a case that the passive voice is more suitable in a particular sentence.

19

Pronoun Use

Pronoun Use Explained

The prefix *pro-* in the word *pronoun* means "in place of." As Chapter 15 explains, pronouns are words that can take the place of nouns. Pronouns function exactly as nouns do in sentences. They are also a kind of shorthand helping to eliminate needless repetition of nouns. As a result, they allow you to communicate your ideas more simply and directly to your reader. To develop mastery of this part of speech, you need to concentrate on

- the correct **case** of the personal pronouns
- agreement in **number** between pronouns and their **antecedents**
- clear relationships between pronouns and their antecedents

This chapter will help you learn how to identify and correct errors in pronoun use.

Considering the Different Cases of Pronouns

The pronouns that refer to specific persons, places, and things—**personal pronouns**—change in form depending on their use. These differences in form are called case, and there

19

are three case types: nominative (also known as subjective), objective, and possessive, shown here separated by number (singular or plural) and case:

PERSONAL PRONOUNS

	NOMINATIVE CASE		OBJECTIVE CASE		POSSESSIVE CASE	
	Singular	Plural	Singular	Plural	Singular	Plural
First Person	I	we	me	us	my/mine	our/ours
Second Person	you	you	you	you	your/yours	your/yours
Third Person	he, she, it	they	him, her, it	them	his, her/hers, its	their/theirs

As the list shows, each case has three divisions, first, second, and third person. You use first-person pronouns when you are talking about yourself. You use second-person pronouns when you address someone directly, and you use third-person pronouns when you discuss other specific people or things.

When a personal pronoun is the subject or predicate nominative, the **nominative case** is the correct choice:

singular nominative
EXAMPLE: **I** understand the question that girl is asking.
subject

plural nominative
EXAMPLE: **They** noticed how confused the patient seemed.
subject

When a personal pronoun is the object in a sentence—a direct object, an indirect object, or an object of a preposition—the **objective case** is the correct choice:

singular objective
EXAMPLE: Lara called **me** for directions to the party.
direct object

plural objective
EXAMPLE: The dean sent **them** letters of congratulations.
indirect object

singular objective
EXAMPLE: That customer had asked for **her.**
object of the preposition

When the personal pronoun shows ownership, the **possessive case** is the correct choice:

singular possessive

EXAMPLE: That accident was the worst tragedy of **his** life.

plural possessive

EXAMPLE: **Our** families spent that whole day together.

The relative/interrogative pronoun *who* also has three forms:

Nominative Case	Objective Case	Possessive Case
who	whom	whose

subject

EXAMPLE: The person **who** has influenced me most is my Uncle Nick.

object of the preposition

EXAMPLE: The person to **whom** I owe a great deal is my Uncle Nick.

sign of ownership

EXAMPLE: One person **whose** influence has helped me is my Uncle Nick.

Personal Pronouns as a Part of Compound Subjects or Objects

Personal pronoun use can be confusing when the pronoun is part of a compound subject or object. Consider the pairs of pronouns in parentheses in the following sentences:

EXAMPLES: Elvin, Joshua, Teisha, and (I/me) meet for lunch every Friday.

Between you and (I/me), this job is unbelievably easy.

To make the correct choice, identify what role the personal pronoun is serving in the sentence. In the first sentence, the pronoun is part of the compound subject, so the correct choice is the nominative form, *I*. In the second sentence, the personal pronoun is part of the compound object of the preposition *Between*, so the correct choice is the objective form, *me*.

19 Personal Pronouns in Elliptical Constructions

Elliptical constructions, shortened forms of sentences beginning with *than* or *as,* can be challenging when it comes to choosing the correct personal pronoun. Elliptical passages aren't spelled out because the missing sections are understood. Consider the pairs of pronouns in parentheses in the following sentences:

EXAMPLES: Don has a much better personality than (he/him).

My parents have worried more about Glenna than (I/me).

To figure out which personal pronoun to use, spell out the understood part of the sentence. With the first sentence, for instance, the complete meaning is, "Don has a better personality than he has," so the correct choice is the nominative case, *he.*

The second sentence represents a more complex problem because the meaning changes depending on which case form you choose. If you choose the nominative form, you are actually saying, "My parents have worried more about Glenna than I have worried about Glenna." If you choose the objective form, you are actually saying, "My parents have worried more about Glenna than my parents have worried about me." Therefore, with this type of elliptical construction, double-check to make sure that you have chosen the correct pronoun to express your actual meaning.

Problems with Possessive Case Pronouns

Confusion between the possessive form of some personal pronouns and contractions that sound like them represents another potential problem for writers. One pair that is commonly confused is the possessive pronoun *its* and *it's,* the contraction for *it is* or *it has.* An apostrophe is needed to create the contraction for *it is* and *it has.* But the possessive pronoun *its* is already possessive, so no apostrophe is needed.

The way to avoid this error is to see if *it is* or *it has* fits the sentence. If it does, you want *it's.* If not, use *its.* Consider the words in parentheses in the following two sentences:

EXAMPLES: (Its/It's) too late for any big adjustments.

The pug puppy drank from (its/it's) water dish.

The first sentence needs *It is* to communicate the meaning, so *It's* is the correct choice. But in the second, *it is* doesn't make sense, so *its* is the correct choice.

Other potentially troublesome pairs are *your/you're, their/they're,* and *whose/who's.* To ensure that you choose the correct word, see if the two words making up the contraction (*you are, they are, who is,* or *who has*) fit the sentence. If so, use the contraction. If not, choose the possessive form of the personal pronoun.

Another problem involving possessives has to do with gerunds, verb forms ending in *-ing* that act as nouns. (See Chapter 15 for more on gerunds.) Anytime you use a pronoun before a gerund, you must use the possessive case, as these examples show:

EXAMPLES: The church volunteer committee appreciated **his working** in the preschool center.

Their complaining about working conditions almost caused them to be fired.

Using Pronouns Consistently in Number

Some **indefinite pronouns**—words that represent nonspecific people, places, things, and ideas—are always singular:

another	everybody	nothing
anybody	everyone	one
anyone	everything	somebody
anything	neither	someone
each	no one	something
either	nobody	

Some of them are always plural:

both, few, many, several

And some of them are either singular or plural depending on the word they refer to, called the antecedent:

all, any, more, most, none, some

Most of these pronouns don't present you with any problem. A handful of them, however, hold the potential for error, in particular the singular indefinite pronouns *everybody* and *everyone.* Because these words suggest or encompass many people, you may find yourself using them as if they were plural, as these examples show:

Faulty: When it comes to teamwork, **everybody** should do *their* best.

Everyone is tired of having *their* suggestions ignored.

These sentences are incorrect. **Everybody** and **everyone** are singular, but the words these pronouns refer to—their antecedents—are plural, creating errors in what is called **pronoun–antecedent agreement.**

To correct these kinds of errors, you simply have to make the two words match in number. Look, for instance, at these versions of the same sentences:

singular

Corrected: When it comes to teamwork, **everybody** should do

singular
his or her best.

or

plural

When it comes to teamwork, **all the players** should

plural
do *their* best.

singular   *singular*

Corrected: **Everyone** is tired of having *his or her* suggestions ignored.

or

plural   *plural*

The workers are all tired of having *their* suggestions ignored.

Both versions of each sentence are correct. In general, however, the better choice with sentences like these is to make both words plural, as the second correct version in each pair shows. As you can see, the plural versions simply flow better.

You may encounter the same kind of difficulty with *anybody, anyone, nobody, no one, somebody,* and *someone.* When you use one of these words, avoid problems the same way: make sure that the pronoun and the word it refers to—its antecedent—are both the same number.

Keeping the Relationship between Pronoun and Antecedent Clear

If your reader is going to understand your ideas, you must also make sure that the relationship between each pronoun and its antecedent is clear. Look at this sentence:

Ambiguous: **Ed** and **Bill** had a fight, and **he** broke **his** nose.

The relationship between the pronouns and their antecedents is ambiguous, and this lack of clarity keeps the reader from understanding who did what to whom.

The easiest way to correct this type of error is to restate the sentence completely to eliminate the ambiguity, as this version shows:

Corrected: During their fight, **Ed** broke **Bill's** nose.

The pronoun *it* holds the same potential for confusion. Look at this example:

Ambiguous: Stephanie made a mess when she poured coffee from the pot into the cup because **it** was cracked.

The pronoun **it** has two potential antecedents: *pot* and *cup*. In order for your reader to understand your point, you need to specify which of the two objects was cracked, as these versions show:

Corrected: Stephanie made a mess when she poured coffee from the pot into the cup because **the pot** was cracked.

or

Stephanie made a mess when she poured coffee from the pot into the cup because **the cup** was cracked.

Be sure to check any sentences in which you have used the pronouns *this, that,* and *which* as well. Make sure that their antecedents are clear and unambiguous so that your reader will understand exactly what you are discussing.

20

Adjective, Adverb, and Other Modifier Use

OVERVIEW

Modifier Use Explained

For a reader to gain a full understanding of a document, the writing must be thorough, detailed, precise, and specific. **Adjectives, adverbs,** and other modifiers play a crucial role in fulfilling this goal. As Chapter 15 illustrates, adjectives and adverbs describe, limit, or illustrate other words. Adjectives modify nouns (and occasionally pronouns), and adverbs modify verbs, adjectives, and other adverbs. To avoid errors with modifiers, you need to consider a number of dimensions of their use, including

- different forms of adjectives and adverbs
- commonly confused and irregular modifiers
- intensifying and absolute modifiers
- dangling and misplaced modifiers

All errors in form are serious matters because they distract your reader from your good ideas. Therefore, it's important to be able to identify and eliminate any mistakes with the modifiers you use.

Using the Correct Forms of Adjectives and Adverbs

20

Adjectives and adverbs have three separate forms: **positive, comparative**, and **superlative**. Regular modifiers follow predictable patterns as they change from one form to the next. The positive form of a regular modifier is the basic version of the word, for example, *bright* or *considerate*.

The comparative form casts one thing against another. For regular one-syllable modifiers, the comparative form consists of the positive form plus *-er*: *brighter*. With regular modifiers of more than two syllables, the comparative form consists of *more* before the modifier: *more considerate*.

The superlative form singles out one item from several as outstanding or extreme. With a regular modifier of one syllable, the superlative form consists of *-est* added to the positive form—*brightest*. With a regular modifier of more than two syllables, the superlative form consists of *most* before the modifier—*most considerate*.

When it comes to regular modifiers of two syllables, no single rule governs the creation of the comparative and superlative forms. Some two-syllable modifiers, for instance, *simple*, consist of the positive form plus *-er* and *-est*: *simpler, simplest*. Other two-syllable modifiers, *handsome*, for example, consist of *more* or *most* in front of the modifier: *more handsome, most handsome*. Therefore, unless you are absolutely sure of the proper form of a two-syllable modifier, always check a dictionary to find the correct version.

Remember this point as well: regardless of the number of syllables, never use both *more* and *-er* or both *most* and *-est* with the same modifier. Modifiers like *more faster* and *most completest* are always wrong.

Things are much simpler with negative comparisons. Except with irregular modifiers, negative comparisons are created the same way: *less* before the modifier with a comparison of two items, situations, individuals, etc., and *least* before the modifier with a comparison of three or more:

EXAMPLES: She seemed *less* **worried** after the discussion with her instructor, but her work suddenly became the *least* **promising** in the class, too.

20 Dealing with Commonly Confused and Irregular Modifiers

A number of modifiers are irregular, so you can't rely on the rules for forming the comparative and superlative forms of regular modifiers to guide you. Here is a list of common irregular modifiers:

Positive	Comparative	Superlative
bad	worse	worst
badly	worse	worst
good	better	best
little	less	least
much	more	most
well	better	best

Actually, deciding between *good* and *well* and between *bad* and *badly* probably causes the most headaches. *Good* and *bad* are adjectives. They describe people, objects, or ideas. *Well* and *badly* are adverbs. They describe how a person or thing performs an action. A person can be a good or bad singer but cannot sing good or bad. When you talk about how someone does something, you need an adverb: She sings *well* but dances *badly*.

Note that *bad* and *badly* share the same comparative and superlative forms, as do *good* and *well*. *Bad* and *good* are adjectives, modifying nouns or pronouns. *Badly* and *well* are adverbs, modifying verbs, adjectives, or other adverbs. *Worse* and *worst* and *better* and *best* can be either adjectives or adverbs, depending on how you use them. Simply remember that *worse* and *better* are the comparative forms and *worst* and *best* are the superlative forms of these irregular modifiers, and you will be all set:

Comparative: Of the two girls on the team, she *ran* **worse**.

Superlative: He suffered the **worst** *injury* of all the people in the accident.

Comparative: The amateur's *portrait* was **better** than the professional artist's.

Superlative: I *enjoyed* their last album **best**.

Dealing with Intensifying and Absolute Modifiers

Two types of modifiers that require a little extra attention are **intensifying modifiers** and **absolute modifiers**. Intensifying modifiers are adverbs used to strengthen or emphasize other modifiers. Common intensifiers include *actually, definitely, much, really, so, too,* and *very.* The problem with these words is that, by themselves, they generally don't provide much added strength or emphasis to the words they modify, as these examples show:

EXAMPLES: The room was **very** *warm.*

The customer was **really** *angry* when his clothing wasn't ready.

The difference between *warm* and *very warm* or *angry* and *really angry* isn't specific or vivid. Rather than using an intensifying modifier, look for a single word that pins down what you are trying to say. Instead of *very warm,* write *stifling* or *sweltering* or *blazing,* and instead of *very angry,* try *furious* or *enraged* or *exasperated.*

Absolute modifiers represent an extreme, something that can't logically be compared to anything else, so they have no comparative or superlative forms. Such words thus can't be accentuated in any way, so don't combine them with intensifying modifiers.

Take a word like *unique,* for instance. *Unique* means "one of a kind." To say that your friend is the *most unique* person you've ever met doesn't make sense because uniqueness is a quality that can't be compared. Something is either *perfect* or imperfect, *impossible* or possible, *round* or not round, *straight* or not straight. A person can't be *very dead* or *somewhat equal* or a *little pregnant.* It's either one or the other. When you use an absolute modifier, be sure you let it stand on its own, without any intensifier.

Avoiding Dangling and Misplaced Modifiers

It's important to place modifiers in your sentences so that they help you communicate your ideas to your reader. In this regard, you need to be concerned about **dangling** and **misplaced modifiers.**

Dangling Modifiers

A dangling modifier is a word or group of words, usually appearing at the beginning of a sentence, that lacks an appropriate word to

20

modify. The sentence may suggest or imply what the dangling modifier is supposed to describe or illustrate, but the word itself is missing. Look, for instance, at these examples, with the dangling modifiers underlined:

Dangling: While taking a shower, the phone rang.

To study effectively, your schedule must be free from distractions.

In this form, these sentences don't make logical sense. In the first example, the phrase *While taking a shower* appears to modify *phone*. In the second, the phrase *To study effectively* appears to modify *your schedule*. Certainly, a reader might be able to figure out what was intended, but your job as a writer is not to make your readers have to figure out what you mean.

To correct a dangling modifier, adjust the phrasing in the sentence so that the modifying phrase clearly describes or limits the appropriate word:

Corrected: While taking a shower, **I heard** the phone **ring.**

or

While **I was** taking a shower, the phone rang.

Corrected: To study effectively, **you should keep** your schedule free from distractions.

or

Keeping your schedule free from distractions **will help you study effectively.**

Recognizing and Correcting Misplaced Modifiers

When you write, you generally know the word you want a modifier to describe or illustrate, regardless of where the modifier appears in the sentence. But your reader doesn't share your insight. Therefore, if the modifiers in your sentences are misplaced—that is, not near the words they modify—your reader won't get the full understanding of your message.

Consider these examples:

Misplaced: As a young child, my great-grandfather often took my youngest sister to the park.

20

> The sales representative demonstrated the tiny
> cell phone for the customer <u>with a fully functional
> keyboard</u>.

Misplaced modifiers prevent sentences from making logical sense. *As a young child* in the first example seems to modify *my great-grandfather*, and *with a fully functional keyboard* in the second example seems to modify *customer.*

But a young child can't be a great-grandfather. *As a young child* is meant to modify *my youngest sister.* And humans don't come *with fully functional keyboards.* This phrase is obviously intended to modify *tiny cell phone.*

To correct these errors, place the modifiers next to the words they modify, or restate the sentence in some way so that it makes logical sense:

Corrected: *As a young child*, **my youngest sister** often went to the park with my great-grandfather.

or

When she was a young child, **my great-grandfather** often took my youngest sister to the park.

Corrected: The sales representative demonstrated the **tiny cell phone** *with a fully functional keyboard* for the customer.

or

The customer asked the sales representative for a demonstration of the **tiny cell phone** *with a fully functional keyboard.*

The use of qualifying modifiers, including *almost, even, just, nearly,* and *only,* can also be challenging. If you don't place these modifiers near the words they modify, they'll change the meaning of your sentence. Look at these examples:

EXAMPLES: The man **nearly** paid $20,000 for the stolen truck.

The man paid **nearly** $20,000 for the stolen truck.

In the first sentence, **nearly** modifies *paid*, indicating that the man was thinking about buying the stolen truck but for some reason changed his mind. But in the second, **nearly** modifies *$20,000*, indicating that the man did buy the stolen truck but paid somewhat less than $20,000 for it.

20

Of the limiting modifiers, *only* is probably the most frequently used and misused. Look at these versions of the same sentence, with *only* in different positions:

EXAMPLE: **Only** Rachael was amused by what the instructor was saying today.

(Of all the students, Rachael alone was amused.)

EXAMPLE: Rachael was **only** amused by what the instructor was saying today.

(Although other reactions were possible, Rachael's reaction was limited to being amused.)

EXAMPLE: Rachael was amused **only** by what the instructor was saying today.

(Nothing on that day except the instructor's comments amused Rachael.)

EXAMPLE: Rachael was amused by what the instructor was saying **only** today.

(The instructor's comments amused Rachael on this one day alone; normally she did not find the comments funny.)

The point is that words like *only* alter the meanings of the words you use them to modify, and that's an advantage to you as a writer. Simply make sure to place them with the words you want them to modify. That way, the message that your reader receives will be the one you intended to send.

21

Spelling

Spelling Explored

For a number of valid reasons, you may find spelling in English complicated. But don't expect any sympathy. Spelling *always* counts—readers always expect correct spelling. Because spelling errors are so noticeable, particularly for people who find spelling easy, these mistakes become major distractions that draw attention away from your good ideas. However, a number of techniques can help you become a better speller, including

- reviewing basic spelling rules, focusing particularly on exceptions
- examining commonly confused words to ensure that you recognize their appropriate uses
- studying frequently misspelled words, identifying words that offer you the most trouble, and developing and maintaining your own personal spelling dictionary

This systematic approach will enhance your ability to find and correct errors in spelling.

21   Remembering the Basic Rules of Spelling

One simple way to enhance your spelling skills is to master the following rules—and the exceptions to these rules.

Forming Plurals

You make most words plural by adding *-s* to the singular form. However, there are numerous exceptions to this basic rule.

- **Nouns that end in *-ch, -sh, -x,* and *-s*** Form the plural of nouns that end in *-ch, -sh, -x,* and *-s* by adding *-es*:

birch birches   box boxes   lash lashes

- **Nouns that end in *-y*** The plural for most nouns ending in *-y* depends on the letter preceding the *-y*. If that letter is a vowel (*a, e, i, o, u*), simply add *-s*:

toy toys   key keys   tray trays

  Exceptions Don't change proper names. *Murphy* becomes *Murphys*, not *Murphies*.
  If the letter before the *-y* is a consonant, change the *-y* to *-i* and add *-es*:

  story stories   duty duties   sky skies

- **Nouns that end in *-o*** For nouns that end in *-o*, look at the preceding letter to decide whether to add *-s* or *-es*. If the letter preceding the final *-o* is a vowel, simply add *-s*:

  radio radios   stereo stereos   trio trios

  If the letter before the *-o* is a *consonant,* you usually add *-es*:

  potato potatoes   echo echoes   veto vetoes

  Exceptions Nouns referring to music, such as *altos, falsettos, solos,* and *sopranos,* do not follow this rule. In addition, with a few nouns ending in *-o* preceded by a consonant, you may add either *-s* or *-es*:

  cargo cargos *or* cargoes   motto mottos *or* mottoes
  zero zeros *or* zeroes

- **Words that end in *-f* or *-fe*** Some nouns that end in *-f* or *-fe* form plurals with a simple *-s*:

safe safes   belief beliefs   chief chiefs

For others, you change the -*f* to -*ves*:

half hal**ves**	knife kni**ves**	leaf lea**ves**

For some nouns ending in -*f* or -*fe*, two forms are acceptable:

scarf scarfs *or* scar**ves**   hoof hoofs *or* hoo**ves**
dwarf dwarfs *or* dwar**ves**

When in doubt, always check a dictionary.

- **Nouns with Latin endings**   In general, make nouns with Latin endings plural in keeping with the original language:

alumnus alumni	crisis crises	analysis analyses

For some of these nouns, however, it is also acceptable to add -*s* or -*es* to form the plural:

appendix	appendixes *or* appendices
memorandum	memoranda *or* memorandums
index	indexes *or* indices

- **Hyphenated and combined nouns**   For hyphenated and combined nouns, form the plural by adding -*s* to the main word:

sisters-in-law	leftovers	attorneys general

- **Irregular plurals**   With some common words, form the plural by changing letters within the word or by adding letters to the end:

woman women	tooth teeth	child children

- **Nouns with the same singular and plural forms**   A few common words have the same form whether they are singular or plural:

one deer several deer   one sheep many sheep
one species five species

- **Nonword plurals and words discussed as words**   For abbreviations, figures, numbers, letters, words discussed as words, and acronyms, form the plural by adding either -*s* or -'*s* (apostrophe + -*s*). Use -'*s* with all lowercase letters, with the capital letters *A, I,* and *U,* or any other time when adding -*s* alone might confuse the reader:

one *A* four *A*'s	one *i* several *i*'s	one *the* many *the*'s

21 Basic Rules for Prefixes and Suffixes

You can change the meaning of words by adding prefixes and suffixes to them. A **prefix** is a unit such as *un-, dis-, mis-,* or *semi-* added to the beginning of a word. A **suffix** is a unit such as *-ness, -ing,* or *-ous* added to the end of a word.

- **Prefixes** When you add a prefix to a word, do not change the spelling of the word:

  believable unbelievable   agree disagree   conscious semiconscious

- **Suffixes *-ly* and *-ness*** In most cases, simply add *-ly* and *-ness* without changing the spelling of the original word:

  usual usually   faithful faithfulness   rare rarely

  For words with more than one syllable that end in *-y*, change the *-y* to *-i* before you add *-ly* or *-ness*:

  lonely loneliness   easy easily   silly silliness

  Exception When you add *-ly* to *true,* you drop the final *-e: truly.*

- **Suffixes for words ending in *-e*** For words ending in *-e*, drop the final *-e* when adding a suffix beginning with a vowel:

  cope coping   disapprove disapproval   fame famous

  Keep the final *-e* if the suffix begins with a consonant:

  care careful   arrange arrangement   safe safety

  Exceptions Drop the final *-e* on words when the suffixes begin with a consonant:

  whole wholly   argue argument   judge judgment

  But keep the final *-e* in a few words, including *mile, peace, notice,* and *courage,* when adding suffixes beginning with a vowel:

  mileage   peaceable   noticeable   courageous

- **Suffixes for words ending in *-y*** For words ending in *-y* preceded by a consonant, change the *-y* to *-i* before you add a suffix, unless the suffix itself begins with *-i*:

  bury buried   simplify simplified

  but

  hurry hurrying   identify identifying

- **Doubling the final consonant when adding a suffix** For one-syllable words that end in a single consonant preceded by a single vowel, double the final consonant before adding a suffix beginning with a vowel:

plan plan**ned**   slip slip**ping**   flat flat**ten**

However, if the final consonant is preceded by another consonant or by more than one vowel, do not double the final consonant. Just add the suffix beginning with a vowel:

wash wash**ed**   warn warn**ing**   fail fail**ure**

If a word of more than one syllable ends in a single consonant preceded by a single vowel, you need to say it out loud to identify where the emphasis or accent belongs. If the emphasis is on the final syllable, double the final consonant before adding the suffix:

begin begin**ning**   admit admit**ted**   occur occur**rence**

But if the accent is not on the final syllable, simply add the suffix:

benefit benefi**ted**   profit profit**able**   abandon abandon**ing**

The Basic Rule for *ie* or *ei*
The basic rule for words with *ie* or *ei* combinations is this:

I before *e*
Except after *c*
And when sounded like *a*
As in *neighbor* or *weigh*

Because the two vowels in the following words create a long *e* sound and do not follow *c*, the correct combination is *ie*:

grief   believe   field   achieve   hygiene

But because the two vowels in the following words do follow *c*, the correct combination is *ei*:

receive   perceive   ceiling   conceive   deceive

And because the two vowels in these words have an *a* sound, the correct combination is also *ei*:

beige   freight   eight   vein   heinous

21

Exceptions   *e* comes before *i* in the words *either, neither, leisure, seize, their,* and *weird,* even though the combination doesn't follow *c* or sound like *a*. And in *species, science, prescient, society,* and *ancient, i* comes before *e* even though the letters do follow *c*.

Basic Rules for -*sede*, -*ceed*, and -*cede*, and Other Endings That Sound Alike

Relying on how a word sounds in English to help you spell it correctly is generally not a good strategy. Sometimes, a syllable or sound occurring within a word has more than one spelling, and sometimes a word or phrase sounds like another that is grammatically incorrect or that logically can't exist.

- **Words that end in -*sede*, -*ceed*, and -*cede***   Only one word in English ends in -*sede*:

  supersede

  Only three words in English end in -*ceed*:

  proceed   exceed   succeed

  All other words with this sound end in -*cede*:

  precede   secede   intercede

- ***Have* versus *of***   The correct forms *could've, should've,* and *would've* sound like the incorrect forms *could of, should of,* and *would of.* Therefore, never trust your ear. Always write the full correct form—*could have, should have,* and *would have*—first. If for some reason you find the contraction form more appropriate, make the change in the final draft.

- ***Used to* and *supposed to***   It is often nearly impossible to hear the final -*d* in the expressions *used to* and *supposed to.* As a result, these two expressions are frequently misspelled as *use to* and *suppose to.* Even if you don't hear the sound of the letter, always add the final -*d*.

- ***A lot* and *all right***   A frequent error is to write the common expressions *a lot* and *all right* as incorrect single-word forms: *alot* and *alright*. Always use the standard two-word versions, *a lot* and *all right.*

Dealing with Commonly Confused Words

21

Some spelling errors aren't actually misspellings. Instead, they are incorrectly chosen words. In some cases, the words in question are incorrect **homonyms** (sometimes called **homophones**), which sound like the appropriate words but have different spellings and meanings. The rest are words that, for a number of reasons, people tend to confuse. To eliminate errors of this kind, familiarize yourself with this list of commonly confused words, focusing in particular on the words that have given you difficulty in the past.

accept—take or receive
except—leave out, excluding, but

EXAMPLES: The family politely declined to **accept** any financial help.

Except for some clothing for their children, they refused all assistance.

advice—opinions, suggestions
advise—give suggestions, guide

EXAMPLES: The lawyer did her best to give me sound **advice**.

But when I asked her to **advise** me, I didn't have all the facts.

affect—influence, stir the emotions
effect—a result, something brought about by a cause

EXAMPLES: Any amount of stress **affects** Paul.

The first **effect** you see is incredible irritability.

all ready—everyone or everything prepared
already—before, previously

EXAMPLES: When she returned from her suspension, the work was **all ready** for her to complete.

She had **already** missed two nights' work when she was suspended.

among—within more than two
between—within two

EXAMPLES: The toddler sat **among** her four best friends.

She grabbed a seat **between** the smallest child and her sister.

brake—device to stop; come to a halt
break—shatter, pause

EXAMPLES: When I saw the dog run across the road, I jammed on the **brake**.

The car skidded and I hit the windshield so hard I thought it would **break**.

can—be physically able to
may—have permission to

EXAMPLES: Once the cast is removed, my son **can** test his leg.

Now, he **may** do more things for himself.

choose—decide or select (present tense)
chose—decided or selected (past tense)

EXAMPLES: During registration, I will **choose** my classes more carefully.

Last semester, I **chose** my classes poorly, and I've found my work much harder than I'm used to.

conscience—inner sense of right and wrong
conscious—aware, awake

EXAMPLES: I can't tell you how often my **conscience** has bothered me about silly things I did when I was a kid.

I'm especially **conscious** of the way I used to be cruel to the younger kids in the neighborhood.

council—a group formally working together
counsel—give advice; legal representative

EXAMPLES: The city **council** reacted angrily to the charge that the real estate agent had bribed them.

The mayor tried to **counsel** the members to be quiet, but she was unsuccessful.

Even when **counsel** for the committee proved that the charges had no legal basis, the members refused to calm down.

21

desert—abandon; dry, arid, sandy place
dessert—final part of a meal

EXAMPLES: The park was as hot and dry as a **desert**.

One by one, the people at the picnic began to **desert** us and head for the beach.

Nobody but one small child even bothered with the **dessert**.

fewer—refers to items that can be counted
less—refers to amounts or quantities that can't be counted

EXAMPLES: During the last month, I've had **fewer** quizzes in accounting.

Unfortunately, I've had **less** time to study.

good—used to describe persons, places, things, and ideas
well—used to specify how something is, was, or would be done

EXAMPLES: My brother has had **good** results with his reconditioned laptop.

He told me that it has run **well** from the moment he plugged it in.

hear—listen
here—refers to specific direction or location

EXAMPLES: Even though the infection is gone, she still finds it hard to **hear** low sounds.

She received treatment **here** at the community clinic.

hole—an empty spot
whole—complete

EXAMPLES: The overturned candle burned a **hole** in the carpet.

Because the damage was severe, the **whole** rug had to be replaced.

its—possessive form of *it*
it's—contraction for *it is* and *it has*

EXAMPLES: The pony broke free from **its** handlers and ran right out into the street.

Whenever something like that happens, **it's** a potential tragedy.

21

knew—understand, past tense
new—recent, not old

EXAMPLES: As soon as I heard the sound from underneath the car, I **knew** what it meant.

Although I couldn't really afford it, I would have to get a **new** muffler.

know—understand
no—negative, the opposite of *yes*
now—at this point

EXAMPLES: You **know** what the main problems at work are.

But the biggest problem is that we get **no** direction from Jerry.

The question **now** is what are we going to do about it?

lay—place down, spread out
lie—rest or recline

EXAMPLES: Once you **lay** the chair on its side, disconnect the arms.

Then **lie** down on the floor and find the seam running up the back of the chair.

lead—go first, direct, present tense (rhymes with *bead*); soft metal, graphite (rhymes with *bed*)
led—go first, direct, past tense

EXAMPLES: The manager told Brian to **lead** the team to victory.

After he took the **lead** weight he used for warm-ups off the bat, he stepped up to the plate.

Then, on the first pitch, he **led** off the inning with a double to center field.

loose—not tight
lose—misplace, fail, not win

EXAMPLES: During the warmer weather, I try to wear **loose** clothing.

I still sweat and **lose** weight, however.

of—stemming from, connected with or to
off—away from, no longer on

EXAMPLES: Peter is fond **of** staying up late and playing online games.

As a result, he often sleeps late, especially on his day **off**.

passed—go beyond or by, past tense
past—time gone by, former time

EXAMPLES: An ambulance suddenly appeared and **passed** us.

From **past** experience, I knew it was going to Parklane Hospital.

personal—individual, private
personnel—employees, office or official in charge of hiring

EXAMPLES: The assistant manager asked for a few hours off to address some **personal** issues.

A clerk in the **personnel** office refused, citing company rules.

precede—come before
proceed—go on

EXAMPLES: A PowerPoint presentation **precedes** the conference activities.

After the presentation, participants **proceed** to different rooms for individual workshops.

principal—individual in charge; primary
principle—rule, law

EXAMPLES: When I was in middle school, the **principal** imposed mandatory after-school study sessions for anyone who failed a course.

Her **principal** goal was to help us become better students.

She made sure to stress the **principles** of study skills and time management.

quiet—not noisy; solitude
quite—very, really

EXAMPLES: After the argument, the room became completely **quiet**.

Everybody was **quite** surprised that such close friends could be so mean to each other.

21

than—used in comparisons
then—next, at that time

EXAMPLES: From a distance, people sometimes think that Bill is younger **than** his brother John.

Then when they get a closer look at Bill's gray hair and lined skin, they can see that he is older than John.

their—the possessive form of *they*
there—refers to a specific direction or location
they're—contraction for *they are*

EXAMPLES: The protesters are devoted to **their** cause.

There have been anonymous threats against the protest leaders, so many police officers are stationed behind the barriers over **there**.

Despite the threats, the protesters say **they're** not going anywhere.

though—despite, however
thought—idea, process of reasoning
tough—difficult, rough, hardy

EXAMPLES: My grandfather didn't seem to understand what I'd said, **though**.

At first, I **thought** he wasn't feeling well.

Then I remembered how **tough** it can be for him to hear with noise in the background.

threw—toss, hurl, past tense of *throw*
through—in one side and out the other, from beginning to end

EXAMPLES: A small boy on the sidewalk **threw** a rock at the car window.

It went **through** the open window and cracked the windshield.

to—in the direction of, toward (also used to form an infinitive)
too—also, excessively
two—more than one, less than three

EXAMPLES: The clerk shook her head and returned the receipt **to** the customer.

She said that the receipt was **too** degraded to read, and the signature was illegible, **too**.

She also pointed out that the warranty had expired **two** months ago.

waist—middle part of the body
waste—use up needlessly; leftover material

EXAMPLES: My uncle constantly worries that his **waist** is getting bigger.

If he'd stick to a diet, he wouldn't **waste** so much time worrying.

weak—not strong, feeble
week—seven days

EXAMPLES: It's a month since I injured my right calf, and the muscle is still **weak**.

Next **week**, I am going to begin a series of exercises to strengthen it.

weather—atmospheric conditions
whether—indicating alternatives or options

EXAMPLES: The **weather** in this region has been unusually mild.

Experts can't seem to decide **whether** the change is temporary or permanent.

were—past tense of *are*
we're—contraction for *we are* or *we were*
where—indicates or raises a question about a specific direction or location
wear—have on

EXAMPLES: Last year, my friends and I **were** going to rent a house on the beach, but we couldn't coordinate our schedules.

We're going to do it this summer, however.

The area **where** we will be staying is about two hours away.

I swear that for a whole week, I will **wear** only my bathing suit and sandals.

21

who—nominative or subjective form, used as a subject
whom—objective form, used as an object

EXAMPLES: After a quick investigation, the police identified the driver **who** had caused the early morning accident.

Meanwhile, I looked through my phone directory to find the name of somebody **whom** I could call to pick me up at nearly 4 a.m.

who's—contraction for *who is* and *who has*
whose—possessive form for *who*

EXAMPLES: **Who's** supposed to arrange for this month's guest speaker?

From month to month, I can never seem to remember **whose** turn it is.

your—possessive form of *you*
you're—contraction for *you are*

EXAMPLES: I left **your** gift in the living room.

I think that **you're** really going to like it.

Mastering the Words That You Most Frequently Misspell

In addition to the commonly misspelled words already presented, many—if not most—of the words that trouble you are probably on the following list of frequently misspelled words. To make this list work for you, read through it with a pen, pencil, or highlighter in hand, and note the words that you have actually misspelled or that are spelled differently than you thought. These words will become the basis for your own personal spelling dictionary.

A computer file is the best place to maintain your personal spelling dictionary because it allows you to make adjustments as often as you need to. First, enter—double-spaced and in alphabetical order—the words you have identified from the list of commonly misspelled words. Then insert any other words that have given you trouble in the past, including homonyms and other words discussed earlier in the chapter. Print out the list and keep it where you do your writing for quick reference.

On a regular basis, update and reprint the list, adding words that you have misspelled in any of your academic papers and in your day-to-day writing. Make it a point to review the list at least once a week, focusing on the spelling of the words you use most often.

FREQUENTLY MISSPELLED WORDS

absence	amount	bachelor	ceiling
academic	analysis	balance	cemetery
acceptance	analyze	bargain	cereal
accident	angel	basically	certain
accidentally	angle	bath	change
accommodate	angry	bathe	characteristic
accompany	anonymous	beautiful	cheap
accomplish	answer	because	chief
accumulate	antarctic	beginning	children
accurate	anxious	belief	church
accustom	apologize	believe	cigarette
ache	apparatus	benefit	circuit
achieve	apparent	biscuits	cocoa
acquaintance	appreciate	bookkeeping	collect
acquired	approach	bottom	colonel
acre	approval	boundaries	color
across	argument	breath	colossal
actual	arrival	breathe	column
actually	article	brilliant	comedy
address	ascended	Britain	comfortable
administration	assented	bureau	commitment
advertise	association	bury	committed
again	athlete	business	committee
agreeable	attacked		company
aisle	attempt	cafeteria	comparative
a lot	attendance	calendar	competent
all right	attorney	campaign	competitive
although	authority	cannot	conceivable
aluminum	auxiliary	careful	condition
always	available	careless	consistent
amateur	awful	catastrophe	continuous
among	awkward	category	convenience

(*continued*)

21

FREQUENTLY MISSPELLED WORDS (Continued)

cooperate	doubt	feminine	illiterate
cooperation	dozen	fictitious	imaginative
corporation	drowned	fiery	immediately
correspondence	duplicate	foreign	immigrant
courteous		forty	important
courtesy	earliest	fourth	incidentally
criticize	efficiency	freight	incredible
curriculum	efficient	frequent	independent
	eligible	fulfill	indictment
daily	embarrass	further	inevitable
daughter	embarrassment	futile	infinite
dealt	emergency		inquiry
debt	emphasis	garden	instead
deceased	emphasize	gauge	intelligence
decision	employee	general	interest
defense	envelop	generally	interfere
definitely	envelope	genuine	interpret
definition	environment	ghost	irresistible
dependent	equip	government	irreverent
describe	equipment	gracious	island
description	equipped	grammar	isle
despair	especially	grateful	
despise	essential	guarantee	jealousy
diameter	exaggerated	guardian	jewelry
diary	excellent	guess	judgment
different	excessive	guest	kitchen
direction	excitable	guidance	knowledge
disappointment	exhausted	gymnasium	knuckles
disastrous	existence		
discipline	experience	handicapped	language
discuss	extraordinary	handkerchief	later
disease	extremely	height	latter
disgust		hoping	laugh
distance	fallacy	humor	leave
distinction	familiar	humorous	legitimate
distinguish	fascinate	hygiene	leisure
dominant	fatigue	hypocrisy	length
dominate	February	hypocrite	lengthen

lesson	muscle	patience	publicity
letter	mustache	peasant	pursuing
liable	mutual	peculiar	pursuit
library	mysterious	perceive	
license		percentage	qualified
lieutenant	naturally	perform	quality
lightning	necessary	performance	quantity
literature	necessity	permanent	quarter
livelihood	negotiate	permitted	question
lounge	nickel	perseverance	questionnaire
luxury	niece	personality	
	noticeable	perspiration	readily
machinery	nuisance	persuade	realize
maintain		phase	really
maintenance	obedience	phenomenon	reasonably
marriage	obstacle	physical	receipt
marry	occasion	physician	receive
marvelous	occurred	picnic	recipient
mathematics	occurrence	piece	recognize
measure	official	pleasant	recommendation
mechanical	often	politics	reference
medicine	omit	possess	referring
medieval	opinion	possibility	regretting
merchandise	opponent	practically	reign
miniature	opportunity	precisely	relevant
minimum	oppose	preferred	relieve
minute	optimism	prejudice	remember
miscellaneous	organization	preparation	remembrance
mischief	original	presence	reminisce
mischievous	ought	pressure	removal
missile		primitive	renewal
misspell	pamphlet	priority	repeat
mistake	parallel	privilege	repetition
moderate	paralyze	probably	requirement
month	parentheses	procedure	reservoir
morning	participant	professor	residence
mortgage	particularly	protein	resistance
mountain	pastime	psychology	responsibility

(*continued*)

21

FREQUENTLY MISSPELLED WORDS (Continued)

restaurant	stature	tendency	vacancy
rhythm	statute	theory	vacuum
ridiculous	stomach	thorough	vain
	straight	thoroughly	valuable
salary	strategy	tomorrow	vane
sandwich	strength	tongue	vegetable
scenery	stretch	tournament	vein
schedule	subsidize	tragedy	vicinity
scissors	substantial	traitor	villain
secretary	substitute	transfer	violence
sensible	subtle	transferring	visibility
separate	sufficient	travel	visitor
sergeant	summarize	traveled	
severely	superior	treasure	warrant
similar	surprise	tremendous	Wednesday
solemn	surprising	truly	writing
sophisticated	susceptible	typical	written
sophomore	suspicion		
souvenir		unanimous	
specimen	technique	urgent	yesterday
statistics	temperament	useful	
statue	temperature	utensil	zealous

22

Parallelism and Punctuation

Structural Aspects Explained

Writing isn't some kind of construction project. Rather, it is a creative activity that involves generating ideas on a subject, identifying and articulating a main point, and adapting, developing, and refining points to support that main point. But writing effectively certainly does involve certain structural elements, mechanical features that guide your reader through your ideas, including.

- **parallelism**—the presentation of pairs or series of ideas in similar form
- **punctuation**—the various symbols that signal starts, stops, separation, and emphasis

As previous chapters have illustrated, your good ideas won't come across for your reader if they aren't expressed in simple, clear, and correct form. Correct use of these structural elements plays a significant role in achieving this goal. At the same time, it underscores for your reader that you have taken the time to develop full mastery of writing.

22 Maintaining Parallelism

Whenever you include a set of ideas, whether they are individual words, phrases, or clauses, you must present them in *parallel*—equivalent or matching—form. You face the same requirement when you make comparisons using *than* or *as*.

Parallelism with Individual Items

When you present a set of individual items, all of these ideas must appear in the same grammatical form. The coordinating conjunctions—*and, but, for, nor, or, so, yet*—are probably the most common means of connecting pairs or series of items, with *and* and *or* serving as the most frequently used connectors. To make sure a series is parallel,

1. *Connect only similar parts of speech*: nouns with nouns (or pronouns), verbs with verbs, adjectives with adjectives, and so forth.

EXAMPLE: The weather so far this summer has been *hot, rainy,*
         steamy
and *a steam bath*.

2. *Connect individual words in a series to other individual words* but not to phrases or clauses.
                                a playwright
EXAMPLE: Steve Martin is an *actor,* a *comedian,* **and** *he writes plays*.

Parallelism with a Series of Phrases

As Chapter 15 explains, a phrase is a group of words without a subject and verb that acts as a single word. Common types of phrases include prepositional phrases and verbal phrases (*-ing* phrases and *to* + *verb* phrases). Phrases connected by *and* or *or* must also follow parallel structure. You can connect prepositional phrases with other prepositional phrases or *to* + *verb* phrases with other *to* + *verb* phrases. But it's incorrect to connect prepositional phrases with verbal phrases and to connect phrases with individual words.

To correct errors in parallelism with phrases, simply change the incorrect element to a phrase that matches the others:

EXAMPLE: The explosion affected people *near the house, around the*
                     throughout the entire city
neighborhood, **and** *the entire city was involved*.

EXAMPLE: When she's not in art class, she keeps busy *sketching*
drawing portraits
animals, painting nature scenes, **or** ~~*to draw portraits*~~.

to send a text message
EXAMPLE: The fastest way to contact him is *to call* **or** ~~*texting*~~.

Parallelism with Items Connected by Correlative Conjunctions

As Chapter 15 notes, correlative conjunctions are pairs of connectors used to join items. Here again is a list of these conjunctions:

both/and	neither/nor	whether/or
either/or	not only/but also	

Each pair indicates two possibilities, alternatives, conditions, and so on, and the words or phrases that these pairs connect must be parallel.

The easiest way to eliminate faulty parallelism involving correlative conjunctions is to make the second item match the first:

EXAMPLE: She impressed the interviewer *by* **both** *arriving early* **and**
dressing conservatively
~~*she dressed in a conservative fashion*~~.

EXAMPLE: The staff at the restaurant was **neither** *polite* **nor**
efficient
~~*did they work efficiently*~~.

Parallelism with Comparisons Connected by *than* or *as*

Maintaining correct parallelism with comparisons connected by *than* or *as* can also be challenging. To correct errors with this type of parallelism, change the second unit linked by *than* or *as* so that it is expressed in the same way as the first unit:

EXAMPLE: Experts agree that harassing a person online is **as bad**
bullying
as ~~*to bully*~~ someone physically.

EXAMPLE: After the fire alarm sounded, that substitute teacher would have found it easier *to run* a marathon **than**
to control
~~*controlling*~~ our fifth-grade class.

22 Using Punctuation Properly

Punctuation is the system of symbols that governs the way language is recorded on paper. It represents the various starts, stops, and changes in tone, pitch, and so on, in conversation, with each mark of punctuation having a specialized use. Punctuation can be divided into three main categories: **end punctuation**, periods, question marks, and exclamation points; **pausing punctuation**, commas, semicolons, and colons; and **enclosing punctuation**, parentheses, dashes, and quotation marks. There is one additional mark of punctuation with a specialized use, the apostrophe.

End Punctuation

In writing, you indicate the stop at the end of a thought by using one of the three marks of end punctuation: the period, the question mark, and the exclamation point.

The Period   The majority of your sentences will express a statement that is not a question or an exclamation. Use a period after this kind of sentence:

EXAMPLE: When the band came out on stage, the crowd began screaming.

Other Uses of the Period   In addition to marking the end of sentences, periods have several other functions:

- between the dollars and cents in monetary amounts—$46.72
- before any decimal—34.4, .623
- as the elements of an **ellipsis**, a series of three spaced periods—...—signifying that part of a direct quotation being used to support or illustrate a point has been left out. It is appropriate to use an ellipsis *only* when leaving the material out does not change the meaning of the original:

Original: As author Mary Roach explains in *Stiff: The Curious Lives of Human Cadavers*, "Chest injuries are the other generous contributor to crash fatalities. (This was true even before the dawn of the automobile; the great anatomist Vesalius, in 1557, described the burst aorta of a man thrown from a horse.) In the days before seat belts, the steering wheel was the most lethal item in a car's interior" (90).

Ellipsis Used: As author Mary Roach explains in *Stiff: The Curious Lives of Human Cadavers*, "Chest injuries are the other generous contributor to crash fatalities. . . . In the days before seat belts, the steering wheel was the most lethal item in a car's interior" (90).

- after most initials and abbreviations—M.R. Kidd, Ph.D., etc., Jr., a.m.

  Exceptions Don't use periods with

- U.S. Postal Service abbreviations for the names of the states—for example, RI (Rhode Island), TX (Texas), DC (District of Columbia)
- the names of organizations that have chosen not to use periods—ESPN, OSHA, USA

The Question Mark When a sentence expresses a direct inquiry of some kind, use a question mark:

Direct Question: What time did the party start?

Direct Question: Is a special notebook required for the term paper?

But use a period, *not* a question mark, with a suggested or indirect question:

Indirect Question: The girls wondered what time the party started.

Indirect Question: The class asked if a special notebook is required for the term paper.

The Exclamation Point When the sentence expresses excitement or some other strong emotion, use an exclamation point:

EXAMPLE: Don't touch that wire!

Keep your use of exclamation points to a minimum, and they'll do what they're supposed to do: signify great excitement or emotion.

22 Pausing Punctuation

In speech, you include natural pauses within your thoughts to make your meaning clear or emphasize some point. In writing, you signify these pauses by using one of three marks of punctuation: the comma, the semicolon, or the colon.

The Comma Of these three marks of punctuation, the comma is definitely the one you'll use most frequently. Commas have five basic functions.

- to indicate a pause between clauses connected by a conjunction

  As Chapter 15 explains, there are three types of conjunctions, each of which can be used to connect clauses: coordinating conjunctions (*and, or, but*, and so on), correlative conjunctions (*either/or, not only/but also, whether/or*, and so on), and subordinating conjunctions (*because, although, until*, and so on). The conjunction joins the clauses, but you also need to include a comma to provide the pause that accompanies the connection:

  coordinating conjunction plus a comma

  EXAMPLE: Those sunglasses are attractive, **and** they are inexpensive.

  correlative conjunctions plus a comma

  EXAMPLE: **Not only** was the speech long, **but** it was **also** poorly delivered.

  subordinating conjunction plus a comma

  EXAMPLE: **After** the thunderstorm was over, the air smelled dusty.

  As the third example shows, you use a comma between clauses connected by subordinating conjunctions even when the conjunction appears at the beginning of the sentence and the pause appears in the middle. If the clause introduced by a subordinating conjunction doesn't appear first in the sentence, however, you don't usually need a comma before it, as this version of the same sentence shows:

  EXAMPLE: The air smelled dusty **after** the thunderstorm was over.

- to separate the items in a series connected by *and* or *or*

  EXAMPLES: Calculus, chemistry, **and** anatomy are required courses for my major.

  Alex spends most of his time playing with his blocks, trucks, **or** stuffed animals.

- to set off words, phrases, and ideas that interrupt the flow of the sentence

22

An element in a sentence is called nonrestrictive if it can be left out without changing its full and accurate meaning, as these examples show:

nonrestrictive element

EXAMPLE: The people in the front of the line, *who had camped out all night on the sidewalk,* got the best seats.

nonrestrictive element

EXAMPLE: These shoes, *which I bought online,* don't fit.

If the material is necessary in order for the sentence to express its complete and actual meaning, however, it's restrictive and you don't enclose it in commas, as these examples show:

restrictive element

EXAMPLE: Cars *that have special stickers* may be parked in the private lot.

restrictive element

EXAMPLE: All items on the Web site *that are marked with an asterisk* are currently unavailable.

When **appositives**—nouns or pronouns that explain or clarify other nouns or pronouns—interrupt the flow of the sentence, set them off with commas:

EXAMPLE: Then the stable, *a rickety old building at the back of the property,* quickly caught on fire.

Exception Don't set off the names of close family members with commas:

My sister Margie is majoring in accounting.

When they interrupt the flow of a sentence, enclose words like *however, for instance, though, too,* and so on, in commas:

EXAMPLE: A bigger problem, *though,* is the lack of support among the public.

But if they don't interrupt the flow of the sentence, include no commas:

EXAMPLE: The environmental organization should *therefore* begin an extensive campaign to show the advantages of geothermal energy.

- to indicate a brief break between introductory material and the sentence itself

This guideline is especially true if the introductory material consists of four or more words or contains a verb form. Look at these examples:

EXAMPLES: *Before paying this bill,* I plan to check my account online.

Next to the finish line, a large crowd was waiting for the winning runner.

Even if a unit has fewer than four words, use a comma to set it off from the rest of the sentence if the comma helps to emphasize the main idea of the sentence or makes the meaning of the sentence clearer for your reader. Words and phrases that fall into this category include clarifying expressions such as *of course, for example,* and *for instance,* and common conjunctive adverbs such as *also, finally, however,* and *instead:*

EXAMPLES: *After all,* the flooding problems began well before the street was relocated.

Instead, the committee decided to give scholarships to both finalists.

- to set off a direct quotation from the rest of the sentence

When you present someone's exact words, you signify this direct quotation by enclosing it in quotation marks. Then you use a comma to separate the direct quotation from the **attribution,** the phrasing that identifies the speaker. You can place the quotation in one of three places in a sentence, each of which requires a different placement of the comma. If you put the quotation first, insert the comma within the closing quotation mark:

EXAMPLE: "My wallet isn't in my bag," Nicole said quietly.

If you place the quotation at the end of the sentence, insert a comma before the opening quotation mark:

EXAMPLE: Nicole said quietly, "My wallet isn't in my bag."

And if you divide the quotation, putting the attribution in the middle of the sentence, use two commas. Place one within the closing quotation mark of the first part of the quotation and a second one before the opening quotation of the second part:

EXAMPLE: "My wallet," Nicole said quietly, "isn't in my bag."

You'll use commas for a few additional purposes, including

- to set off the salutation of a personal letter—Dear Jacqueline,
- to separate elements in a date—March 31, 1982, was her birthday.
- to divide parts of an address—Mr. Gus Shanok, 325 Middle Street, Jacksonville, TX 67431
- to signify hundreds within numbers of more than four digits, except decimals—1,254 or 5,400,768
- to set off a name in a direct address—But, Alex, don't forget that I warned you.

The Semicolon   As Chapter 16 explains, a semicolon has the power to provide connections. A semicolon is generally equivalent to a comma plus a conjunction—**, and**—but it signals that the relationship between the units is so strong or significant that no word is needed to link them.

EXAMPLES: Cliff couldn't have been involved in that hit-and-run accident; he was miles away from the scene at that time.

All I wanted was to go home and take a shower at the end of that miserable day; things didn't work out that way.

You can add emphasis to the relationship between clauses by adding a conjunctive adverb like *besides, finally,* and *therefore,* followed by a comma, after the semicolon:

EXAMPLE: All I wanted was to go home and take a shower at the end of that miserable day; *however,* things didn't work out that way.

You can also use semicolons rather than commas to separate series of items such as names, dates, addresses, and so on, that contain commas themselves:

EXAMPLE: The award-winning volunteers include Joseph Michaels, 327 Spencer Street, Barrel, AK; Sarah Clairmont, 57 Princeton Place West, Central Falls, NE; and Lizzie Tonson, 50 Earle Avenue, Kasmir, VA.

22

When clauses connected by a coordinating conjunction contain commas themselves, you may use a semicolon rather than a comma before the conjunction:

EXAMPLE: At 9 a.m. they drove out to the state reservation, the area where they had regularly hiked, camped, and fished; and they spent several hours helping to remove trash, clear overgrown brush, and repair the signs marking the trails.

The Colon   In writing, a colon announces that something important—for example, an explanation, a list, a formal quotation of more than one sentence, and so on—is to follow:

EXAMPLE: She did have something special to offer the company: three years of experience with the newest accounting software.

Notice that the part of the sentence that precedes the colon could stand as a complete sentence.

Use colons in a few other instances, including

- after the salutation of a formal letter—Dear Dr. Arakelian:
- between hours and minutes—10:45
- between the city of publication and the publishing company in bibliographic citations and footnotes—New York: Pearson Education
- between biblical chapter and verse—Genesis 4:11

Enclosing Punctuation

In writing, you occasionally need to keep some ideas in your writing separate from the rest of the information. When this is the case, you'll rely on one of the marks of enclosing punctuation: parentheses, dashes, and quotation marks.

Parentheses   With information that not every reader necessarily needs—for instance, a definition, an explanation, or an expression of personal feelings—enclose it within parentheses:

EXAMPLES: The people at the front of the line (all were wearing team jerseys) were hoping to obtain playoff tickets.

Hypoglycemia (low blood sugar) is a frequent issue for some diabetics.

If the unit within the parentheses is a complete sentence, include a mark of terminal punctuation:

22

EXAMPLE: The recent mayoral election cost the candidates a total of $2.5 million, a staggering amount for a job that pays $55,000. (The salary was established by the city council a decade ago.)

The Dash   One way to make sure that an idea stands out is to set it off with dashes. You form a dash by hitting the hyphen key twice and not leaving a space between the words preceding it and following it. When you use dashes, you tell your reader that the information deserves special attention:

EXAMPLES: When the electricity went out for the third time— resulting in both the smoke and burglar alarms going off—my parents just went to the front desk and checked out.

But she had the one thing I didn't have—self-confidence—so she had a flawless interview.

Quotation Marks   When you include someone's exact words, you signify that the material is a direct quotation by enclosing it within quotation marks. To do so, you put quotation marks at the beginning of the passage and at the end, even if the quotation runs for several sentences.

If the quotation appears first in the sentence, separate it from the attribution—the phrase indicating the speaker—and the rest of the sentence by using a comma at the end of the quoted passage. If the quotation expresses strong surprise or a question, use an exclamation point or a question mark instead of this closing comma. Then put the appropriate mark of end punctuation after the rest of the sentence:

EXAMPLES: "The problem with that laptop is the ridiculously short battery life!" Jacqueline exclaimed.

"The problem with that laptop is the ridiculously short battery life," Jacqueline stated.

If the direct quotation appears at the end of the sentence, use a comma to set it apart from the attribution, but keep this comma

22

outside the opening quotation mark. The mark of end punctuation in the direct quotation serves the entire sentence, so you keep it within the closing quotation mark.

EXAMPLES: Jacqueline exclaimed, "The problem with that laptop is the ridiculously short battery life!"

Jacqueline stated, "The problem with that laptop is the ridiculously short battery life."

And if the direct quotation is interrupted so that part of it appears at the beginning and part of it at the end, treat the opening portion the way you would treat an entire quoted passage at the beginning of a sentence, and treat the second portion the way you would treat an entire quoted passage at the end of a sentence.

EXAMPLES: "The problem with that laptop," Jacqueline exclaimed, "is the ridiculously short battery life!"

"The problem with that laptop," Jacqueline stated, "is the ridiculously short battery life."

Incidentally, should you prepare a passage that records the exact words of two or more speakers, called **dialogue**, begin a new paragraph each time you switch speakers.

When you merely explain or state what a person said without using the person's exact words, a construction called an indirect quotation, don't enclose the passage in quotation marks, as these two versions of the same sentence show:

Direct   *exact words spoken*
Quotation: The embarrassed driver said, "I didn't even see the yield sign."

Indirect   *report of the words spoken*
Quotation: The embarrassed driver said **that** he didn't even see the yield sign.

As this second example shows, be sure to double-check any sentence in which *that* introduces what a person has said. Chances are good that such a passage will be an indirect quotation, meaning that no quotation marks are necessary.

Quotation marks have a couple of other uses as well, including

- to enclose the titles of shorter works that can be thought of as parts of something larger:

    Article Title—"Shopping at the App Store"
    Chapter Title—"Concussions: The Broad Implications"
    Short Story Title—"Fast Company"
    Song Title—"Things Have Changed"
    Episode of a TV show—"Secret Santa"

    But put in *italics* the titles of the longer works from which they come:
    Magazine Name—*Newsweek*
    Book Title—*The Body Human*
    Short Story Collection—*Crawdad: A Quarterly Journal*
    CD Title—*The Essential Bob Dylan*
    TV Show—*The Office*

- to discuss the definition, origin, or specialized use or meaning of a word:

EXAMPLE: When the coach referred to me as a "newbee," I felt my face turning red.

The Apostrophe

One of the most useful—and most frequently used—marks of punctuation is the **apostrophe**. It serves two primary functions: to show ownership, or possession, in nouns, and to form contractions.

Apostrophes to Show Possession   For the most part, making words possessive is pretty easy.

- To change a singular noun into a possessive form, add an apostrophe and -*s*:

EXAMPLE: artist's easel   girl's wallet   business's assets

Add an apostrophe and -*s* even for singular words that already end in -*s*:

EXAMPLE: Jonas's response boss's concerns   witness's response

If the resulting possessive form is awkward, you have another option. Use a prepositional phrase to replace it. Rather than writing *Jonas's response*, write *the response of Jonas*.

322 PART IV Dealing with Matters of Form

- To make most plural nouns possessive, simply add an apostrophe:

EXAMPLE: artists' easels   girls' wallets   leopards' spots

Some plural words don't end in -s. Make these words possessive by adding an apostrophe and -s to the plural noun:

EXAMPLE: men's shirts   people's attitudes   children's toys

- To make indefinite pronouns such as *anybody, everybody, anyone, everyone,* and *nobody* possessive, add an apostrophe and -s:

EXAMPLE: everyone's schedule   anybody's attention
          nobody's fault

- To make a compound subject possessive, identify whether the item is possessed jointly or by only one of the subjects. If the subjects jointly possess something, you put an apostrophe and -s after the last subject:

EXAMPLE: Muriel and Billy's house [*One item jointly owned*]

If each subject possesses his or her own item, add an apostrophe and -s to each subject:

EXAMPLE: Muriel's and Billy's paychecks [*Two items separately owned*]

- To form the possessive of compound words like *maid of honor* and *father-in-law,* add an apostrophe and -s to the end of the last word. Do the same for names of businesses and corporations that are compound:

EXAMPLE: brother-in-law's car   District Attorney's office
          Lord & Taylor's sale

Apostrophes to Form Contractions Contractions are words you create by combining two words. In a contraction, an apostrophe takes the place of the letters left out when the words are combined, as the following sentences show:

EXAMPLES: The new key **wouldn't** open the lock. (*would + not*)

           We'll never forget the blizzard of 2010. (*We + will*)

Here is a list of common contractions:

COMMON CONTRACTIONS

aren't—are not	he's—he is, he has	should've—should have
can't—cannot	I'd—I would	that's—that is
couldn't—could not	I'll—I will	they'll—they will
didn't—did not	I'm—I am	they're—they are
doesn't—does not	isn't—is not	who's—who is, who has
don't—do not	it'll—it will	won't—will not
hadn't—had not	it's—it is, it has	you'd—you would
hasn't—has not	she'd—she would	you'll—you will
haven't—have not	she'll—she will	you're—you are
he'd—he would	she's—she is, she has	
he'll—he will	shouldn't—should not	

Notice that the letters in contractions follow the same order as in the original two words. The exception is *won't,* the contraction for *will not.*

As Chapter 21 indicates, the following contractions are among the words often confused:

it's—its

they're—their—there

who's—whose

you're—your

To make sure you choose the proper homonym, change the contraction back to the original two words, for example, *you're* to *you are* or *it's* to *it is* or *it has,* and read the sentence aloud. You'll be able to tell right away whether the contraction is correct or not.

Apostrophes serve a few additional functions, including

- to replace numbers omitted in dates—the '60s (1960s)
- to mark time that is expressed in word form—five o'clock
- to create informal contractions—ID'd, OK'd
- to form the plurals of the capital letters *A, I,* and *U—A*'s, *I*'s, and *U*'s
- to form the plurals of lowercase letters—*i*'s, *b*'s, *e*'s

Credits

Stanley Aronson, "The Sweet Fresh Smell of Morning." Reprinted with permission by Stanley Aronson. Copyright © July 15, 2002.

David Bodanis, "What's in Your Toothpaste?" From *The Secret House* by David Bodanis. Reprinted by permission of International Creative Management. Copyright © 1986 by David Bodanis.

Margery Eagan, "Holidays Help Remind Us of All That Has Changed." Reprinted with permission of the *Boston Herald*.

Jill Griffin, "Growing a Loyal Customer." From Jill Griffin, *Customer Loyalty*. Copyright © 2002 by Jill Griffin. This material is used by permission of John Wiley & Sons, Inc.

Jill Griffin and Griffin Group. "The Profit Generator." 512/469-1757. Copyright © 1991 by Jill Griffin.

Liliana Ibara, "Treading Thoughtfully." Copyright © 2005 by Liliana Ibara. Reprinted by permission of Liliana Ibara.

Bernice Kanner, "The Nose Knows after All." Copyright © McClatchy-Tribune Information Services. All Rights Reserved. Reprinted by permission.

Jack Olsen, "The Night of the Grizzlies." Copyright © 1996 G.P. Putnam's Sons. Reprinted by permission.

Joe Rogers, "Yellow Skies, Blue Trees." From *Newsweek*, November 30, 1998. Newsweek, Inc. All rights reserved. Used by permission and protected by the Copyright Laws of the United States. The printing, copying, redistribution, or retransmission of the Material without express written permission is prohibited.

Michael Schirber, "What Ever Happened to Energy Conservation?" Reprinted by permission of Michael Schirber.

Index